How to Rent
Vacation
Properties
By Owner

3RD EDITION

The Complete Guide to Buy, Manage, Furnish, Rent, Maintain and Advertise your VACATION RENTAL INVESTMENT

Christine Hrib Karpinski

Kinney
Press
Pollack

Softcover edition ISBN: 978-0-9748249-7-0
Kindle edition ISBN: 978-0-9748249-6-3

Cover design by George Foster
Interior design by Desktop Miracles, Inc.

Publisher's Cataloging-in-Publication Data
(Prepared by The Donohue Group, Inc.)

Karpinski, Christine Hrib.
    How to rent vacation properties by owner / Christine Hrib
Karpinski. —3rd ed.
        p. : ill., forms ; cm.
    "The complete guide to buy, manage, furnish, rent, maintain, and
advertise your vacation rental investment."
    Issued also in Kindle format.
    Includes bibliographical references and index.
    ISBN: 978-0-9748249-7-0 (softcover)
1. Vacation rentals—Handbooks, manuals, etc.   2. Vacation homes.
3. Real estate development.   I. Title.   II. Title: Vacation properties
HD7289.2 .K37   2013

                                                              643.25

Printed in the United States of America

to Tom with all my love . . .

Table of Contents

Foreword

Seconds Anyone?

BY BRODERICK PERKINS

Right now is a good time to buy a second home for play or for profit.

Why?

Several solid reasons.

Interest rates are at record lows.

Prices are down or flat, making properties more affordable.

And more foreign travelers and domestic tourists are looking for the kind of travel accommodation bargains you just can't get anywhere else.

Reports from the National Association of Realtors (NAR) and others reveal the housing market recovery is underway. Along for the ride is the second home sector—vacation homes and investment properties.

Credit is tight, but a well-kept property in a good location with a proven track record of appreciation during good times and solid rental income can help get you over the financing hurdle.

Lenders still know a good deal when they see it and the deals are plentiful, but a rush for vacation properties soon could be underway.

The "2013 NAR Investment And Vacation Home Buyers Survey," reveals vacation home sales rose over the past two years. In 2011, vacation home sales rose 7.0 percent to 502,000 in 2011 from 469,000 in 2010 as owner-occupied home purchases fell 15.5 percent to 2.78 million. However in 2012 the entire housing market is showing signs of recovery with owner-occupied purchases up 17.4 percent to 3.27 million in 2012 and vacation homes sales up 10.1 percent to 553,000.

At the time of the 2012 report, increased sales had not translated into higher prices. NAR reported the median sales price for a vacation property was $121,300 in 2011, down 19 percent from 2010. However in the 2013 report, the NAR reported that the median price jumped 23.6 percent from the previous year to $150,000.

While you might be thinking the window of opportunity is beginning to close on vacation home deals, you have to look at the big picture. Even with a price jump in 2012, prices are still considerably lower than they were in 2004.

Vacation Home Prices
2004–2012

Source: NAR® Investment and Vacation Home 2013 Home Buyers Survey

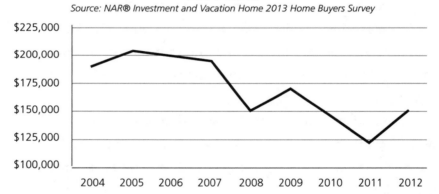

Vacation home purchases are largely tied to lifestyle considerations. An additional home in a desirable location makes for a great family getaway. When the owner doesn't use the home, there's also an opportunity for potentially lucrative short or long term rental income.

HomeAway.com research released in 2012 found that 70 percent of those listing their vacation rentals on HomeAway.com's U.S. vacation home rental sites generated enough rental income to cover half or more of their mortgage, and 51 percent covered at least three-fourths of their mortgage.

Much of that income is coming from abroad, especially Canada, in the first quarter 2013, where the weaker U.S. Dollar was attracting travelers looking for more bang for their bucks.

The U.S. Travel Association forecasts travel expenditures in the U.S. from abroad will rise by 7.1 percent this year, compared to 2012, while U.S. travel expenditures at home will rise only 3.0.

The writing's on the wall.

Join a real estate investment group and pool your money. Tap retirement money. Get a second job. Get a third job. Just do what it takes.

If you've ever considered purchasing a second home for fun, retirement or as a vacation rental investment, you might not get a better deal than you can right now.

Emerging supply-and-demand economics will continue to drive the lucrative vacation home market and along with it, the returns on vacation home investments.

But you can't rely on the market alone. Along with information about the basic economic forces that drive the vacation home market, you'll need to develop a strategy to actively manage your investment.

You're in luck. You hold that strategy in your hands.

Just don't forget to kick back once in a while, vacation in your vacation home and reap all the benefits.

Broderick Perkins, is founder and executive editor of San Jose, CA-based DeadlineNews.Com, a real estate news-based editorial content provider, who also offers editorial content consulting. Perkins is a Pulitzer Prize winning journalist and has been a consumer and real estate journalist for 35 years.

Preface

Over fifteen years ago, I bought my first vacation home. Back then, I could not afford to buy a vacation property, but I wanted one anyway. During my quest, I stumbled upon a vital loophole that rarely surfaces when looking to purchase vacation property—"Renting by Owner." Unfortunately, there aren't many resources out there to provide much-needed answers on how to take advantage of this oft-overlooked, and as I found out, important method of vacation home ownership. I wrote this book to fill that void.

I bought the vacation home of my dreams, and I spent more for it than I did for my primary residence. I have never regretted it. I had positive cash flow from day one. From there I ended up purchasing more vacation rental homes. Others became curious and asked if I would share my knowledge. I did. Word spread, and I started giving seminars to teach people how to own a vacation property and rent it themselves. To date, over 10,000 vacation rental owners have attended my seminars.

I have always rented my homes "by owner" without the use of any local property managers. In the more than fifteen years of renting my vacation homes, I have replied to more than 30,000 emails and phone calls from travelers, taken more than 5,000 reservations, and hosted more than 15,500 guests. It's those interactions and conversations that have given me much fodder for this book.

These pages are filled with not only my own observations and experiences, but also with true stories I've compiled from conversations with tens of thousands of vacation property owners. Over the years, they have opened up and shared with me their challenges and triumphs. I've changed their names for privacy reasons, but you will find a treasure trove of wisdom in their anecdotes. Whatever your situation, don't worry . . . you're not alone. The people I've worked with have found innovative strategies that really work. Now you can benefit from their experiences.

What's New in this Third Edition?

Many things have changed since the second edition of this book was published in 2008. The third edition of *How To Rent Vacation Properties By Owner* brings not only updated information, but also many new topics that have emerged over the past couple of years.

Industry changes. There have been dramatic changes in the vacation rental industry. Most importantly, it seems that the vacation rental industry has moved into the mainstream for prospective travelers. When I wrote the first edition, I used to have to explain what a vacation rental was before I could explain anything else; many people would say, "A vacation rental? I think you mean a timeshare." Thankfully that's not the case any longer.

Credit card and sales tax laws have changed. Short-term rental bans and ordinances, natural disasters and so-called phishing scams are on the rise. Mortgage rates are much lower but difficult to obtain. Insurance is getting a bit easier to acquire. And the general costs of buying and owning vacation homes is on the lower because of the foreclosures and general economic downturn in the real estate industry.

With the increased popularity of vacation home buying, there is now much more hard and fast information available to anyone looking to buy or rent a second home. When I wrote the first edition, news stories about vacation rentals were few and far between. Today, you'll find stories almost daily in various newspapers throughout the country and in some select markets they even have sections devoted especially to vacation home industry news and information.

The National Association of Realtors ®(NAR) continues to make great strides in the vacation home sector of their industry. They have designed a special course to teach agents about selling properties in second home markets. They have been conducting and publishing regular studies of the second home and vacation rental markets for nearly ten years now, which give solid facts, figures and trends to reference.

Personal changes. Many things have changed for me as well. First off, I continue to purchase, manage and rent vacation homes. I have gained new insights in buying in this new market, renovating (from afar), and renting different types of properties.

Secondly, in February of 2010, I left my job at HomeAway, Inc. (the company that owns VRBO.com, VacationRentals.com and HomeAway.com). I'm working independently again and loving every bit of it.

Inside the book. Inside the book, you'll find changes and clarifications to things that were written in past editions. In some instances, the information I provided is no longer true, in other instances advancements in technologies have broadened procedures. And then I have made changes in areas where perhaps I didn't explain things clearly enough the first time around.

I hope you enjoy reading this book as much as I enjoyed writing it. Owning a vacation home and managing it yourself is an exciting adventure. And I want to be there to help you every step of the way. Happy Renting By Owner!

Christine

Acknowledgements

Wow ... finally complete a third time around. This book took much more work than I anticipated. It has been a long, arduous and fun journey. I can't take all the credit—there are many people without whose help and support this book would not have been accomplished.

For The Personal Help and Encouragement

First and foremost to my loving husband and best friend, Tom. Thanks for the constant encouragement and loving support. Thanks for believing in me. Tom, I love you.

To my son Zachary, thanks for understanding Mom's work. Throughout writing this book, you have been in the forefront of my mind—may this book serve as a guide for you when you are ready to join the family business. I cannot express how proud I am of you and your accomplishments (but let's not take it too far, I'm still not going to fly with you in that little, bitty airplane!) Zach I love you!

To my father Mihaly Hrib, through your own actions you taught me how much hard work and perseverance can achieve. I'm sure that you are walking around heaven saying, "See I did not have the opportunity to go to school, I never learned to read, but my daughter (fer), I made sure she had a good education." Dad, I wish you could have lived to see this book come to fruition. I know you are proud.

To my mom, Judy Hrib Kowalewski, you made me who I am today. No words can explain the impact you have on me. You are my hero. I miss you every day. I am sure you are looking down, smiling at the irony of your little girl that was always in trouble at school for talking too much. Look Mom, I am speaking for a living now!

To my in-laws, Ed and Shirley Karpinski, thanks for your encouragement and assistance. You are wonderful parents to both Tom and me.

To Pappa John Kowalewski, you encouraged me to take the risk to do what I love. I miss you!

To Andrew Harris, while you are sorely missed, the wisdom and guidance you shared with me will be cherished forever.

To all my family and good friends, especially, Sue, Gabe, Mike, Kathy, Sherry, Danny, Jill, Lisa, Dianne, Dede, Gabbi, Gai Lynn, Jane, The Kathy's, The Lisa's, Marybeth, Maria, Tania and The Vanessa's.

For The Professional Help and Encouragement

To my friend Dianne Dhanani, who helped us buy and rent our first vacation property. Without your honest candor, we would have never purchased. And there would be no story to write.

Thanks to all the vacation property owners who attended my seminars and encouraged me to write this book. Thanks too to those who took the time to answer my survey and shared their stories, experiences, ideas and tips.

And to the vacation property website owners, thanks for your input and assistance. Your dedication to the industry has made it possible for each individual owner to successfully rent his or her vacation homes.

For the Information Contributors

A special thanks to Jack Simpson, thanks for the many articles you allowed me to quote. You were the pioneer of "By Owner" in the Destin area.

To Amy Ashcroft Greener, thanks for your experiences and talents and sharing them in this book.

To Andy Sirkin, my gratitude extended for your information on the newest trend in buying—co-ownership.

To Tom Kelly, my favorite person from Bainbridge Island, Washington, thanks for sharing your knowledge about international property buying.

To Danielle Workman, thanks for your assistance on the ever-so-important insurance chapter.

To Jeff Cutler, Jeff Desich, George Jaremko, and Gai Lynn McCarthy, thanks for your articles and input.

And a special thank you to Broderick Perkins for the insightful foreword.

For the Time and Talents Shared

Gratitude to all my great friends and colleagues who, for the meager salary of one red pen, agreed to proofread this book. Dave Clouse, Edward Karpinski, Kim Land, Hunter Melville, Karen Pollack, Sheryl Pollack, Fred Quinn, and Jennifer Shriver.

Thanks to all who helped me put my book together. Cover designer George Foster of Foster and Foster. Barry Kerrigan, Del LeMond, and the interior design team at Desktop Miracles. Copy editor Jeff Smith. Transcriber Maria Pembrook.

For Sales Support

A special thanks to all those who helped this book sell out many editions and reprints, and helped this book sit on the best sellers list on Amazon.com for over ten years! Dottie DeHart, Paige Hendren and the entire team at DeHart and Company.

Thanks to all the Vacation Rental By Owner portal sites who helped spread the word about this book. The links are appreciated.

To all of the media professionals, especially my NAREE friends, thanks for remembering me when you're writing about the vacation rental industry.

Most importantly, I thank the Lord for the gifts and blessings bestowed upon me.

CHAPTER

1

Getting Started

It always sounded like a great idea, didn't it? Owning a vacation home. You heard your friends talking about the possibilities. "It pays for itself," they said, and that part of it really appealed to you. After all, it only makes sense. Why spend thousands of dollars on hotels when you can own the vacation home of your dreams, spend as many weeks as you want every year enjoying it, then rent it out the rest of the year, and rake in all that income. Well, I'm here to tell you that you've made an excellent decision. But (you knew there would be a "but") don't delude yourself into thinking this will be simple, easy, or without risks. You need someone to guide you through the process, to show you the ins and outs of how it all works, the pitfalls to avoid, and how to

25

earn maximum profits. If you do things the right way—by educating yourself before jumping in blindly—you will be much better off in the long run.

The first question you need to answer is this: are you buying a vacation property for your own personal use or for an investment? Before you answer, I want to let you in on a little secret: you can do both! In fact, people who otherwise would not be able to buy a vacation home can indeed if they learn the right techniques of renting by owner. This is not for the wealthy only, and it's certainly not a get-rich-quick scheme. This is a long term investment opportunity, with a time proven strategy that almost any middle-income family can use effectively. I will show you how your property can pay for itself (see my "break-even formula" in Chapter 3). It's not as difficult as you might think. My goal is to teach you how to own a vacation home that will be a financial asset rather than a liability.

Think of this new venture you're embarking on as a unique hybrid. You're uniting the idea of owning a vacation home for yourself with the idea of renting it out to others and keeping it as a long-term investment. So, when you do decide to move forward, the decisions you make will be both financial and emotional. Remember back when you bought the home you live in now? Was it just a financial decision? Of course not. You knew that everything had to be right, had to have a certain feel to it before you took the big plunge and made an offer. The location was a key, for sure, but there were other factors: the number of bedrooms, the size and condition of the lot, the garage, the basement, fireplaces, the kitchen cabinets, the wallpaper, paint . . . the list is almost endless. But all of these things mattered tremendously to you, because, after all, this was going to be where you lived, the place you came home to after a long day's work to unburden yourself and relax, the place where you entertained friends, and, quite possibly, the place where you raised your children and gathered your family for holidays for many years. So a lot more went into your decision than just the asking price.

It's much the same when it comes to buying vacation property. A lot of thinking has to go into it. And while it's true that you spend a certain amount of time planning your vacation trips (deciding on the best airfares, hotels, rental cars, etc.) don't think of buying a vacation home as simply a minor extension of that process. It is, in fact, an entirely different process. It's not just a one-shot vacation where you go for a week, hopefully have a good time, and then head home. Buying a vacation home, whether for an investment or for personal use, usually means a long-term commitment. And, if it is for personal use, the stakes are a lot higher. It becomes more than a simple matter of what kind of return you get on your investment.

Whatever you do, don't think of this as similar to dabbling in stocks or any other kind of investing. Instead, think of it in the same terms as when you were buying your primary residence. I know you won't be living there year round, but in all likelihood, you will still be making a large emotional investment in this property. It is not just some impersonal hotel where you hang out for a little while, and then you're gone. This is the place you'll be going for that much needed rest and relaxation over and over again every year, probably several times each year. Its location, size, and condition are important, serious issues. These decisions cannot be made lightly.

Try to cover all of your bases. What about personal emergencies? What if there is a major problem with your primary home (the septic system goes, you are flooded, etc.)? What if you or your spouse loses a job? It's not an unrealistic possibility in today's hard-to-predict economic environment. For the most part, there is no such thing as a stable job these days.

I'm not asking these questions to scare you. I just want you to go into this new venture with your eyes wide open. But there's no reason to worry that this is somehow the equivalent of going to Vegas and betting your life's savings at the craps table. Far from it. Here's what real estate expert Jack Simpson said on the subject, "Trying to eliminate risks often creates other risks. Some people put all their money in a 'safe' insured account only to see their buying power taken away by taxes and inflation. Ask yourself, what is the worst that can happen? To me, the worst thing is seeing your life slip by without risk and reward. That's sad."

Are there challenges to owning a vacation home? Yes, and they will vary greatly from one person to another. Be sure to bring your family situation into the picture. Do you have children? Do you or your spouse have demanding jobs? People are so busy these days, many of us don't even have enough time to mow one lawn, never mind two! Even if you hire landscapers and other helpers (and the money can add up fast) to assist with maintaining the property, when it comes right down to it, you, as the owner, will still have to spend at least a few weekends a year at the home making sure everything is in proper order. Do you have that kind of time? Even if you do, is that something you're willing to do? Maybe you're just too darned tired to spend your time that way. Be honest with yourself about these things before making any decisions. I'm sure you've heard the term "sweat equity." Well, it really plays an important role when it comes to owning a vacation home and renting it yourself. This is something you have to rely on yourself to do. Nobody else can do it for you. Size up the situation carefully before taking the next step. The challenges are not by any means overwhelming . . . if you have the right information for dealing with them, which is why, in the following chapters, I will arm you with all of the facts you will ever need to know about vacation home ownership and renting by owner.

Well, I see you're still reading so you must have decided to keep going. Good. Remember, this is supposed to be fun, even though it involves hard work. But if you've gone this far, you're ready to answer another very important question: where will this vacation home be? The old real estate cliché—"location, location, location"—is extremely pertinent at this point. Don't jump to an overly simplistic conclusion such as, "Well, I live in Michigan, and I hate these horrible, snowy, freezing winters we have every year. I'll buy a vacation home in sunny south Florida where I can escape with the kids every February vacation. Man, that'll be the life!"

Well . . . maybe. Have you really thought that plan through? You're talking about a trip of over 1,000 miles. You can't get there easily by car. Every time you need to visit your property, for any reason, chances are you'll have to fly. And while there may be lots of cut-rate airfares these days, it's still not cheap, and it's certainly not convenient. Getting a direct flight can be nearly impossible. Tedious layovers and connections, not to mention all of the post–9/11 security hassles and long lines that can leave you exhausted well before you even arrive at your home away from home's doorstep. Is that what you want? I'm not exaggerating. Having a vacation home in some exotic locale far from home may have a strong appeal, but it may not be too practical for your individual situation.

According to a survey by the National Association of Realtors, vacation homeowners live an average of 220 miles from their property, and 34 percent live more than 500 miles away.

In the first edition I wrote, "I recommend your prospects be places within a six-hour drive of where you live." Boy did I get a lot of questions on that statement. While this recommendation is still true, it doesn't forbid you from buying farther away. It's just a guideline. The main drawback to buying and owning further away is it could make your visits to your property much less frequently.

We bought our Smokey Mountain cabins while we lived in Atlanta, we used to visit the cabins once every six to eight weeks. From door to door it was 230 miles, a quick three and a half hour drive.

Now that we live in Austin, it's over 1,100 miles or an 18-hour drive. Now we're lucky if we get there once a year, which means we can't enjoy them as frequently and have to make a concerted effort to travel there for maintenance. So for this reason, I still recommend buying a property closer to your home, but it's not a set in stone rule.

You also need to do a good deal of research about the location before making a selection. It's not like you can throw a dart at the map and just take your chances. Even if you're buying the vacation home primarily for personal use, you have to know and understand the market. Just because it is located on a beautiful lake or has a breathtaking view of the ocean, doesn't necessarily mean it is a good deal. What is the rental history of the house? What is the competition like? Is the area glutted with vacation homes? How long is the busy rental season? Does the area have vacation rental restrictions or bans (see chapter 19)? These and many other questions are crucial to ask—and answer—before you make any decisions. Do your homework!

Again, personal choices will play a large role. Think about the vacations you have taken for the last 10 years. Actually, write them down; it will make it easier to keep track of things. Where did you go? The mountains? The oceans? The woods? Did you go to quiet places? Somewhere you could lie in a hammock all day and read a book? Or, did you go to exciting places with lots of nightlife and fun attractions to visit? Now imagine you had to choose just one of those locations, and that is where you will, from now on, be spending your vacations. Does anywhere in particular come to mind? Hopefully, this winnowing process will give you some clues as to the kind of places you should be searching for.

OK, so we've gone through the preliminaries: your motivations for buying, and whether your circumstances make this a sensible move for you. Let's assume you've determined that vacation home ownership is indeed the right way to go. Now you have to get ready for the long haul, which means you need to come to the realization that this is a long-term commitment. This isn't the kind of deal where you are going to do a quick flip, i.e., invest a little money, make a few improvements, and cash out way ahead of the game. I'm not saying that it can't be done; in some cases I've seen people do it quite successfully. But for the average vacation homebuyer, that is not going to be the route you take.

Instead, you should look at it this way: the investment that you'll be making will enable you to afford a property that you couldn't otherwise afford. The one constant in real estate is that it almost always appreciates, and sometimes it does so very quickly. If you play it smart, you may build up a good deal of equity in just a few short years. Yes, at first you might have to rent it out for most of the year just to break even. It probably won't be a cash cow, so don't set your expectations too high. However, with a little patience, as the years go by and the equity continues to build and rents increase, you will be able to rent the property less often and still stay ahead of the game. It will eventually become profitable, and in the meantime, you have a wonderful place where you can spend your future vacations. No reservation required.

Before we go too far, let me add a word of caution. They say politics is the art of compromise. Well, the same could be said of the real estate game, especially when it comes to vacation home ownership. We discussed earlier how this is not only a financial investment, but also an emotional investment. In other words, you have to really like the place before you sign on the dotted line. And while that is certainly true, liking the place isn't the same as loving it. Yes, you want to be satisfied with it. You want it to be a place you are proud of and eager to visit. But you have to be realistic and acknowledge that sometimes you can't have everything you want. For example, let's say you have a large family, and you really have your heart set on a five-bedroom house. However, through your extensive research of rentals in the area, you've discovered that three bedrooms rent much better. Time for a compromise. Buy the three-bedroom (some of the kids will have to share, but they'll survive just fine), and put yourself in the best possible position for renting. Go with the situation that will really keep the cash flow up. The same thing happens when it comes to issues such as buying a furnished or unfurnished home. The latter means more work, of course, but in the end it could be worth it. Explore all your options, and you will be glad you put in the extra effort. Compromises such as these will be necessary every step of the way—beach vs. just off the beach, condo vs. house, and many others.

Just be prepared for these compromises, and you will be more likely to make intelligent, well-informed choices.

The bottom line to all of this, and a good credo to keep in mind as you begin this new adventure, is ... you must be an actively involved owner! Get all the facts. You have to know what exactly it is you're buying, what the competition is, and who your potential renters are. This background work is well worth the effort because you'll soon be enjoying a vacation home that pays for itself. You may very well turn a profit, but you must do your homework first. So keep reading.

2

Financing Your Vacation Home

Everybody knows how to buy things. Most of us know how to find a bargain. When it comes to financing a home, suddenly all of our consumer savviness seems to disappear. Just mention the word mortgage and a great doubt descends on us like a huge dark cloud. Mortgages are the mysterious domain of bankers and other financial people—all that stuff about interest rates, fixed and flexible rates, closing costs, loan-to-debt ratios, fees and points, and the whole foreign language that goes with it. But there is indeed a way to cut through all of the confusion.

Let's look at it as if you were going to purchase a car. We've all done that before. Gives you a chill, doesn't it? But instead of letting the car salesman talk you into a car, you do your research before you go to the car dealership. Like cars, there are many different mortgage products out there. Finding the right one, the one that best fits your needs, depends on the amount of research you are willing to do. But first, let me give you some psychology about getting a loan.

The first thing to realize is that your loan officer, counselor, broker, etc., whatever he or she calls him or herself, is a salesperson. The salesperson's main goal is to earn him or herself and the organization the biggest commission possible. I'm not telling you this so you will hate the salesperson. Just as you educate yourself about cars prior to going to the dealership, you should do the same with your mortgage. Know all your options. By presenting yourself as an educated consumer, you will lessen your chances of being ripped off. The smarter you are, the less likely you are to be taken for a ride.

The next thing is that most people never think in terms of buying a mortgage. It's always, "getting a loan" or "getting financed." Have you ever heard anyone say, "I'm buying a mortgage?" In this mindset of getting a loan, you, as the customer, are vulnerable and at a disadvantage. You probably feel that you have to convince the loan officer that you are worthy of a loan, as if he or she is doing you a favor. It is very important to have the correct mindset! Remember the loan officer needs your business as much as you need the loan.

The first thing that people always shop for is rates. Mortgage rates are determined through some very in-depth formulas based on all sorts of numbers that we as consumers really do not need to understand. Bottom line, you just want to know what's the best rate available for you. Mortgage rates are quoted in increments of eighths or 0.125 increments, for example: 3.00, 3.125, 3.25, and 3.375, or 3, 3⅛, 3¼, and 3⅜.

Now let's say you shop around, check the rates on a particular day, and find that various mortgage companies have all different rates for the same type of loan. Why is this? Well, if you view mortgages just like any other consumer product, say cars, then depending on where dealers purchase the car (from the manufacturer, used car auctions, wholesale, etc.) dealers can price the cars according to the discounts they may receive when they purchase the vehicles. This gives car dealers the leverage to charge more or less for the same exact vehicle as their competitors. The same is true for mortgages. Certain mortgage companies do more volume in one product so their lender (supplier) sells that product at a discount rate, thus making it easier for the mortgage company to sell it to the consumer for less.

But I caution you, rate is not the only thing to consider when shopping "to buy" a loan. You need to consider rates, products, and fees, the same as you would consider different makes, models, and accessory packages for a car. Don't make the mistake of thinking that there is anything standard about fees. No, absolutely not! There are many fees that are fixed, such as doc stamps on a deed, taxes, and title insurance. However, there are many fees that are not fixed and will vary from lender to lender, such as loan origination fees, discount fees, appraisals, credit reports, underwriting fees, processing fees, and wire fees, etc. Along with shopping the source, you will also have to shop the total costs of the loan, including interest rate, broker fees, points (each point is 1% of the amount you borrow), prepayment penalties, loan term, application fees, credit report fee, appraisals, and a host of other items. Just as the car salesperson can sell you that worthless warranty, loan officers and mortgage brokers can rip you off by charging junk fees at the closing table. So the bottom line is . . . check out your mortgage broker. Make a few calls. Be sure to have some references. Look for a company that has been in business for at least three years. There are many very good, honest, up-right mortgage brokers in the business. You just have to work a bit harder to find them.

Which Loan Program?

There isn't a simple answer to the question of "which loan program?" The right type of mortgage for you depends on many different factors:

- Your current financial picture
- How you expect your finances to change
- How long you intend to keep your house
- How comfortable you are with your mortgage payment and the possibility of it changing
- How many weeks you intend to rent your property
- Reasonable rental income potential
- The property's past rental history
- If you intend on "renting by owner" or using a management company to rent (which means you will have to pay commissions)
- If you expect to pay the property off through principal payments or if you are banking on property appreciation to make you money

One rule of thumb to remember is that the more risk for the bank, the more you will have to pay (i.e., higher interest rates and more closing costs).

Term of the Loan

One thing to consider is the term, or length of the loan, and how it will affect your bottom line. For example, a 15-year fixed-rate mortgage instead of a 30-year loan can save you thousands of dollars in interest payments over the life of your loan, but your monthly payments will be higher and make it more difficult for you to break even with your rental income. An adjustable rate mortgage may get you started with a lower monthly payment than a fixed-rate mortgage and may make it easier for your property to pay for itself with your rental income . . . but your payment could increase when the interest rate changes. Get comfortable using one of the many mortgage calculators available for free online (my favorite is www.hughchou.org/calc/mort.html). Also try to determine your goals from the day you purchase and set the term of your loan accordingly

Before we discuss products, I want you to understand that there are two separate qualification guidelines that must be considered when purchasing each particular product—conforming and non-conforming loans. The products are the same, but the qualification factors are different. A conforming mortgage is just that, the normal, usual way to purchase. Under a conforming mortgage, there are industry-standard, set rules, though the guidelines may still vary from lender to lender. Conforming loans generally require that you fit into the government standards of Fannie Mae and Freddie Mac guidelines*, which may or may not include maximum loan amounts, certain debt-to-income ratios, and minimum credit scores. A non-conforming mortgage is used when you or your property does not fit into that perfect little box. So if you need a huge loan, are self-employed, your credit score is low, or your debt-to-income ratio is high, you may be required to purchase through non-conforming guidelines. Non-conforming loans, as a rule, have an up-charge of 0.75%–1.5% more than conforming loan rates.

* For information on conforming loans figures and facts, visit www.mortgage-x.com.

Second Home or Investment Property?

You need to determine whether you will be using your vacation home as a second home or as an investment property. This makes a big difference in the kind of mortgage you should buy and the rates that you would be able to get with your loan. It also has significant income tax implications, but those are separate issues that we won't discuss here (discuss it with your tax adviser). You must realize that this is only a question for mortgage purchases; how you claim your property on your income taxes is a completely different issue. Let's take a look at the different mortgage products available.

Second Home Mortgage

When you go this route, rates are the same as a primary property mortgage, with minimal down payment. Second mortgages are my favorite way to purchase a vacation home. There are no "up charges," i.e., higher rates (since the bank has less risk than with an investor mortgage explained below). This is also the type of loan that the average person is most familiar with. It works exactly the same way the loan on your primary residence works. Basically, if you made it through the loan process on your primary residence, then you can get through the process of a second home mortgage. And for income tax purposes, you can convert your property from a second home to an investment property *after** you purchase the loan, which will maximize all of your income tax deductions.

The only caveat is that you must be able to qualify under the second home's terms. What does this mean? You have to be able to afford it just as you would your first home. Under this loan, there is *no consideration for potential rental income.* So if your primary residence mortgage is $300,000 and your second home mortgage is $225,000, then you must to be able to qualify for $525,000 worth of debt. Therefore, if you maxed out your debt on your primary residence, this is not the type of loan for you. But have no fear; there are many more options.

> * Be sure to read the fine print in your mortgage documents to make sure there are no restrictions against renting your property. Some mortgages require one to three-year owner occupancy prior to renting.

Investor Mortgage

This is a mortgage where everyone concerned knows you are buying the property strictly as an investment. Accordingly, certain factors come into play. The bank will want to know the rental history of the property, which will be taken into consideration for your affordability factor. For many people looking to purchase a second home, investor mortgages will be the best option. Also, these types of loans are considered by the lender to be higher risk. So the risk for the bank translates into higher interest rates and higher fees for you.

In today's financing market investor loans are extremely difficult to obtain regardless of your credit worthiness or your down payment. During the housing market crisis, the banks got crushed by speculators. For this reason, they are very gun-shy with investor loans.

In 2011, I started purchasing properties again (I took a hiatus during the economic downturn). While searching for new properties to purchase, I also investigated mortgages. I have awesome credit (over 800), a sizable cash portfolio, and an extremely low debt to income ratio. Despite an exceptionally good financial position, I couldn't get a bank or lending institution to provide an investor mortgage for any properties.

Thankfully, there are other mortgaging options available that I will discuss a little bit later.

Fixed-Rate, Fixed-Term

The most commonly used type of mortgage product is a fixed-rate mortgage. With these mortgages, your interest rate and monthly payments never change. Property taxes and homeowner's insurance may increase, but your monthly payments will otherwise remain stable.

These mortgages are available for 30 years, 20 years, 15 years, and even 10 years. Under a fixed-rate fully amortizing loan, a large percentage of the monthly payment is used for paying the interest during the early amortization period. As the loan is paid down, more of the monthly payment is applied to principal. A typical 30-year fixed-rate mortgage takes 22.5 years of level payments to pay half of the original loan amount.

Note: Most investment advisors will suggest a loan for an investment property for the longest term. You will have to decide for yourself whether this makes sense for your particular situation.

Adjustable Rate Mortgages (ARM)

These loans generally begin with an interest rate that is below a comparable fixed-rate mortgage and could allow you to buy a more expensive home because the monthly payment will be lower.

However, the interest rate changes at specified intervals (i.e., every year) depending on changing market conditions. If interest rates go up, your monthly mortgage payment will too. But if rates go down, your mortgage payment will drop.

There are also mortgages that combine aspects of fixed and adjustable rate mortgages starting at a low fixed-rate for 7–10 years, for example, then adjusting to market conditions.

Interest-Only Loans

Interest-only loans were a popular mortgage option available in the past, in which the mortgagee paid only the interest on the mortgage in monthly payments for a fixed term. With this loan no equity was built from the payments unless you made additional principal payments.

But after the mortgage crisis of 2008, interest-only loans are virtually non-existent any longer. In January 2013, new regulations were passed which specifically regulate interest-only mortgages. I suggest you just stay away from these types of loans.

Jumbo Loans

A Jumbo Loan, is exactly what it sounds like: a loan for a big amount of money. Mortgages for large loan amounts are set into a different category—basically for the buyer it means tougher qualification factors and higher interest rates.

As a rule, the loan amount is considered to be "jumbo" by a predetermined standard which is set each January by Fannie Mae (the Federal National Mortgage Association) or Freddie Mac (the Federal Home Loan Mortgage Corporation.) They set what is known as "conforming loan limits" and anything over that limit is considered a Jumbo Loan.

At the start of 2008, the conforming loan limits were $417,000 for homes in the contiguous United States (in Alaska, Guam, Hawaii, and the U.S. Virgin Islands, the maximum conforming loan limit was $625,000.)

The Economic Stimulus Act of 2008, signed into law on February 13, 2008, established a temporary increase to Fannie Mae's conventional loan limits in high-cost areas, for loans originated on April 1, 2008 through December 31, 2008. In the areas defined as "high-cost areas," the conforming loan amount in the contiguous United States was $729,750.

The last time the jumbo loan limits were set was October 1, 2011, which reset them right back to the same jumbo limits as 2008.

Because many vacation homes are located in areas where the real estate prices are quite high, many vacation home buyers are forced to purchase jumbo loans.

Mortgage Payments

Here are some examples of how payments can differ depending on the product you choose:

Payment calculated per $100,000		
Product	Rate*	Payment
30 yr. fixed	3.59%	$454
15 yr. fixed	2.89%	$685
5/1 ARM	2.82%	$412

 * Rates according to BankRate.com on 02/07/2013

On the chart above, you'll notice no significant differences in the interest rates. The savings will be realized only when you investigate it together with the term of the loan. For example, with a loan for $300,000, comparing a 30-year to a 15-year loan, there's only a .70% difference in the interest rate. But look at interest you'll pay over 30 years which is $190,410, compared to only $70,064 with the 15-year loan. As you can see, that is significantly different.

With the 5/1 Arm, the interest rate and payment are going to be less for the first five years, however once the five year period is over your payment can increase or decrease. The school of thought right now is ARMs are not a big gamble since mortgage rates are at nearly an all-time low. If you are absolutely certain that you will be selling the property (or paying off the mortgage) within five years, then go for the ARM. But if there is a chance (even the slightest chance) that you'll keep the property longer than five years then you'll likely want to just go for one of the fixed rate mortgage products. Be sure to discuss all options with your mortgage broker and investment advisor.

Securities Backed Lending

Did you know that you can use your current stock portfolio to finance a property? Financial companies such as Wells Fargo, Merrill Lynch, Charles Schwab and Morgan Stanley have these products available to property investors. You can use a portion of your portfolio as collateral.

There are many advantages to using your investment portfolio to purchase a vacation rental home. First, your investment company is much more confident about your credit worthiness so they are more willing to loan you money. Secondly, they are using your portfolio as collateral.

You don't need a down payment, and you don't even have to cash in your stocks! You can still buy, sell, and defer capital gains on liquidated securities and still use pledged securities. Of course, there may be trading restrictions on the collateralized stocks. One thing to remember here is that your mortgage interest may not be deductible if you are using tax-deferred stocks. In some cases, you can pay the principal back according to your own income schedule.

Self-Directed IRA

All of your stocks tied up in your IRAs? Did you know that you can buy real estate, including vacation properties, with your IRA? Jeffrey Desich is a vice president and principal with Equity Trust Company. He is actively involved in real estate and the financial service industry, and an expert on real estate investing with self-directed retirement accounts. Here is what he said on the subject:

> With a self-directed IRA, you have the ability to take control of your retirement savings. A self-directed IRA is an Individual Retirement Account in which you call the shots, and you choose your own investments. By investing your IRA in real estate you have the ability to shelter your profits from taxes! Both rental income and appreciation of the property grows either tax-deferred or tax-free!
>
> With these self-directed accounts you have the ability to invest in stocks, bonds, mutual funds, and special assets, such as vacation properties. If you choose to use your IRA to purchase property, you must select a custodian for your self-directed IRA. When selecting a custodian for your self-directed IRA, you want to make sure you ask a few questions:
>
> + Does this custodian offer one low flat fee with no hidden costs?
> + Am I allowed to invest in non-traditional assets like vacation properties?

+ Does the custodian have experience and knowledge in real estate?

+ Is the firm federally regulated?

+ Will I have the ability to speak with knowledgeable individuals and not just an automated service?

Once your IRA owns the property, all expenses related to this investment will be paid from the funds in your self-directed IRA, per your direction. In addition, all income made from the investment will be sent into your IRA, where it grows tax-deferred or tax-free depending on the account type.

Note: This program has strict government guidelines.

Cash Purchases and Down Payments

In today's market, cash is king! According to *2013 Investment and Vacation Home Buyers Survey* published by the NAR®, a staggering 46 percent of buyers who purchased vacation homes in 2012 paid with cash! While second homes buyers have always had higher percentage of people purchasing with cash (in 2006 it was 25%) than the primary residence sector, the number of people who purchased with cash has increased significantly in the past couple of years. This is mainly because of the residual effects of the housing market crash—banks just don't want to take the risk of loaning money on a non-primary residence.

Let's face it; not everyone can purchase with cash. For those who are able to obtain a mortgage, banks are now requiring much larger down payments, in most cases, 20–30% down. Of those who mortgaged in 2012, nearly 70% put more than 20% down (I purchased my first vacation home in the 1990's with only 3% down payment). So the bottom line is whether you intend to obtain or mortgage or not, you'll have to have a significant cash position to purchase a vacation home today.

Let's fast forward. You're ready to buy. What is the best way to approach the seller? Well, there are a couple of ways. On the one hand you can be pre-qualified for a loan, but even better is to come to the table armed with a pre-approval letter. Here is the difference between the two:

Pre-Qualification

In this case, you go to the loan officer and tell him or her your income and expenses. He or she will punch in a few numbers, maybe run a quick credit report, and then tell you how much you can afford. This is just a preliminary approximation and comes with no guarantees that you will qualify for the loan.

While a pre-qualification can help you approximate how much you can afford, it does not offer the same advantages as being pre-approved.

Pre-Approved Pending Property

In the case of a pre-approved loan, you have not only gone to the loan officer for pre-qualification, he or she has actually sent your file to processing and underwriting, and you are completely approved for a specific loan amount. With this, the lender is just waiting for the sales contract and property to fill in the blanks on the closing documents. Pre-approval pending property is like having a blank check in your pocket just waiting to be filled out! Why do this? It gives you leverage as a buyer.

Realize that vacation homes and investment properties can be located in two significantly different markets: seller's markets or buyer's markets. Believe it or not, there are some areas that have become sellers markets again.

Take for instance Destin, Florida where I constantly watch the market because I invest in vacation rental properties there.

Destin saw a deep decline in sales (and prices) with the real estate market crash that started in 2008. In Florida, as in many judicial foreclosure states, the court systems were backlogged with so many foreclosures that it took two to three years to complete the foreclosure process. As properties started to come onto the market in 2011 and 2012 bidding wars ensued. The bidding wars were mainly due to foreclosed properties coming onto the market at very low prices. This is created a "seller's market" many properties. By the summer of 2013 most of the foreclosed properties were sold and the market normalized. *Now let me be clear, just because a lot of properties sold in Destin during 2010 and 2011 properties went into multiple offer situations, often selling above the asking price, you have to realize the asking price was significantly lower than the going market price.*

Now to get back to our point at hand, should you get prequalified for a mortgage or preapproved pending property? Each time a property goes up for sale there may be multiple buyers fighting to purchase it. If you were the seller, which offer would you accept? Sell to the person who does not have a loan yet, and take the risk that that buyer will not qualify for the loan? Or, would you sell to the buyer who has already gone through whole mortgage process and has full loan approval? Of course you would pick the sure deal.

In 2010 I started to feel that the real estate market in Destin had finally reached the floor, giving me confidence to start purchasing properties again (I took a hiatus from buying from 2003 through 2010). I put offers on three different places where I ended up getting outbid by another buyer. In one situation I offered an over the asking price bid and still got outbid. I realized that I needed to change strategy. Rather than using price as a benefit, I knew that I had to start offering quick closing and cash deals.

Then there is the other type of vacation property market, the buyer's markets, where there are several dozen, maybe even hundreds of properties for buyers to choose from. In a buyer's market, homes may be on the market for longer periods of time. As the savvy buyer with your pre-approval in your pocket, you can go to the seller and offer considerably less than the asking price and have a better chance of the seller accepting your offer.

This is the way I purchased our first property in Destin, Florida, back in the 1990s. I got pre-approved for a loan. I went and looked at numerous properties priced within my pre-approval dollar amount. I then narrowed my choices down to 10 properties. My plan was to give low-ball offers and keep going down the line until I found a seller who would take my offer. I put an offer on the first property and told the sellers that I could close in two weeks! Back then, two weeks was unheard of for closing. Most mortgages took four to six weeks to process.

The sellers were not as offended as my real estate agent thought they might be. The property had been on the market for more than six months, and they had already had two contracts fall through due to buyers not being able to qualify for the loan. So the sellers made a counter offer, and I agreed to split the difference. I called the appraiser and inspector, asked if they could have the property ready to close in a week, and they went along with it. In the end, I purchased the property at 86% of the market value and closed in one week! I started off with 14% equity in the property from day one! That's pretty tough to beat (but I want you to try).

The bottom line when it comes to mortgages is . . . learn how to be a wise consumer. Again, the car analogy is appropriate. When was the last time you paid the sticker price or test drove only one car? It just doesn't work that way. You did a lot of shopping around before signing on the dotted line. Well mortgages are a much bigger purchase than an automobile, and there is so much more at stake. Don't be afraid to ask questions. Kick the tires, check with previous customers, and do a good deal of comparison-shopping. Chances are there is an excellent mortgage product available that will specifically address your situation and your needs. But it won't leap into your arms. It's up to you to go out there and find it.

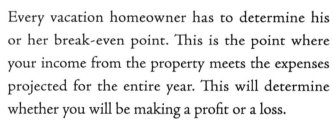

CHAPTER

3

Crunch the Numbers

Every vacation homeowner has to determine his or her break-even point. This is the point where your income from the property meets the expenses projected for the entire year. This will determine whether you will be making a profit or a loss.

Let me explain why this is so important. One of the goals when you purchased your vacation home was, of course, to achieve a break-even cash flow (on a year-to-year basis), coupled with a maximum tax shelter on other earned income.

My definition of the break-even point is when all the income (rent) from your property is enough to pay all of the bills associated with ownership of the property. In other words, your property should not cost you another dime after your down payment. Now, that's not necessarily the definition you will get from financial analysts. Let's face it; they talk in ways that most of us cannot understand. They would say that break-even is a point at which your income is equal to the initial investment with all factors included, such as investments, depreciation, tax benefits, losses, and liabilities. The total revenue for your small business with all factors considered: total direct expenses incurred, revenues minus direct expense, contribution of revenue, total fixed establishment expenses, and so on.

I am not an accountant and chances are, neither are you, so we'll talk in terms that you and I can understand and not worry about the things that your accountant will take into consideration when he or she handles your income taxes (which by the way will make your investment look much more lucrative).

Now, I said your property should not cost you another dime after your down payment. You're probably asking, is that realistic? Absolutely! Let me show you how.

The Break-Even Formula

Here's my copyrighted formula which I came up with many years ago: If your monthly mortgage payment is less than or equal to one peak week rental, and you rent approximately 17 weeks per year, you should have break-even cash flow on your vacation home.

- Your mortgage payments (including taxes and insurance) should be roughly equal to, or less than, one peak week's earnings.
- Peak weeks—the highest earning weeks of the rental season. Usually there are 12 peak weeks in a rental year. So if you rent these 12 weeks, you will have enough revenue to pay your mortgage payments for the entire year.
- Other costs, including bills for your phone, power, cable, and association dues, are paid by your earnings from approximately five off-week rentals. So, even by renting only 17 weeks out of the year, you can still break even. These other costs, as you can see, are also paid for.

> • Here's how: Take a property that rents for $1,000 per week during the peak season with a monthly mortgage payment of $1,000. There are 12 peak weeks most or all of which are generally occupied. Then 12 weeks rented = 1 year's mortgage payments. Then you'll need to rent 5 other weeks to pay for incidentals such as power, phone, association dues, minor maintenance etc. Rent by owner and have 17 (33% occupancy) weeks booked and you have break-even cash flow. Rent more and you have positive cash flow.

This formula is not absolute of course, but it will at least give you a good feel for where the numbers should be.

During the peak of the housing market, in 2003–2005, many reporters and potential buyers asked, "How, with the increased cost of vacation real estate today, can you purchase a home that will fit into this formula?" While the formula held true, the challenge was finding a property that would fit the formula because vacation property prices rose significantly in the previous 5–10 years. It was very difficult to find a home that would fit the formula, especially with minimal down payments. In today's market, we have reached the sweet spot again. It's very easy to find properties that have good cash flow and you can even find properties that will actually have positive cash flow.

So what if the property does not fit into the formula? So does that mean that this would not be a good property to purchase or one that might not have positive cash flow? Not necessarily. It might be pretty close, but not unachievable. Remember, this formula is the *most* conservative way to look at the numbers.

For example, what if your mortgage payment is $3,000 per month, but similar properties in your area only rent for $2,000 per week? This property would need to bring in approximately $51,000 in rental revenue in order to break even ($36,000 to pay the full year's mortgage payments and $15,000 to pay for other costs of ownership). You would need to rent 25.5 weeks (49% occupancy) at $2,000 per week in order to break even.

With this property you would have three factors that would assist you in determining whether it could earn break-even cash flow.

Number of weeks rented. The first would be how many weeks can you actually rent it? When I researched for the first edition of this book, I found that the average occupancy rate for vacation homes was around 33% or 17 weeks. Today, with travelers' increased propensity to rent vacation homes, most owners rent their properties for more than 17 weeks per year (I average 65% occupancy rate). While you would need to determine the exact potential occupancy rate for your area, 25.5 weeks booked would be achievable for more than one third of the properties out there.

Rental rates. The second factor would be the rental rates. In many areas throughout the country, the rental rates for vacation rentals have lagged behind the appreciation rate. For example, in Destin, Florida, in 1996 an average condo was around $150,000, whereas in 2006 that same property would run upwards of $450,000. Even though the cost to purchase had tripled, the rental rates have lagged very slowly behind, not even doubling. While you do have some control in raising your rental rates, you can't raise them significantly overnight.

While rental rates lagged behind the appreciation rates from 1996 to 2006, the good news is from 2008 to 2013 the rental rates were stable and in many cases actually increased. Or to put it more simply, while the prices to purchase property can fluctuate significantly, rental rates are generally much more stable, rarely decreasing and most often increasing slowly over time.

Other costs. And the last factor would be the extra costs associated with ownership of the property. While $36,000 is a true number (the $3000 monthly mortgage payment from the example multiplied by 12 months), the $15,000 for other costs of ownership is an arbitrary amount. The other costs such as power, phone, cable, etc., are generally minimal and likely wouldn't add up to $15,000 annually. In most cases, however, you may reach this large sum by adding your homeowners association (HOA) dues. If this property is not in an HOA, then the chances for positive cash flow are significantly greater.

So now let's look at this same example from a different perspective, one that will *not* have break-even cash flow. Say your mortgage payment is $3,000 per month and similar properties in your area only rent for $1,400 per week. Therefore you would need to rent 36.4 weeks or have 70% occupancy in order to break even (annual mortgage payments plus annual expenses, divided by the weekly rental rate). Is that feasible? It's much less achievable since very few vacation rental properties are rented at 70% occupancy.

But say you have your mind set on buying this property anyway, or you already own it. You can use this formula to determine how much this property would likely cost you in out of pocket expenses on an annual basis. If you rent it for 17 weeks per year, it would bring in $23,800 worth of rental revenue (rental rate multiplied by 17 weeks). The rental revenue of $23,800 would then be applied against the annual estimated expenses of $51,000 per year. Without renting this property, it would cost $4,250 per month (estimated annual expenses divided by 12 months), with renting it would cost $2,268 per month or $27,200 annually out of your pocket.

ROI on Cash Purchases

Figuring out your "Return On Investment" (ROI) with cash purchases can be looked at in two significantly different ways. You can look at it from an accountant's point of view where they would weigh all factors including depreciation, tax advantages, losses, and liabilities. Or you can simply look at the actual numbers, cash in versus cash out. Again, I take the simplistic approach.

Let's say you have cash that you want to invest. You can invest it in the stock market, securities market, bond market, commodities market. Or you can invest it in real estate.

I purchased a pre-foreclosure condo in Destin in April of 2012 for $156,000. I put $24,000 worth of improvements into it when I purchased it for a total investment of $180,000. My expenses (HOA dues, taxes, insurance, cleaning, power, phone, advertising, etc.) were $9,100. The actual net rental revenue from May through the end of the year was $34,000. With those numbers, my first partial year, I earned 14.3% return on investment (and that was only 8 months of rental revenue—May through December).

When you factor in appreciation, the ROI looks even better. Let's say that the improvements I made to the property increased the property value to $200,000 and I decided to sell it. The ROI would be 25.5%. You can't get those kind of numbers in the stock market!

4

Insurance

If you were to ask me what was the biggest motivation to write a second edition of this book, this topic would be it. Insurance is by far the most common concern of vacation rental property owners today. In early 2004, when the first edition was published, insuring a vacation rental property wasn't too difficult. You would have simply called your current insurance agent and added your new property to your existing portfolio.

Today, calling your insurance agent and just adding your property is no longer the case. As soon as you mention the mere words "vacation rental home" you'll find it difficult to come across an insurance agent who will give you the time of day, much less write an insurance policy on your vacation rental home. After much research, speaking with various agents and insurance commissioners, and reading new insurance laws, I have brought together some information that will hopefully help you find affordable insurance solutions for your vacation rental homes.

Before I tell you how to find insurance, it is important for you to realize what has changed in the insurance landscape and why. Knowing about these changes will assist you when you're shopping for insurance. Factors that have radically changed the ability to obtain insurance are:

Catastrophic weather. Starting with the four major hurricanes in 2004, Charley, Frances, Ivan and Jeanne followed by five major hurricanes in 2005, Dennis, Emily, Katrina, Rita and Wilma, Ike in 2008 and Sandy in 2012. These eleven hurricanes alone have created hundreds of billions of dollars in insurance claims. Add to this the damages from tropical storms, wild fires, hail, floods, tornadoes, earthquakes, mudslides, snow storms or everyday mishaps.

The stock market. Because many insurance companies are publicly traded stock companies, or their asset portfolios are heavily traded, the insurance companies rely on their assets growing. When the stock market doesn't do well, it affects your premiums. The stock market crash of 2008 had a significant impact on insurance companies.

Whether or not you own in an area that has been affected by any of these natural disasters, your insurance premiums or ability to obtain insurance has likely been impacted. Insurance companies throughout the country are dropping homes like hot potatoes. In Florida alone, one well-known insurance company dropped 9,500 policies and another dropped 35,000 customers in 2005. And forget about new policies, they were not writing any.

Which homes do insurance companies drop first? Always the homes that are the highest risk for claims. Unfortunately, vacation homes most often fall into this category. Furthermore, many state insurance regulatory commissions and laws do not always protect vacation homes because these homes are not primary residences. So all the chatter about state-backed insurance likely will not apply to vacation rental and second-home owners (Florida does indeed have a state insurance program that can be written on vacation rentals—it's called Insurance of Last Resort and can be obtained through local agents).

Vacation homes are considered high risk because, frankly, they are high risk (from an insurance perspective). Think about it: Where are our properties? Most often in or around areas where natural disasters are more likely to occur—near the ocean (hurricanes), in ski areas (wild fires and snow), on lakes (flooding), and so on.

Another risk factor, which is equally important to insurance companies, is our homes are not occupied full time. To an insurance company an empty house equals increased risk—an unoccupied home means there is no one to address problems immediately, which intensifies the risk of further damages.

> ### *Insurance vocabulary lesson number one:*
>
> While speaking with insurance specialists, I found that there are a few words that we commonly use in the vacation rental world that have very different meanings with regards to insurance. For instance, the word *vacant* to vacation rental owners just means nights that our property is not rented. But to your insurance agent, *vacant* means the property has no furnishings and no one is ever occupying it. What we really have in a vacation rental situation is off-peak seasons when our properties are unoccupied. So strike the word *vacant* from your vocabulary when you are speaking with your insurance agents.

Then there are always the liability risks of having different people occupy your property nightly or weekly. To an insurance company the risks are much higher when you have strangers occupying your property as we do with vacation rentals.

As for the premiums, they have gone through the roof for everyone, even primary residences in major metropolitan areas. While second home owners who don't rent their properties will pay a premium above primary home insurance policies, vacation rental owners can expect to pay even more than second-home owners simply because we rent them out.

Qualification Factors

There are many things that affect the cost of your insurance policy but with vacation rental properties, sometimes these cost factors will also affect whether a company will write your policy at all. If you apply for insurance and are denied, unfortunately the insurance companies don't always tell you why you were denied. Below are just a few explanations of qualifications and cost setting factors for underwriting insurance and how they apply to vacation rental homes. Knowing these important facts could assist you in obtaining insurance.

Disclosure. Upon the application and the discovery process, you'll be asked many questions regarding your vacation rental home. It is imperative that you disclose all information to your insurance agents. Because it can be difficult to find insurance, many vacation rental owners are tempted to withhold information in order to obtain insurance. For example, some owners are tempted to omit information regarding renting their homes. It's important to note, if you misrepresent anything while obtaining insurance, you can possibly void your coverage should you have a claim, or worse yet be charged with a crime (for example, in Florida it's a felony). While the application will likely ask if the property is owner or tenant occupied, is it used for primary use or seasonal use, it may not specifically ask about renting your property on a nightly or weekly basis. It's imperative that you disclose this information.

Portfolio. While many people combine homeowner's, auto, umbrella, wind and flood insurance policies under one company in order to receive a discount on their premiums, combining your policies might be a necessity in order to obtain insurance for vacation rental homes. Your current company may not have a product available that will insure your vacation rental property, so this means you may have to leave your current insurance agent.

Deductibles. With a primary home policy, the amount of your deductible would affect the cost of your policy. Traditionally by increasing your deductible from $250 to $1000 your premiums will be reduced by as much as 25%. While the same thing holds true with vacation rental properties, you will see a decrease in cost with the increase of deductible, I doubt you'll find a company willing to write a policy with $250 deductible. They'll more likely ask if you want deductibles in the $1000 to $5000 ranges.

Claims. The number of claims you have made under *any* homeowners insurance policy, including your primary residence, will definitely affect your ability to obtain insurance for your vacation rental home. Any claims within the past three to five years will have the heaviest weight, though some insurance companies may look as far back as seven years. To me this is the most counterintuitive thing I have ever heard. You have insurance to cover damages, but if you make a claim you won't be able to get insurance? Thankfully in some states this is regulated; some companies will still offer coverage but may impose surcharges for past claims.

Management. Most insurance companies will not write your policy if you do not have a housekeeper, caretaker or handyman checking up on your property regularly.

Insurance vocabulary lesson number two:

When I was going through the insurance application process one of the questions they asked me was: Who *manages* your property?—We need the name of your property manager.

Of course I was stunned. I don't pull rank often, but this caught me off guard. Defensively I protested, "Property manager?!? I don't have a property manager! I wrote the book on managing vacation rental properties by owner."

The insurance company was looking for something a little different than what I define as property manager. To me, a property manager is a company that organizes and handles everything including housekeeping, maintenance and reservations. But from an insurance company's perspective they're more concerned about ongoing property maintenance. For insurance terminology, most vacation property owners do have a rental *manager*, but we're calling them something else—housekeeper, caretaker or handyman.

Business activity. While many vacation rental owners don't consider their homes a business, if you are renting out your property the insurance company considers it a business. If you only rent any more than two weeks per year, it's considered a rental business.

Security. Most insurance companies will ask if you have smoke detectors, dead bolts, fire extinguishers, gated-communities, monitored fire and burglar alarms, security guard on the premises, hurricane glass windows, or earthquake braces. If your answer to most of these is no, you may have a tough time obtaining insurance or it will severely affect the pricing of the policy. I would definitely consider adding some of these items.

Fire station. Other factors insurance companies take into account are how far away your home is from a fire station and water source, the accessibility of your property with regards to emergency response time and whether the fire fighters are paid or volunteer. Homes more than 5 miles from a fire station, and more than 1,000 feet from a fire hydrant need to have a pumpable pond, lake or stream nearby. Also, in absence of a year round accessible water source, the insurance company may inquire about the fire station's capabilities to bring water to the scene. It's helpful if you track down the phone number for the fire department and have it handy should the insurance company ask.

Credit history. The insurance company may use information in your credit history to determine your insurance score. While for primary residences your insurance score may raise or lower your premium, for vacation rental owners this could be another reason a company would deny insurance. (You should check your credit report and score before applying for insurance and settle any disputes or inaccuracies before applying for insurance. The free service is available through www.AnnualCreditReport.com—be careful, there are a lot of other sites that "claim" free reports, but this one is the official one). Some states have strict laws regarding how insurance companies use credit history. Check your state's insurance regulatory website or call the insurance commissioner's office for details.

Mortgage. If your property is paid in full or has a very low mortgage left, this could help you obtain insurance. While paying off your property isn't really feasible for most, when faced with the choice between making extra principal payments on your primary home or vacation home, from an insurance perspective, you might be better off paying it to your vacation home.

Year built. There are some insurance companies that will only insure new homes and others that will not insure older homes. Older homes, if recently updated to code with electrical, heating and plumbing systems, would be much easier to insure than ones without these renovations. In areas where hurricanes are prevalent, newer wind resistant windows and sliding glass doors, and hurricane shutters will play a major factor in the cost of your policy.

Smoking. If you allow your renters to smoke inside your property, this could also be a check mark against you. In today's society most smokers are accustomed to going outside to smoke anyway, so don't let them smoke in your home.

Types of Insurance Agents

When shopping for insurance you'll have three types of insurance agents to choose from. I suggest you start from the top of this list and work your way down. Be prepared to do a fair amount of searching for an agent who will insure your property. Whatever you do, don't give up until you find an agent ready and willing to find insurance that fits your needs.

Captive agents. Typically sell insurance for one company. An example would be State Farm or Nationwide agents; while these agents will likely be your starting point, captive agents often will not insure vacation rental homes. The problem is most captive agents have policies that are intended for owner occupied properties or second residences that are used solely by the owner. The short-term rental aspect will eliminate 95 percent of the traditional insurance companies.

Independent agent. Represents a multitude of insurance companies. Most often this is where you will find the insurance you will need. You'll probably have the most success when you go through an agent who writes policies for these companies: Chubb, Fireman's Fund, or Citizen's Property Insurance. To find an independent agent, you can go to their websites and look for an agent in your area. If you'll be consolidating your insurance portfolio, it'll be best to find an agent in your hometown.

Surplus line companies. To access a surplus lines company, you must go through an appointed independent agent. These agents sell a specialty product mainly for businesses called surplus lines insurance. Surplus lines insurance is commonly referred to the "insurance of last resort." Lloyds of London is one of the largest insurance providers of surplus lines insurance. The main disadvantages to this type of agent are the policies they sell are usually pretty expensive and state insurance protection programs do not back them. What this means to you is if there is a disaster that makes them go insolvent (bankrupt), and they're unable to make their claim obligations, the states have no bail out program which would pay your claim. For this reason, it's very important to check the financial status of any insurance company you're going to work with, especially surplus lines companies.

Note: It's very important to check the financial status of any insurance company you're going to work with. To check financial status, go to www.ambest.com and type in the name of the insurance company. You'll be able to pull up a little history of that insurance company, how long they've been in business, what their financial status is. What you'll really want to focus on is the company rating. Look for companies with a rating of "A," "A+" or "A++."

The Policy

A homeowner's policy will have four main components of coverage: Structure or dwelling, personal property and contents, loss of use and liability. When evaluating these individual sections of your policy here are some things to pay close attention to:

Dwelling. Pay close attention to the exemptions. For example, some policies will exclude wind (hurricane), mold, earthquakes or flood damages. If you are in an area prone to these perils, you will need to separately purchase policies that specifically cover these types of catastrophes.

Some vacation property owners, however, make a conscious decision not to purchase catastrophe insurance. For example, they own a condo on the 7th floor of a 20-story building and the homeowner's association (HOA) carries insurance for the building (commonly up to the inside sheetrock). While the HOA insurance policy would not cover your interior (furnishing, fixtures, appliances), the chances of total loss due to hurricane or flood damages to your home would be highly unlikely. Moreover, the estimated cost to repair or replace your interior fixtures and furnishing might not be worth the cost of obtaining coverage. Be aware though, should there be catastrophic damages, your HOA insurance policy might have a high deductible or may not cover all of the damages. After many of the 2004 and 2005 hurricanes, many condo owners were faced with tens of thousands of dollars in special assessments. If you have an individual wind or flood policy an added benefit may be coverage for special assessments imposed by your HOA.

Personal property. This is one part of your policy that you may be able to decrease the limits and save a little money. Most homeowner's policies factor in your personal belongings beyond furnishings, clothing, computers, jewelry, etc. Since this is not your primary residence you don't have as many things that would need to be replaced in case of a loss.

Loss of use or loss of rental income. The loss of use section of the policy is primarily for living expense should anything happen to your home. In most vacation rental policies, this will not be an allowable claim since this is not your primary residence. However, some policies will have a loss of rental income in place of living expenses portion of your policy. In this case, if any insurable damage occurs, you will be reimbursed a certain percentage (defined in your policy) of your average gross income for the time period that your home is not up and running as a rental.

Liability. The liability insurance written into your homeowner's policy is likely to be somewhere in the $100K–$300K range. Most insurance experts recommend vacation rental owners closely evaluate the need to extend liability limits via an umbrella policy. Most insurance experts advise that you ask for the maximum coverage possible.

In addition to the liability insurance that is written into your policy, many vacation rental owners opt to purchase a separate liability insurance policy—most often through an umbrella policy. The good news is umbrella policies are relatively inexpensive for the amount of coverage extended, usually running $200–$800 per one million dollars of coverage.

While researching for this chapter, I asked every insurance specialist the recommended amount for the liability insurance. They all said, "However much you get sued for." While I was a bit annoyed with their "skirting the question" response, I can understand it. The answer varies so much depending on the individual's financial assets and risk exposure. Simply put, the more money you have, they more you have to lose. They did highly recommend that everyone speak with their agents to individually determine the exact exposure in order to determine how much liability insurance they'll likely need.

Personal injury. Be sure to look at the exclusions in the personal injury section of your policy. While liability coverage will likely cover bodily injury and property damage to others, personal injury often includes wrongful evictions, entry or arrests.

Conclusion

Obtaining insurance for your vacation rental property might be a difficult task. You'll have to determine which types of insurance you'll need and you may have to look for other types of agents beyond the traditional captive agents that you are accustomed to calling. The key is finding the right agent who writes policies that fit all of your needs. Though I have heard a lot of complaints from owners who have said they've had difficulty finding insurance for their vacation rentals homes, I have yet to hear one who ran out of options entirely.

When obtaining insurance for your vacation rental home:

- Find an agent who can fit all your insurance needs;
- Start with your current insurance agent. If he or she cannot assist you, seek an independent agent;
- Call the insurance commissioner's office if you have specific questions regarding insurance within your state;
- Check the financial status of any insurance company you're going to work with (www.ambest.com).

When speaking with your agents:

- Disclose all information about the rental aspect of your vacation home;
- Be sure to discuss your liability exposure to assess the need for an umbrella policy;
- When they ask you if you have a property manager—as long as you have a housekeeper, caretaker or maintenance person, the answer to this question is yes;
- If they ask you if your property is vacant—as long as your property is furnished and you're actively renting your home even only a few weeks per year, the answer to this question is no;
- If they ask about business activity—as long as you are renting your property, the answer to this question is yes, short-term rental.

When reviewing your policy:

- Be sure your policy has sufficient coverage to replace or rebuild your home in the event of total loss;

+ Double check exclusions within the policy;
+ Determine your risks of catastrophic events and purchase wind (hurricane), flood, earthquake and/or extended liability insurance separately.

After you have acquired insurance, be sure to:

+ Read, understand and know your policy;
+ Maintain a record of personal property within your vacation rental home (photos and videos work well);
+ Keep good records of your rental income;
+ Review your policy annually;
+ Make sure your coverage keeps pace with appreciation;
+ Pay your policy on time and whatever you do, don't ever let it lapse.

In closing, I'll leave your with a "learn from my mistake" lesson on insurance:

When I lived in Atlanta, I had my liability insurance for my vacation rental homes through an umbrella policy with my primary residence. When we moved from Atlanta to Austin, we took the normal course of action: sell the current home, then buy the new one.

We sold our home quickly but we decided we would build a home so that meant renting a house for nine months to a year—since we didn't own a home, no need for homeowner's insurance. We never gave the "umbrella" portion of our insurance a thought when we cancelled our policy. Bad move! Try to find insurance after your policy has had an interruption in coverage. It's not easy.

Furthermore, we had our hurricane insurance through a different company. Unfortunately, hurricane insurance also wasn't at the top of my mind when I was filling out all of those change of address forms.

The hurricane insurance was through a surplus lines agent. Their billing process was to send out one bill (which I did receive but somehow got buried in the boxes and mess of moving). I never received a follow up bill or a call from my agent. The next thing I got was a cancellation notice (because of the change of address and rerouting of my mail, unfortunately the cancellation notice came after it was cancelled). Super bad move!

When I realized that my insurance lapsed, I called the insurance company, explained my dilemma and after many years with them without a single claim, they used that opportunity to drop me like a hot potato.

Finding another insurance company that would insure my properties was a huge pain in the neck—it took weeks of phone calls. In the end, I did find a company that would insure me, but I went from paying approximately $600 per year per property to $1375 per year per property. The good thing is I have much better coverage than I originally had and I learned enough about insurance to write this whole chapter.

CHAPTER

5

Buying the Right Place ... For You

We're now at the point where you've made certain critical decisions. You have carefully analyzed your personal situation, you've crunched the numbers, and you've decided that buying a vacation property does indeed make sense for you. Now what? How exactly do you go about the process of buying the right place for you? The choices you make at this stage of the game will impact your finances and lifestyle for many years to come.

Let's start by eliminating the "don't wanters," those aspects of a vacation property that you don't want, under any circumstances. First, you do not want to purchase a home where there are laws or restrictions prohibiting short-term or transient rentals. Wait, let me say that again—do NOT purchase

69

where there are restrictions against short term rentals. Check the local laws and neighborhood or complex rules.

Another category you would want to eliminate is neighborhoods that have specific rules and rental exclusives. For example, condominium complexes are notorious for having rules about renting for less than thirty days. Some condo complexes exclusive in-house rental management companies which would prohibit you from renting by owner—if your objective is to cash flow on your property, I would stay away from these types of properties.

Some municipalities have very strict guidelines as to when you can and cannot rent, some do not allow rentals at all. Properties on government owned land, such as Army Corp of Engineers, or state and nationally protected lands often carry very strict rules also. This is where a licensed local real estate agent would most likely be a valuable source for information.

Fixer-upper. As for the structure itself, I would not recommend you purchase a property that requires a lot of maintenance. Even if you are the handyman type, this new venture will be quite different than fixing things up around your own residence once in a while. It's not just a quick trip to the local home improvement mega store to pick up a new storm door or a washer for that pesky leaky kitchen faucet. No, if you buy a high maintenance house, costly repairs will require frequent attention. And here's the key—you'll be doing it *at a distance*. Chances are, your vacation property is not going to be right up the street from where you live (otherwise, going there wouldn't be much of a vacation!). So every time the vacation home needs maintenance, you will have to get in the car and make a long drive, arriving worn and tired before you even begin the work. The alternative—hiring workers to do the job—can be quite expensive. And, you won't be there to supervise the work they do and to make sure they don't run up the bill. Not a good idea. There's a good deal of truth in the old adage: "If you want something done right, do it yourself." But it can be rather difficult when you live many miles away.

The solution? Buy a low-maintenance property. I know that sounds incredibly simple, but you might be surprised at how easy it can be to overlook things that should be obvious. After all, this is probably something you've never done before, and nothing is ever simple until you have some experience with it. The best way to find out the condition of a house is by employing a home inspector. It's always money well spent. Of particular interest in the home inspector's report will be the condition of the roof, electrical wiring, heating system, and the plumbing. These are all non-cosmetic items that often are not readily apparent to the naked eye. But they are some of the major areas of a house that tend to erode with time, and repairing them can be expensive and time consuming. Buy a home without these problems to begin with, and you will save yourself many days of headaches in the years ahead.

Here's another consideration to take into account. Many people think it's a great bargain to do the exact opposite of what I've just said. They intentionally buy a house with many problems because the price will be lower. Then, they rehab this diamond in the rough and end up with a lavish home for a cheap price. While that may sound good in theory, and there certainly are cases where people have made money this way, doing a successful rehab is much more difficult than most people imagine. Did you ever see the movie *The Money Pit?* It may be a Hollywood comedy, and an exaggeration, but it also contains a valuable lesson. Just like when the you get an estimate on any project, when the final numbers are added up, it inevitably seems that the project comes in over budget. The same tends to be true when you try to rehab a house with a number of repair issues. Moreover, during the period that you are making your repairs you will not be able to rent it out. Your cash flow will be put on hold indefinitely. I'm not ruling the idea out completely, but carefully consider these potential problems before going the rehab route.

Now that all being said, there are some great "fixer-upper" deals out there right now.

Last year I purchased a condo that needed some work. Perhaps that's an understatement—it needed to be gutted and totally rebuilt. When we purchased it we calculated that it would cost around $40,000 to renovate. Once we started tearing down the sheetrock and exposing the wiring and plumbing we opened up Pandora's Box. In the end we ended up $35,000 over budget. But, since we purchased the property for such a ridiculously low price, even factoring in the extra costs, the total investment was still below market price and significantly below the peak market price.

Aesthetic rehab. In viewing properties, many people overlook purchasing properties that just need a measure of TLC—tender loving care. Those who can see past the blemishes and visualize a polished result—and willingly add their own sweat equity—are able to pay less money and realize quick appreciation.

The following owner actually looked for a property that needed cosmetic upgrades.

Already owning and successfully renting an investment property, Erin was ready to purchase another. She could see possibilities of beauty among the scruffiest properties and shopped for properties selling for less than market value. One she found was $20,000 less than comparable properties. But you guessed it—it was ugly. It had outdated 1970s décor, little curb appeal, and the need for some TLC. But she went for it. She and her husband worked for two solid weeks painting, pulling up carpeting, installing hardwood floors, extending decks and installing a hot tub, landscaping, and tossing old furnishings and adding new ones. They spent $12,000 plus their two weeks of hard work, and had a diamond to show for it.

Condominiums. I personally love condominiums. For starters, maintenance is much easier. There is no roof to repair, no lawn to mow (you probably do enough of that at your residence!), no snow to shovel, and no leaves to rake. Moreover, a condominium complex in all likelihood will include a bunch of nice extras that you probably won't get in a single family dwelling, such as Olympic-size pools, hot tubs, golf courses, health clubs, and more.

And one of the best advantages of condos is that they usually are situated in the very best locations—right on the beach, right next to that big ski mountain, or directly on the lake. Developers know all of the ideal spots to buy up real estate, and they always manage to get their hands on the most coveted land and turn it into something beautiful.

Here's what real estate pro Jack Simpson said on the subject: "You should always consider the view value of a property before buying. Maybe view isn't the only thing to you personally, or perhaps you aren't even going to live there. But, you should still consider view. Properties with a good view will rent better and be worth more when it's time to sell." Moreover your prospective renters will more often ask about the view first.

Now the downside. Some condo associations limit the use of the property. For example, in some towns you may be required to occupy the premises yourself for a certain number of weeks per year. This means, of course, that you can't rent as much as you want. They can also impose various rules about renting, such as age restrictions, minimum rental periods and "quiet times." They can sometimes charge "special assessments" that you would never have to pay with a single-family home.

Lastly, condos generally have homeowner's fees that are due either monthly or quarterly. When evaluating a condo purchase these fees must also be incorporated in the costs. If you have never owned a condo, this could be a mental barrier. Evaluating the costs of the association dues versus the properties that do not have association dues, the properties that are not covered by the homeowners associations cost more. The maintenance and upkeep of the exterior and grounds add up much faster than you realize.

Still, when you look at the big picture, I think the benefits of condo ownership outweigh the drawbacks. They may not be the perfect solution for a vacation home, but I think purchasing a vacation condo will be a decision you won't regret.

Build or Buy Existing?

Another area that you need to explore before making your final decision about a purchase is the question: do you build (buy pre-construction) or buy a home that is already built? There is a whole set of factors to consider. First, you need to realize that in most cases buying pre-construction can be more expensive up front. You usually have to come up with a larger down payment. You also have to buy all of the furnishings. This is in sharp contrast to purchasing a vacation home that has already been built, as these homes typically are sold fully furnished. Not only does buying the furnishings mean paying additional money, it also means additional work. Be prepared to spend a good deal of time cruising furniture stores, looking for sales, making sure what you want is in stock, setting up delivery dates, and handling a number of other hassles. On the other hand, you won't have to worry about buying a home that you love that comes with a set of furniture that you hate!

I should also mention that although buying a pre-construction home can be expensive initially, in the long run you might be better off financially. The reason is appreciation. In all likelihood, you will see better appreciation in your first three years of ownership with a pre-construction. This is because of the delay between the day you purchase a pre-construction and the day it is actually built. Typically, that can be three years for a condo and one year for a house. The builder needs to sell at a reduced price so he or she can get the project off the ground, so he or she sells pre-constructions at a reduced rate, which later works to your benefit in the form of accelerated appreciation in the years immediately following your purchase.

For a more detailed look at just how this process works, read what Jack Simpson, owner of Holiday Isle Properties, a real estate company, said in a recent article:

First, the developer acquires the land and applies for a construction loan. To reduce risk, lenders typically require the developer to sell at least half of the condo units with a binding contract before funding the construction loan. Since it is harder to sell sky and paper than something that you can actually see and feel, the developer discounts the purchase price to achieve the required pre-sales. Pre-sales are usually done first on a non-binding reservation agreement with a few thousand dollars as a good faith deposit. This is called the reservation stage. Buyers can opt out anytime in this stage and receive a full refund.

After the lender-required units are reserved, the developer delivers the final condominium documents to the buyers. These documents describe the condominium project in great detail. This is called the contract stage. Buyers then have 15 days to look over the documents and decide whether to "go hard on the contract" or to back out and have their reservation deposits refunded. Going hard on the contract normally requires buyers to make an additional deposit, which combined with the reservation fee, will be 20% of the purchase price. At hard contract stage, the deposit becomes non-refundable. Some fallout may occur as the result of a few buyers opting out. With the required number of firm contracts in hand, the developer has the construction loan funded and building begins. Buyers do not close and start making payments until the project is completed with a certificate of occupancy.

Timing. Like so many other aspects of business, when it comes to deciding exactly when to purchase your vacation home, timing is everything. Please don't waste your money by making your purchase at the wrong time. And when would that be? At the height of the rental season. That may not have been the answer you expected, but there is a good reason for it. That is the time when there are the fewest available vacation homes for sale, which makes it a seller's market. As the buyer, it's not a good deal for you. The opposite, of course, is true during the off-season. At that time there are many more available vacation homes for sale to choose from, which tends to lower prices and create more of a buyer's market.

Another reason why buying during the off-season makes sense will become clear to you when you become more familiar with how the vacation rental cycle works. Most renters book their vacations 60 to 90 days ahead of time. So if you buy in February, for example (the middle of the off-season in most U.S. locations), you will be in an excellent position to lock in renters for May and beyond. By contrast, if you made the mistake of buying during the peak of the season (let's say July) by the time you were ready to start accepting new renters you would have already missed out on some of the prime months for vacationers. That would mean more of the expenses right up front would have to be paid out of your pocket rather than by the renters. See why timing is so important?

Price. When you're finally ready to buy, the critical issue of price rises to the forefront. First, let me say that today the real estate market is still a bit unstable in some markets. There are markets that have not yet seen their proverbial "bottom" and there are other markets that are in recovery mode—the prices have stabilized and/or are increasing. While this is a great time to buy, we are by no means in a "quick-flip" market. You should expect to buy and hold the property two to five years to see any significant appreciation. As long as your decisions are based on a longer-term strategy, you should be safe during the holding period. You can rent out the property and generate revenue from it—the property should pay for itself. In other words, the cash flow from the rentals will make you impervious to even cataclysmic fluctuations in real estate prices.

Do Your Research

Gone are the days of going on vacation and coming home with a second home. You need to do a lot of research and homework so that you can protect yourself and ensure you're making a sound long-term investment.

Here are some tips you can quickly reference when shopping for a vacation home.

Start with a plan. Whether you're buying for personal use or for investment, you should start with a business plan, just as you would if you were starting any new business. To be confident in a sound investment takes a lot of research.

Buy with your wallet not your heart. Make sure you're buying a smart investment. It's especially difficult for vacation homebuyers because we tend to use our emotions more than our heads. It's easy to get caught up and sign on the dotted line when you see that gorgeous beach home or perfect ski resort. Why do you think so many people own timeshares? Because they get caught in the moment and only see the romantic side of ownership without doing the due diligence.

Research the area. Is this a new, emerging area? Or is it an older, more developed area? If you are looking to purchase in an area that's well developed, such as Cape Cod, then there's less to worry about. The supply is so low in these areas that historically they indeed hold their value. But in an emerging market such as Southeast Florida, you should exercise caution to be sure that there are not too many new developments such that the inventory exceeds demand.

Utilize your real estate agent. Pick your agent's brain. Ask tons of questions, scour through his or her website and absorb as much information as possible. After all, your agent is getting paid to be knowledgeable in this area. Use his or her expertise to your advantage.

Look for large credible developers. Developers do more research than any single buyer could ever dream of doing or affording. They sink thousands of dollars into researching the market, tourism, growth, and inventory. If you find credible developers your chances of failing are significantly less.

Beware of overextending with adjustable rate mortgages. Yes you can afford that payment with a 2.85% interest rate, but be realistic. That interest rate will not last forever. In five to seven years the interest rates and your payment is likely to go up. You might be saying, I'll just sell when the rates rise, but so might thousands of others. You might be stuck with a property that's difficult to sell and you cannot afford.

Leave your options open. You may be saying, "I want to buy a vacation home for personal use. I never intend on renting it out." Well that is perfectly fine but "never say never". Today it may be financially feasible to NOT rent your home, but what will tomorrow bring? What will change in your finances over the years? Will you be retiring? Will your children be attending college? Will the tax rate for the property skyrocket? What about the simple costs of ownership? Buy in an area where you know you can utilize, as a safety net, the option to rent your property.

Stay away from areas with short-term rental bans. The best way to protect yourself from market fluctuation is to leave your options open to rent your property on a nightly or weekly basis when you are not using it. Some complexes, towns or cities may have areas where covenants or laws restrict renting on a short-term basis. If you stay away from purchasing in these areas, then you're leaving your options open to turn your vacation home into an income-producing asset.

All in all, vacation homes are still good long-term investments. If you make well-researched and educated decisions you'll be setting yourself up for success rather than failure. Smart investing is all about eliminating your risks from the start.

Make an Offer

The best position to be in is to be pre-approved for a mortgage (in writing) before you pick up the phone and talk to the first real estate broker. This can, in many cases, put you in the driver's seat, setting the stage for buying a vacation home significantly below its market value. When you are pre-approved, you are automatically much more attractive to sellers. It all depends, of course, on the market conditions. In a tight market, the sellers are more likely to get their asking price, or close to it. So you have to know how to adapt your bids to changing conditions (much the way you would with the stock market). If it is a buyer's market, not only should you not accept the asking price, you should go for a much lower price.

Many people are afraid or intimidated to bid lower than the asking price. Don't be. No one is going to be offended. This isn't personal (it's not like you're saying, "I think your house is lousy."). This is a business transaction. You don't know the sellers' circumstances. They might be going through a divorce, bankruptcy, or some other hardship and are desperate to sell. Your significantly lower bid might be perfectly acceptable to them. Besides, you have nothing to lose by trying. The worst they can say is "No," usually with a counter-offer, and then you can continue to negotiate. There is no reason in the world why you shouldn't try to get the best possible deal for yourself.

I put an offer for $50,000 less than the asking price on one of the properties I recently purchased. My real estate agent was very reluctant to submit such a low offer because this property was already priced around $25,000 lower than market price—they wanted to sell it quickly. I was buying with cash and offered a quick closing. Much to everyone's surprise, the seller countered back at $40,000 less than the asking price.

Case Studies

Let me share a few case studies with you to give you a better understanding of some of the different scenarios we've been discussing. All of these stories are true, but the names have been changed for privacy reasons.

> Lauren bought a two-bedroom, two-bath pre-construction, beachfront condo in Florida. She bought during the pre-sale stage. The purchase price at pre-sale was $195,000. At the time of hard contract, she had to put down 20% of the purchase price; she put 10% down ($19,500) and had a secured letter of credit for the remainder of the 20% deposit. The construction took three years to complete. Lauren closed on the property the day it was built and sold it two hours later for $325,000. So her initial cash investment of $19,500 became $130,000 earning her $110,500 in three years! That's an annualized return of 88.2% and a return for the entire three year period of 566.59%.

Here's another story that I think you will find informative.

> Gabe bought the same two-bedroom, two-bath home as Lauren, at the same price, and at the same time. He chose to furnish his unit and rent it (furnishings cost him $16,000). In the first year, his rentals were slow and sparse, and he had to pay out $5,000 out-of-pocket to pay the mortgage and expenses. The second year he had better rental business and just barely managed break-even cash flow, having to pay $1,000

out-of-pocket. He sold his unit, after two years of renting, for $400,000. Coupled with the two years of rental loss and the cost to furnish the property, it cost him around $22,000 in extra cash investment. Now, let's break down precisely what happened. Gabe invested a total of $41,500 (down payment + furnishings + negative cash flow for the first two years) over five years, and it became $164,500! That's an annualized return of 52.61% and a return for the entire five-year period of 727.78%!

While these numbers are certainly high and are best-case scenarios, these kinds of investments really do exist in the marketplace. You just have to do some research to find them.

Here's another example.

Ashley purchased an existing, furnished beachfront condo for $165,000. She put down $8,250. She had positive cash flow from day one, earning $23,000 (above and beyond all the expenses) over the five-year period. She earned $2,000 the first year, $3,500 the second year, $4,100 the third year, $6,000 the fourth year, and $7,400 the last year. She sold the condo for $300,000. That's an annualized return of 40.58%, with return for the entire period of 449.06%.

Let me show you yet another perspective.

I spoke with Sean, who co-owns a cabin with his two siblings in Illinois. The three siblings live in different areas all over the country. In 1996, they had an interesting idea. Their father owns and lives on a beautiful 100-acre property (the family homestead). Their initial intent was to build a cabin that they all could use for family gatherings. Although they did not need to make the initial investment for the land, they still incurred building and furnishing costs. They decided that the best way to offset those cost was to rent out their cabin part of the time. Being in an obscure area with no real tourism and no option to use a management company, they decided to rent their cabin themselves (by owner). They were not sure how successful they would be but figured any amount, even small, could help offset their costs and still enable them to use the property themselves. Well, they put their property on the internet, and much to their surprise, people wanted to rent it. Their property rents mostly on weekends, and they rent a few full weeks per year. This family found that the rentals not only paid for their bank note but also allowed them some extra income to upgrade (hot tub, swing set, etc.) and maintain their cabin. For maintenance, they get together at least one week per year at their cabin. During that week, they designate one workday. Sean said, "We all pitch in and work together to accomplish our deep clean and maintenance list." Naturally, they are very pleased with their decision to build and rent their cabin.

OK, here's another example of some folks who purchased their vacation house for self use and are renting it out to help pay for it.

Zachary and his wife own property in a popular Colorado ski resort. They purchased it 15 years ago. They live two hours away. They rent it 10–16 weeks per year but use their property a whopping 60 nights a year themselves! They are very selective about their renters and actually turn down rentals. They strictly rent only to offset the costs for personal use. They find most of their renters through the internet, but also find the local ski magazines/brochures a useful advertising tool. They have found that renting in a ski area, all of their renters expect a hot tub. Zachary is a member of the condominium board, and he pushed for the complex to build a hot tub on the premises. They stated that this was a very wise investment for the complex. And now it has one.

One last note about your adventure in buying: you don't have to do it alone. You may initially think that if you work directly with the seller, cutting out the middleman, you will save money. The risks may outweigh the benefits. Especially if you are buying in an area you are not familiar with, there are so many things a qualified professional real estate agent can help you with. If you are buying in a different state, for example, often the laws governing real estate are different than the laws in your home state. You need someone who is thoroughly familiar with the area and its vacation scene, someone who can readily answer the dozens of questions you're likely to have. But don't become completely reliant on your real estate agent. Make sure you do your homework each step of the way. After all, you're the one who will be signing all of those papers at closing. And you're the one who will be enjoying your wonderful new vacation home for years to come. Happy hunting!

6

Buying with Family, Friends or Strangers

Because the second home market boom has affected the affordability of vacation properties in many areas, a growing trend in acquiring second homes is co-ownership. Buyers are purchasing their second homes together with other people—family, friends, or complete strangers. When done properly, co-ownership can work very well for all, but when done poorly, it can be an absolute nightmare.

For information on co-ownership, I have turned to the expert in this field—Andy Sirkin. He is an accredited instructor with the California Department of Real Estate, and frequently conducts co-ownership workshops for attorneys, real estate agents, corporations, and prospective homebuyers. You can find his contact information in Appendix 5.

Co-Ownership 101

By Andy Sirkin

What is Co-Ownership?

Vacation home co-ownership (sometimes also known as vacation home partnership or fractional ownership) is an arrangement where several individuals or families buy vacation property together and share the costs and use of the property. Typically, each of the co-owners owns a percentage of the property, is shown on the title and deed as an owner, and acts as a co-borrower on a mortgage. In some cases, particularly where the property is located outside the United States but the owners reside in the United States, the property will be owned by a company (foreign, domestic or sometimes both) formed for the purpose of holding title, and the co-owners will own the company. A detailed co-ownership agreement (sometimes also known as an operating agreement, shareholder's agreement or bylaws) allocates usage rights, costs and responsibilities among the co-owners.

Why Co-Own a Vacation Home?

Although many people dream of owning vacation property, most either can't afford the type of property they want, or reason that they would not use the vacation home often enough to justify the expense. Fractional ownership provides a solution to these problems by allowing you to pay only a fraction of the costs and ongoing expenses of vacation home ownership, and share the risks of unforeseen maintenance problems and value depreciation with others. Of course, in exchange for spreading the costs and risks, you give up some of the usage rights and freedoms that you would have if you owned the property alone. But job and school commitments prevent most people from using a vacation home for more than a few weeks or months each year, and some loss of freedom and control is often an acceptable sacrifice for the huge cost savings.

Is It a Time Share?

Although the ownership structures of arrangements known generally as "time shares" vary from place to place and among different developments, these arrangements always involve a large group of owner/users, an organizer who put the deal together, and an outside management company that will operate the property. By contrast, vacation home co-ownership generally involves only 2–12 families, no organizer or developer, and the option of self-management. Although it is impossible to make a generalization about which type of arrangement is best, here are some issues to consider when comparing possibilities:

- What is my per-night cost when I add up all of my annual costs (including management fees and dues) and divide them by the number of days I can use the property?
- Will I have any control over how my costs (particularly management fees and dues) increase over time?
- To what extent am I free to rent out the vacation home and control the rent charged?
- If I want to vacation somewhere else, how easy is it to get the location I want at the time I want it?
- How readily can I re-sell, and is there actually a market for my interest?

How to Allocate Usage?

Deciding how the vacation home will be used is usually the first step in structuring the co-ownership arrangement. Focusing on usage first usually makes the rest of the organizational process easier. This is because a co-owner's right to use the home, or his/her right to earn rental income, are the most important and valuable benefits of ownership.

There are two basic models for allocating usage rights. In the "Usage Assignment Approach," each owner is assigned the exclusive right to use the home during a specified number of days, weeks or months each year. The usage periods can be fixed (such as "the month of February" or "the first two weeks of February and July") or variable (meaning they are selected each year based on a rotation system adjusted for holidays and seasonal variations). During each co-owner's assigned usage period, he/she can live in the home, allow family and friends to use it, rent it out (and keep the rental income), swap it, or leave it empty. When the Usage Assignment Approach is used, the purchase price of the home is generally shared among the co-owners based on the amount of usage allocated to each co-owner. When usage periods are permanently fixed, price allocation may also be influenced by the quality of each owner's assigned usage dates.

The second basic model for allocating usage rights is the "Pay-To-Use Approach." In this arrangement, co-owners pay a pre-agreed "usage fee" for each day or week of usage. The usage fees, along with any rental income generated if the home is also rented to non-owners, are used to pay the expenses of ownership. If the usage fees and rental income together exceed the expenses, the surplus is divided among the owners; if there is a shortfall, each owner must contribute. Here again, there are a variety of methods (discussed below) for determining when and how often each owner will be permitted to use the home, and how usage will be allocated if two or more owners wish to use the home at the same time. When the Pay-To-Use Approach is used, the purchase price and ownership of the home can be divided based on what each co-owner can afford, their investment goals, or any other criteria the group finds useful, but purchase price and ownership need not have any relationship to usage.

There are a large number of variations and hybrids on these basic usage rights allocation models, and each group needs to find an approach that works for them and their property. For example, it is possible to employ the Usage Assignment Approach, but still allocate a certain number of weeks each year as "Pay-To-Use" weeks, meaning that during those times the home will be rented out to owners or to non-owners and the resulting income split among the owners in proportion to ownership. In another variation, it is possible to employ the Pay-To-Use Approach but still give co-owners preferences or discounts for a certain number of weeks each year.

How Are Fractional Vacation Home Co-Ownerships Financed?

Historically, vacation home co-ownership groups that needed bank financing had to obtain a mortgage as a group. Although this is still the most popular financing method for vacation fractional co-ownership arrangements, some lenders have recently begun offering fractional financing which allows each co-owner to obtain a separate loan secured only by his/her fractional ownership interest. Individual financing remains difficult to locate and significantly more expensive than group financing.

If there will be a group mortgage, the group will need to calculate how to divide the mortgage payments. If the down payment is shared in the same proportion as the price, the mortgage will also be divided in proportion to price. So, for example, if five families each buy an equal share of a $500,000 home, and each put down $20,000, they will divide the mortgage payments equally. Where the mortgage will be divided in proportion to ownership, the mortgage payments can be lumped together with the operating expenses and handled as described in the preceding paragraph.

On the other hand, if some co-owners contribute more down payment than others (relative to their price), the mortgage division will be different than the ownership division. To illustrate, imagine five families want to share equally a $500,000 home, and plan to buy it with a $100,000 down payment and a $400,000 mortgage. Now suppose Family #1 has only $10,000 for down payment, Family #2 has $30,000 for down payment, and the other families each have $20,000. Family #1 will be buying a $100,000 share of the property with a $10,000 down payment, meaning they will need to borrow $90,000 of the $400,000 mortgage or 22.5% (90/400). Family #2 will be buying a $100,000 share of the property with a $30,000 down payment, meaning they will need to borrow $70,000 of the $400,000 mortgage or 17.5% (70/400). Each of the other families will be buying a $100,000 share of the property with $20,000 down payments, meaning they will each need to borrow $80,000 of the $400,000 mortgage or 20% (80/400). In this situation, all mortgage payments will be divided according to amount borrowed, meaning Family #1 will pay 22.5%, Family #2 will pay 17.5%, and each of the other families will pay 20%. Where the mortgage will be not divided in proportion to ownership, the mortgage payments should be calculated separately from the operating expenses.

How Do Vacation Home Co-Owners Share Expenses?

The starting point for allocating property tax among the co-owners should be the amount that each co-owner paid for his/her interest. When the property tax is increased as the result of the resale of a fractional share, the buyer should pay the entirety of the increase. A resale by one co-owner should never increase a non-selling co-owner's property tax burden.

Other operating expenses such as insurance, maintenance, repairs, improvements, utilities and management are usually divided in proportion to ownership, so that a 20% owner will pay 20% of each of these expenses. When using the Pay-To-Use Approach, owner usage fees and rental income would be offset against expenses, and the 20% owner (after paying the usage fees for any days or weeks he/she spent in the home) would get 20% of any surplus if income exceeds expenses, or pay 20% of any deficit if expenses exceed income.

The Usage Assignment Approach

As noted above, one variation of the Usage Assignment Approach is to permanently assign specific dates to particular owners. Inevitably, certain usage dates are more desirable than others because of seasonal climate, school vacations, local events and other factors, and these differences should be taken into consideration when allocating price. It is important to remember that there is no particular advantage to allocating things equally, particularly when such an allocation would lead to unfair results.

Co-owner groups employing the Usage Assignment Approach without permanently assigned usage dates need to establish a fair and predictable system for determining when each owner will be able to use his/her days, weeks or months. It is important that each of the co-owners have the ability to plan vacations well in advance. I suggest that the usage period assignment system have the following elements:

- Usage blocks should have minimum and maximum lengths, and rules to govern whether a particular co-owner can take consecutive blocks, or multiple blocks within a particular season. Both the blocks, and the aggregation rules, can vary depending on time of year, so that the rules during a less popular time of year could be less strict.
- There should be a specific time of each year when usage assignments for the following year will be established. Once the usage assignments are established for the year, they cannot be changed except when willing co-owners trade with each other.

- There should be a rotating preference system to determine the order in which co-owners will choose their usage blocks each year.
- There should be a central website, log or file where all of the usage assignments and trades are recorded, so that there is a record to resolve usage disputes.

The Pay-To-Use Approach

The Pay-To-Use Approach is considerably more difficult to administer than the Usage Assignment Approach, and care must be taken to ensure maximum occupancy and avoid conflicts. I suggest that the usage allocation system have the following elements:

- There should be a manager (who could be a group member) or management company in charge of reservations and collections.
- As with the Usage Assignment Approach, usage blocks and aggregation rules should be established to make sure all co-owners get a fair chance to use the vacation home at the most desirable times of year.
- Usage costs/rental rates must be established for each year in advance. These could vary depending on length of stay, time of year, and whether or not the user is a co-owner. If co-owners pay less than rental tenants, it can be useful to allocate a maximum number of "discounted" days, weeks or months that each co-owner can use (which can also be seasonal), and whether co-owners can assign these "discounted" periods to family or friends.
- There should be a specific time of each year when co-owners can reserve usage blocks for the following year, based on a rotating preference system. The co-owner reservation period should occur before the home is offered for rent to non-owners. Of

course, co-owners should be allowed to use the home during periods that have not previously been reserved by other owners or renters, generally on a first-reserved-first-served basis.

Management

It is useful to divide fractional vacation home management tasks into four categories: usage allocation, accounting, cleaning, and repair. Any of these jobs can be handled by either co-owners or outside professionals, can involve compensation or not, and can be combined as needed for efficiency or convenience.

The tasks involved in usage management will be different depending on whether the group is using a Usage Assignment Approach or a Pay-To-Use Approach. If the Usage Assignment Approach is employed, usage management will involve administering the usage assignment system for each year and keeping track of the results. If the Pay-To-Use Approach is employed, usage management will involve administering the advance co-owner reservation system, soliciting and managing rentals by non-owners, and tracking (and possibly collecting) co-owner usage fees and rental payments.

Accounting management will involve collecting payments from co-owners (and possibly from rental tenants), paying bills, and keeping records. To avoid disputes and cash shortfalls which could result in credit blemishes and even loss of the property, it is absolutely essential to collect co-owner payments based on a budget and regular assessment system rather than "as needed." This means that at the end of each year, the accounting manager estimates all of the expenses for the following year, including mortgage, property tax, insurance, maintenance, repairs, improvements, utilities and management, offsets those expenses against any anticipated income from co-owner usage fees or rental income, and determines the amount, if any, that will be needed from each co-owner to pay the bills. The anticipated expenses should include some reserves for long-term recurring expenses such as painting, roofing, system upkeep, and furniture and appliance replacement. The amount required from each co-owner should then be divided into equal monthly or quarterly payments, and each owner should be required to contribute his/her payment on schedule. In this way, each co-owner knows with a fairly high degree of precision what will be expected of him/her in the coming year, and it is easy to track whether a co-owner is meeting his/her obligations before a significant problem develops. Obviously, unforeseen expenses can always arise, but it is still critical to budget for the expenses you know you will have. It is very risky, and an awful lot of work, to wait until funds are needed and then attempt to reach each owner to try to collect.

Cleaning is a management task with a surprisingly high potential to cause displeasure and discord within the group. Most co-owners enjoy using their vacation home much more when they arrive to find it clean and orderly, and cleanliness is essential for successful rental to non-owners. Unless an unusually consistent and high standard of cleanliness and order prevails among all of the co-owners in the group (and their families and friends), it is likely that resentment and even anger will develop over the condition of the home when certain users leave. It is also true that you are supposed to be on vacation when you use the home, and you may not want to have to spend the last day of your vacation cleaning. For all of these reasons, I strongly advise vacation home co-owner groups to employ a cleaner or cleaning service to clean the property on a regular basis. This can be done most efficiently when the usage blocks are fairly uniform in length, and the cleaning corresponds with the end of the blocks. The cleaning person can also monitor the condition of the property, and inform the co-owners when a particular co-owner or guest has damaged, broken or stolen something. One of the best things about vacation home co-ownership is that you can spread the cost of this type of service over the entire group, rather than paying for it yourself.

Repair management is important because without it, no one person is responsible for keeping the home in good repair, and small inexpensive problems can develop into large expensive ones. The repair manager should be responsible for periodically inspecting the property, fielding comments and complaints from co-owners, and arranging for and supervising repairs. If the repair manager will be doing any major repairs him/herself, it is important to establish, before beginning work, whether the repair manager will be compensated and, if so, how much. "Time and materials" compensation should be avoided because it often leads to disputes, particularly where the repair manager is not a professional contractor and may not use his/her time and/or the materials efficiently. A much better approach is to establish a scope of work, time for completion, and payment amount in advance. This avoids most potential disputes and allows the group to compare the repair manager's proposal to bids from outside contractors.

How to Make Decisions

Regardless of how many co-owners will be in the group, it is useful to establish certain mandatory duties, things the group will be required to do unless all owners otherwise agree. These mandatory duties should include allocating usage, paying the recurring operating expenses, and maintaining the building in good condition. Establishing mandatory duties prevents an individual owner (in a group of only two owners), or a majority of owners (in a group of three or more owners), from taking actions that endanger the group investment.

For actions that are not mandated by the co-ownership agreement, the group needs to vote. In groups of only two co-owners, voting is obviously problematic. If the co-owners do not agree, the outcome depends on how the co-ownership agreement treats the item under consideration. If the agreement states that the action under consideration requires the consent of both owners, no action will be taken since the owners did not consent. If the agreement is silent on the issue, the co-owners will need dispute resolution assistance, typically mediation and/or binding arbitration.

Groups of three or more co-owners typically have tiered voting systems where certain decisions are made by a majority or a subgroup such as a board of directors, and certain decisions require unanimity (or alternatively, a larger majority). Decisions requiring a higher level of approval are typically those involving major physical changes to the property, large expenditures, changing usage rights allocations, selling the entire property, and borrowing money against the property, and could also include anything else the group thinks is particularly important. When analyzing how decisions should be made, keep in mind that allowing a decision to be made by a majority allows the majority to take usage rights away from, or add cost burdens to, the minority (and you could be that minority). On the other hand, requiring a decision to be made by consensus can paralyze the group if there is a co-owner who is uninterested, unreasonable or angry. The personalities and relationships of the original co-owners may change over time, and new people may come into the group through resale or death, so don't assume that the level of cooperation, ease of consensus-building, and rationality you experience now will continue into the future.

One particularly important but often overlooked area of decision making and potential dispute is the layout and furnishing of the shared vacation home. The property can become an overly cluttered repository for all of the co-owners' unwanted furnishings, or an unpleasant maze of clashing tastes. I suggest that the co-owners initially agree on a furniture layout and, if items must be purchased, a budget and plan for how purchasing decisions will be made. Once the initial furnishing and decorating is completed, any additions or changes should require group approval.

Tax Deductions

Tax treatment of vacation homes depends on how often the property is used for "personal use" and how often it is used as a "rental." There are three possible tax treatments, each with their own rules on tax deductions: "Pure Second Home," "Pure Rental Property," and "Second Home/Hobby Rental."

You qualify for "Pure Second Home" tax treatment if the property is a "rental" for no more than 14 days in a particular tax year. With this tax treatment, mortgage interest and property taxes are generally tax deductible, but other expenses are not. Rent income is entirely tax free.

You qualify for "Pure Rental Property" tax treatment if both of the following two things are true: (i) the property is a "rental" for more than 14 days in a particular tax year, and (ii) the total number of "personal use" days is either no more than 14 or no more than 10% of the total number of "rental" days. (For example, if there were 220 "rental" days, you could have up to 22 "personal use" days; if there were 100 "rental" days, you could have up to 14 "personal use" days.) With this tax treatment, you need to divide the year in two parts, "rental" and "personal use", and allocate each expense proportionally. For the "rental" portion, expenses (including mortgage interest, property tax, insurance, maintenance, repairs, improvements, utilities, management, and even depreciation) are deductible to the extent they exceed rental income, but the deduction cannot be taken against all types of income, and in some cases must be carried forward and deducted in future years. For the "personal use" portion, only property tax is reliably deductible; other expenses, including mortgage interest, generally are not.

You qualify for "Second Home/Hobby Rental" tax treatment if you do not qualify for either of the other categories. With this tax treatment, you again need to divide the year in two parts, "rental" and "personal use," and allocate each expense proportionally. For the "rental" portion, expenses (again including mortgage interest, property tax, insurance, maintenance, repairs, improvements, utilities, management, and even depreciation) can offset income, but are not otherwise deductible. For the "personal use" portion, mortgage interest and property taxes are generally deductible, but other expenses are not.

When determining how often the property is used for "personal use" and how often it is used as a "rental," these rules apply:

- Use by a co-owner, even when the co-owner pays a usage fee, is "personal use."
- Use by a relative of an owner, even if the relative pays full rent, is "personal use."
- Use by a non-owner under a vacation home exchange or swap arrangement is "personal use."
- Days spent primarily repairing or maintaining the vacation home are not "personal use," but need not be counted as "rental" days either.
- A day when the home is available for rent but is not actually rented cannot be counted as a "rental" day.

When vacation property is co-owned, usage of all the co-owners (and their relatives, non-paying friends, and swappers) should be added together to determine the total number of "personal use" days, and the days when the property was rented to paying tenants who are not owners or relatives (regardless of whether the rent went to an individual owner or was shared by the group) should be added together to determine the total number of "rental" days. The tax treatment should then be determined. If the home qualifies as a Pure Second Home, each owner can then generally deduct all of the mortgage interest and property tax he/she paid. If the home does not qualify as a Pure Second Home, the group will need to determine the collective "rental"/"personal use" expense allocation ratio. Each owner will then need to apply that ratio to the expenses he/she has paid, offset any income he/she received, and apply the appropriate tax deduction rules as outlined above. This discussion of tax issues is intended as an introduction to the general rules only. You should consult a qualified attorney or accountant for complete and personalized tax information.

Capital Gains

Unless you have occupied the property as your primary residence for two of the five years immediately preceding the sale, you will not qualify for the $250,000 single/$500,000 married exclusion from capital gains tax. But you are likely to qualify to have any profit taxed at the lower long-term capital gains rates, and you may qualify to complete a tax-deferred exchange. In general, the tax treatment of your profit or loss on resale will depend upon how the property was used in the 12 months preceding the sale. If you are contemplating a sale of a vacation property (or just your share of one), it is wise to consult a tax expert at least a year before the planned sale.

Limited Liability Company or Limited Partnership

Owning a vacation home as a limited liability company, limited partnership, corporation, or other entity (rather than in the names of the co-owners) can offer several advantages, including (i) protecting your other assets from liabilities arising from ownership of the vacation home, (ii) protecting the vacation home from seizure by your creditors (or the creditors of other co-owners), (iii) increasing flexibility for ownership changes, and (iv) adding the structure created by the large body of law that is applicable to these entities (but doesn't otherwise apply to co-ownership).

But owning a vacation home as an entity also has drawbacks. Creating and maintaining the entity structure involves costs that you would not otherwise incur, including formation fees, special taxes, and the annual cost of preparing tax returns for the entity (which is required even if the entity doesn't owe any tax). In addition, owning the group vacation home as an entity may deprive the co-owners of some of the income tax benefits of vacation home ownership, such as the ability to deduct mortgage interest and property tax as a second home. Ultimately, the question of whether to hold a vacation home as an entity must be answered based on a case by case basis in light of the particular circumstances of your group and your property.

Selling Shares

Most people who purchase a vacation home with others are very careful in selecting their partner(s), and are legitimately concerned that allowing co-owners to re-sell their shares will cause incompatible or unqualified co-owners to enter the group. But prohibiting individual re-sales, or requiring unanimous consent for them (which is really the same thing), may mean that there is no way for a co-owner to exit the group without selling his/her interest to another co-owner. The problem with this situation is that no other co-owner may be interested in purchasing an additional share. Moreover, even if another co-owner or group of co-owners is willing to purchase, there is little incentive for them to pay fair market price since the seller has no choice but to take whatever is offered. (Requiring that the price be based on an appraisal will not be helpful if the effect is to dissuade the other co-owners from purchasing.)

An important thing to keep in mind when considering this issue is that personalities and lives change in ways that no one expects or can predict, and it is inevitable that people will need or want to leave the group over time. Examine the issue both from the perspective of someone who might be forced to accept a new co-owner, and from the perspective of someone who might need to sell because of financial difficulties or illness. Also remember that it generally hurts the group dynamic, and makes decision making and management much more difficult, to force someone to stay in the group when he/she needs or wants to leave.

I strongly recommend that individual re-sales be allowed, subject to restrictions intended to protect the group from incompatible or unqualified buyers. These protections typically include rights of first refusal (the right of one or more of the existing co-owners to purchase the seller's interest at market price) and rights of rejection (the right of the other co-owners to reject a proposed buyer if they can articulate a reasonable basis for rejection).

A Guaranteed Exit Strategy

As I mention above, it is critical to recognize that the lives of each of the co-owners will change in ways they do not expect, and there must be a way for co-owners to leave the group. Allowing co-owners to sell individual shares is one way to make leaving possible, but selling partial interests may be difficult or impossible due to market conditions, bad group dynamics, the condition of the property, or other unpredictable factors. So even if individual sales are permitted, it makes sense to create a realistic, guaranteed exit strategy. Typically, this means picking a time in the future when it will become possible for any of the co-owners to insist that the others either buy them out based on fair market value, or sell the entire property.

Risks

Fractional co-ownership involves the risks of sharing use of property with others and relying on them to fulfill their obligations to you. Sharing use means that you will not be able to do what you want when you want, and that others may do things that displease you. Sharing obligations means that necessary maintenance and management might not be completed, or worse, that as the result of a co-owner failing to make a payment, a mortgage lender could foreclose on the entire building causing all of the other co-owners to lose use of the vacation home and possibly all of the money they have invested. There is no way to eliminate these risks, but there are ways to lower them. Perhaps the single most important thing you can do to lower the risk of co-ownership is to have a thorough, written, signed co-ownership agreement that deals with all of the issues, including events you don't expect to happen, the possibility that people you don't know will be in the group as the result of a death or re-sale, and the reality that people change and you might not get along with the other co-owners as well as you do now.

Besides having an agreement, these steps will help diminish the risk of co-ownership:

- Carefully investigate the background and financial qualification of potential co-owners.
- Use a monthly assessment system for collecting payments from the group, and pay all bills from a group account.
- Assign each of the essential management tasks to a specific person either within or outside the group.
- Have each co-owner contribute to a default reserve fund that will be used to pay mortgage interest, property tax or insurance if a co-owner fails to contribute his/her share, and make sure you don't accidentally spend the money on maintenance or repairs.
- Give the group the power to quickly force out a co-owner who is not fulfilling his/her obligations, and use that power before the group is in serious financial trouble.

Properties Located in a Foreign Country

When the co-owned vacation home is located abroad, enforcement of the co-ownership agreement can be more difficult. Even where all of the parties agree to have their relationship governed by U.S. law, the property itself is governed by the law of the country where the property is located. For example, if the group needs to recover possession of the property from an unauthorized user (tenant or co-owner), or remove a co-owner from title in connection with a forced sale of the co-owner's interest after a default, local law will apply. To make sure the co-ownership arrangements can be effectively enforced, it is essential to involve both a U.S. attorney, and an attorney licensed in the country where the property is located, in the formulation of the co-ownership agreement and ownership structure.

Written Agreement

People and circumstances change in unforeseeable ways, and new people can come into a co-ownership group at any time as a result of death or other unexpected events. When these changes occur, even the best of friends, the closest of families, and the most agreeable and easy-going people in the world can disagree. The purpose of an agreement is to help resolve these conflicts quickly, inexpensively, and without ruining the personal relationships of the group members.

Even a well-prepared co-ownership agreement should be used only in the event friendly relations among group members break down. While it is useful to have owners' rights and duties well defined, relying on the agreement to dictate a response to actual events is unwise. Even the best agreement will rarely anticipate all circumstances, and applying a formulaic response that does not quite fit the situation may not reveal the best course of action. Such an approach encourages group members to adopt firm positions based on agreement interpretations, and an impasse may develop. A better strategy is to rely first on discussion. The goal should be to develop a consensus that all owners can accept even though some may believe that the agreement dictates a more personally advantageous decision.

If a consensus cannot be reached, the co-ownership agreement can provide a final resolution.

No one reads a co-ownership agreement for pleasure. The only time you are likely to read the agreement is if you have a conflict that you can't otherwise resolve. In that situation, you want the agreement to provide a specific and clear resolution. The shorter a co-ownership agreement is, the less likely it is to address the specific problem that caused you to look at the agreement. The advantage of length is that it allows you to cover more issues, and makes the agreement more likely to be helpful if you need it. There is no disadvantage to length, as long as the agreement has a complete table of contents so that you can find what you need quickly. Simplicity is desirable, as long as it doesn't come at the expense of breadth.

Co-Owner Defaults

While co-owner default is a major potential risk of co-ownership, it is important to keep the problem in perspective. In my experience, the type of default that co-owners are most worried about, failure to make a required payment, is extremely rare. Far more common, but still rare, are defaults related to usage of the property, such as damaging the property, failing to keep it clean, using it at unauthorized times or in improper ways, and altering or cluttering it without group approval.

While it is necessary (from both a legal and an ethical point of view) to protect the rights and equity of each co-owner even if he/she has defaulted, it is also important that a co-ownership agreement give the group the power to deal with a default quickly and effectively. The group can always decide not to use all of its power if the circumstances warrant leniency, but the group should not be forced to be lenient if one member is ignoring the rules or putting the property or the investment at risk.

A typical co-ownership agreement will provide that an owner who has been accused of a violation be given notice of the accusation and a limited time to either contest it or cure it. If the accused co-owner chooses to contest the allegation, the matter is submitted to dispute resolution, which is typically mediation, or if that is unsuccessful, binding arbitration. If the accused co-owner does not cure the violation or initiate dispute resolution within the specified time, his/her interest in the property is sold at market price using a carefully described procedure. Sale proceeds are applied to pay any arrearages, transaction costs, legal fees and penalties, and any remaining amounts go to the defaulting co-owner. Note that a procedure which causes a co-owner to simply forfeit his/her ownership, investment or equity, is generally unenforceable and therefore useless to the group.

As mentioned above, it is advisable for co-owner groups to establish a default reserve fund that will be used to pay mortgage interest, property tax or insurance if a co-owner fails to contribute his/her share. But it is important to understand that this fund is not intended to be a pool from which a defaulting co-owner can borrow at will. If a co-owner fails to make a payment, and the group chooses to use a portion of the fund to make up the shortfall, the defaulting co-owner has still defaulted and the group should still have the power to take the same remedial action that it would be entitled to take if the default reserve fund had not been used. In other words, the defaulting owner should not be able to escape responsibility by claiming that since it was his/her own money in the default reserve fund that was used, he/she has not really defaulted.

7

Buying Multiple Vacation Homes

If you have ever attended one of my seminars, you have probably laughed about the slide in the presentation pointing out the "cons of owning vacation rental homes." The slide says, "Be Careful it's contagious! Once you buy one, you want to buy more and more and . . . more."

If you'd like to join this phenomenon of multiple vacation rental ownership, here are a few guidelines that might help you get there.

Deciding Where to Purchase

When you're looking to purchase another property probably one of the biggest dilemmas you'll face is where to purchase your second vacation rental home. There are two simple choices: Buy where you already own or purchase in an entirely different area. We'll explore both.

Buying where you already own. There are many advantages to purchasing a second vacation rental property in the area where you already own your first vacation rental property. The most obvious reason is you're already quite familiar with the area. Because you know the prices of homes in your area, you'll know right off the bat how much you'll need to spend.

Looking for a property that you are confident will rent is easier because you've spoken with enough guests over the years to become familiar with the kind of properties renters are most attracted to. Having all of this expertise under your belt certainly makes it an easier transition into the next property.

Another motivation for buying right where you are is you already have all of your outsourcing challenges accomplished. Finding good help is no easy task and the thought of having to find *new* good help is daunting. If you purchase where you already own, you'll likely be able to use the same housekeepers, maintenance staff, plumbers, heating and air service professionals for your new property as you use for your current one. And for the maintenance you do on your own, it's easier to kill two birds with one stone—just one trip to one city.

You also gain an advantage by being able to piggyback off the inquiries you already receive. If you get a call from someone looking for your property and it's already booked, you'll have an opportunity to convince them to explore your other property.

Buying elsewhere. While all of these reasons seem to be convincing for purchasing in an area where you currently own, let's explore the advantages of purchasing somewhere else. One advantage is not having all of your eggs in one basket. If there is anything that dramatically or rapidly affects the market conditions, your risk exposure will probably be limited to one property. For example, say you have a property on Florida's Gulf Coast and a property at a ski area in Vermont. When a devastating hurricane hits Florida, you'll only have one property impacted, not two.

Having properties in two entirely different areas could also be attractive from your personal use perspective.

For example, I own condos on the beach and cabins in the mountains. It's nice to have both. While the beach is a place that I usually stay for a week at a time, I often use my cabins for weekend trips.

While both areas have similar occupancy rates of 60–70 percent, the two areas have completely different booking patterns and peak seasons, both work to my advantage for time management and cash flow purposes. Both properties have great summer rental seasons—the beach properties are mostly weeklong rentals that are booked solid from January to August, while the cabins are mostly sporadic three to four night rentals during that same time period. The cabins are my cash cows during the time of the year when our beach properties aren't rented much, from August to December. It's really nice to have the constant flow of rental revenue throughout the year rather than the "now you have it, now you don't" cash flow of the beach properties alone.

While you would think that there's little advertising or marketing advantages, surprisingly, I have had renters who have rented both my beach and mountain properties.

Financing Another Vacation Home

After you decide where to buy, the next thing you'll have to think about is how you will pay for another property. Do you remember Caroline from my second book, *Profit From Your Vacation Home Dream*? Caroline really wanted to buy a vacation home but her annual income was only around $70K per year. With some strategic planning and financing measures, she ended up buying a cabin. Guess what? Caroline was so successful generating positive cash flow with her first vacation rental property, now she's ready to take the plunge and buy another. How in the world can she afford another vacation property when she could barely afford that first one?

Let's evaluate her situation. She has owned her current vacation rental property for two years. In that time period, the property has appreciated nearly 30%. Caroline has 3 basic options for financing another property. She can purchase it straight out as an investment property, leverage the current equity to use as a down payment on the second, or sell her first property, using a 1031 tax free exchange to purchase two properties. Let's explore each option:

Buy the second vacation home outright. While you think that you might not be able to qualify for another mortgage there is a distinct possibility that you could. Here's how. If you have been renting out your vacation home on a positive cash flow basis and claiming all of the income on your income taxes for at least two years, then the rental income will offset the expenses. To further explain, to the mortgage company, as long as you show your property as either a break even or an income asset then the expenses associated with your first property are negated by the income that it produces.

Here's an example that might help you understand better. On your existing vacation home, say you have $2000 per month rental income and your expenses are $2000 per month. What's your income minus your debt? Zero. That's how the mortgage company looks at the debt on your vacation home, as zero. For qualification factors, the mortgage company will analyze the bigger picture and see that you'll likely be in the same financial position (or better) as when you purchased your first vacation property. While this is an overly simplistic view, it gives you a good picture. It is likely your vacation home will be deducted on your taxes as a loss (even if your income exceeded your expenses) because you'll have other aspects of the property that are tax deductible. But when mortgage underwriters look at your whole financial picture, often they take into account the write offs, which then bring you back to zero or a positive, and in turn makes it possible for you to get another mortgage.

Leverage. A second option you would have is commonly referred to as leveraging. To leverage is to use your existing property's equity in a way that you can increase the profits in a manner that would ultimately give you greater return than if you just owned one property.

There are two ways that you can leverage your existing property. The first way would be to borrow money against the equity in order to purchase or use as a down payment for your second property. You could borrow it in the form of a second mortgage, or a home equity line. The goal would be to purchase another property that will make more money in appreciation and rental income.

The second way you can leverage is by selling your existing vacation home and leverage to equity to use as a down payment to purchase two properties. While this sometimes complicates the process because you'll have two new properties to get up and running for rentals, sometimes it's the best option, especially when your existing property has appreciated a great deal or you have owned it long enough to significantly pay down the mortgage. The best way to avoid capital gains when you are selling an investment that has appreciated is to do a 1031 Exchange.

1031 Exchange

Before 1979, it was complicated to buy and sell properties in a way that deferred paying capital gains tax. That year, the Starker decision in the U.S. 9th Circuit Court of Appeals changed the rules and made it possible for investors to have more time to find a desirable property after selling one. The transaction, properly executed, would qualify for tax-deferred status. Treasury Regulations passed in 1991 validated and simplified this process. As a result, the Internal Revenue Code Section 1031 (commonly referred to by property owners as a 1031 exchange) states: "No gain or loss shall be recognized if property held for productive use in a trade or business or for investment purposes is exchanged solely for property of a like-kind."

For real estate investors in particular, the 1031 exchange code allows them latitude in their choice of investments. The rules for 1031 exchanges require that a replacement property be identified within 45 days of the sale of the first property to realize the tax-deferred benefits.

Your real estate agent and/or tax advisor will give you full details on how 1031 exchanges can work to your benefit as a vacation home investor. You can also go to www.starker.com. With the funds you thought you'd have to pay in taxes, you can invest in your next property or even two!

Common Mistakes

There are a few common mistakes that people who own multiple properties make. The mistakes almost always pertain to advertising. While owning two vacation rental properties will give the benefit of being able to cross sell your properties from one ad to another, you need to make sure you are giving equal exposure to both of your properties.

Here's an example of a common mistake. Say you have two condos in the same complex. You only list one of your condos thinking that single ad will give enough exposure for both properties. While you'll likely be able to benefit from the overflow of one ad, it's important to advertise both properties in separate ads because it gives them equal exposure as well as giving you slightly more shelf space on the vacation rental portal websites.

Another common mistake is not listing all your properties on all the major portal websites, as in the following scenario: Your first property is listed on VRBO.com and Flipkey.com, and your second property is listed on AirBNB.com and PetFriendlyTravel.com. While you think that the exposure you'll get would be ample because collectively you have four ads, you are really shortchanging both of your properties. You need to have ads for each property on each of the listing sites.

And the last most common advertising mistake has to do with your calendars. Most often, multiple property owners don't keep calendars up to date. I understand the thought process and have heard all of the arguments—you don't mark dates as booked until both properties are booked for a particular time period with the mindset that you can "sell" the other property. While sometimes you'll be able to convince the renter to look at your second property, often the renters want to rent the property they are looking at, and have a different back-up property in mind. They also want to know instantly whether or not it's available. It's been proven that properties with up-to-date calendars book better than properties with no dates shown as booked. So not marking your booked dates on both ads can be a greater disadvantage to both of your properties.

Sell Your Vacation Home

Whether you're selling a vacation rental home to buy a bigger property, a property in a different location, to do a 1031 exchange or simply to unload your property altogether, when listing your property for sale, it's important that you think like a buyer who is going to own it from afar. What are some of the things that you would love to have in your new vacation home? Set up your property so that it looks attractive from all aspects of ownership—personal use, rental ease, and maintenance.

Sell it as a business. If you have been renting out your vacation home, selling it as vacation rental business could be very attractive to buyers. Ask your real estate agent to quote your last year or two of rental revenue history. Many buyers seek vacation homes that they can rent out for part of the year to defray expenses—just as you do. Buyers may even pay more for a property with proven rental income.

If you use a rental organizer, such as the one I have developed, you can easily show the buyer all of your past rental records proving your rental history. Now you're selling an established business rather than just another property.

Sell your advertising. Another thing you can do that would help your property sell is include in your sales listing all of your advertising channels. This means transferring any personal website domains and portal website subscriptions. Some portal websites will allow you to transfer your listing to the new owner. Think of the advantage of saying, "Property with a great rental history *and* complete website is included."

Note: The word on the street is VRBO.com no longer allows you to transfer listings when you sell the property. So before you "advertise" that your listing on VRBO.com is a part of the sale, be sure to verify it can be done. I tried to verify this information with VRBO.com and even with my direct connections (I used to work there!); I couldn't get a straight answer out of them.

Transferring rentals. While it's a good idea to continue to take bookings while your property is on the market in the event it takes a long time to sell, you'll want to start thinking about where you'll place your future bookings if the new buyer does *not* want the rentals. This would mean that any future bookings would have to be transferred to another property. Some owners are tempted to just refund the money and cancel the bookings, but I would not recommend it. Remember, your renters may have already scheduled time off from work, booked air travel, car rentals, etc. Canceling their trip altogether just isn't ethical. As a matter of fact, it may even be illegal. In some states it is the law that you must accommodate any rentals on the books.

If you are faced with the dilemma of having to place your rentals in another property, it's usually best to call other owners with properties similar to yours and ask if they would like your bookings. Of course it's important to also communicate with the renters to give them the option to transfer or simply cancel the booking. You can also call a property management company and see if they would like your bookings. Many owners have actually sold the bookings for a percentage of the revenue to management companies.

If the new owners would like the bookings, be sure to work out how you'll transfer them with the sale. It's usually best if the new owner takes over completely and writes up a new contract and has each renter sign the contract. If you wish to handle the rentals, then it's best to have a written "property management" contract written between you and the seller. It could get very sticky if you have a situation where one of the renters damages, steals or has a liability claim after the ownership has transferred.

Sell your home fully furnished. If you are not selling your property fully furnished, you may be at a disadvantage. Many buyers like to buy a vacation homes "turn-key," with sheets on the beds, silverware in the drawer, and artwork on the walls. While it's acceptable to omit some of the furnishings in the sale, such as a valuable piece of artwork or an heirloom piece of furniture, I think it's better to take those items out and replace them before you put your property on the market.

Stage your vacation home. Sellers often overlook the importance of staging their second homes. Buyers are turned off by clutter, outdated decor and old furnishings. A fresh coat of paint, a new comforter on the bed and some nice accessories can cost less than $1,000 and can often yield a faster sale or command a higher price.

Do the maintenance. It's best to take care of any repairs or maintenance up front; vacation home buyers don't want the hassle of dealing with these issues especially because they are buying from afar.

Share your resources. For many vacation home buyers, the thought of finding service providers in an unfamiliar area is daunting. Mention in your sales flyer that you have housekeepers, maintenance workers, or property managers all lined up. When you sell your property, be sure to give that list to the new owners.

Make sure you have the right agent. It is very important that you choose the correct agent when selling your vacation home. Does your agent understand the difference between selling second homes and primary residences? Good agents will facilitate opportunities for their buying clients to visit for weekends and remain available to communicate with the sellers. Real estate firms that also do property management can sometimes generate interest from their rental clients or attract investors. Also, look for Realtors® with the "Resort and Second-Home Property Specialist" certification.

Post scads of photos. Because vacation homes are often purchased from a distance, buyers usually shop on the internet prior to visiting the area. Some properties are even bought sight unseen. To attract buyers, provide as many high-quality photographs of your property as possible.

Write a great description. Vacation home descriptions differ from those of primary homes. Your description should emphasize the "get away from it all" nature of the vacation home, using words like private, peaceful, quiet and escape. Be sure to list amenities such as swimming pools, tennis courts, close to the beach, near bike trail, etc.

Offer a trial run. Vacation home buyers often visit and stay in the area while they're looking for a property to purchase. Tell your real estate agent that potential buyers can stay in your vacation home for a nominal fee. What better way for a buyer to fall in love with your property than to stay there for a weekend?

Be patient. Vacation homes sometimes take twice as long to sell as primary homes. Demand for second homes and retirement homes by aging baby boomers, however, should keep the vacation home market strong for some time to come. Realize that the average buyer takes 18 to 30 months to shop and research before they actually purchase—a process that requires persistence as well as patience.

International Buying

A new vacation home trend is buying properties outside the United States. Some people are buying simply because they fall in love with an area. For instance, if you saw the movie, *Under the Tuscan Sun*, it likely prompted you to dream of owning a home in Tuscany. Other motivations for purchasing are affordability, untouched beauty, or familial connections in the countries.

Regardless of the reasons, people are snatching up vacation homes all over the world. They're buying in areas including the traditional hot spots of Mexico, Costa Rica, France, Italy and Spain, to the less conventional but increasingly popular areas of Dubai, Bulgaria, Nicaragua, and Sri Lanka.

Purchasing outside the United States will present some challenges for buyers. For instance some countries will not allow foreigners to hold title to the land, requiring foreigners to have the title held in trust. Another challenge is financing, some countries require buyers to use their banks or financing companies, sometimes at high percentage rates, they may require large deposits, or some will not allow the properties to be mortgaged at all.

If you intend to purchase a property outside the United States, it's imperative that you do a lot of research. While this research might become quite time consuming, often it is well worth the time and challenges involved.

The next section is written by Tom Kelly, the author of *Cashing in on Second Homes in Mexico*, the first book in a multi-book series of buying properties throughout the world.

Property Outside the United States Provides Adventure AND Diversification

By Tom Kelly

Remember the popular advertising line: "This Is Not Your Father's Oldsmobile"?

International property, except for some longtime retirees who saw the light early, "is not your father's idea of a second home spot." Florida was the vacation home spot of the past, however now a touch too common for the bouncing baby boomers and adventuresome Generation X and Generation Yers who are now driving the move toward second homes both here and abroad.

One of the most widespread and vivid images of owning property abroad comes from the Frances Mayes book (and the movie made from it) *Under the Tuscan Sun* the highly romanticized tale of an academic who undertakes the renovation of a villa near Cortona, Italy. Her adventures in dealing with Italian laws, culture and craftsman are an unforgettable chronicle of the wonders of living in Tuscany. On top of this, the glories of Italian food and wines, the intriguing travel videos of Rick Steves and our fascination with Roman history have all preconditioned us to love Italy and regard it as the best place to own a home abroad. That feeling holds until we hear other stories or see compelling videos of an equally enchanting place.

While accurate estimates of the number of U.S. citizens living abroad are nearly impossible to pin down, the State Department believes that between three and six million people lived outside our borders in 2012. Why do the numbers vary so greatly? First, our government puts a very low priority on tracking ownership of real estate in other countries. Second, how do you classify and measure part-time residents, second-home owners and investors?

Never before has there been more information available to the buying public concerning real estate around the world. Websites have become more plentiful, with real estate agents displaying more pertinent information and available property listings. In many markets, a local multi-listing service (MLS) is available, and often a significant number of agents participate in professional organizations at the municipal, state and national levels. Some countries require that all who endeavor and earn commissions in the sale of real property be registered and comply with specified guidelines on education and professional ethics. There is greater awareness of property conveyance, tax and legal matters, and greater attention is being placed on safeguarding foreign investment through the use of neutral third-party escrow agreements.

In addition, agents are now recommending that buyers obtain a commitment for title insurance, acquire coverage at the time of closing and follow through with the subsequent title insurance policy once the deed is recorded.

With the number of U.S. people alone looking to real estate to acquire wealth and leisure time, the resale prospects for well-situated second homes abroad appear to be extremely bright. And for at least the next 20 years, the numbers are overwhelming. According to the U.S. Bureau of the Census and the National Center for Health Statistics, the 50-plus population is growing by 10,000 people every day, and this trend is expected to continue for the next 20 years. Right now, an American turns 50 every seven seconds.

Why is this important to the outlook for international real estate? The baby boom generation is the largest, healthiest and wealthiest group ever appearing on the U.S. growth landscape and it is just beginning to grasp the concept of actually living a part of the year in a foreign country (or having the bravado to say you own a piece of Provence).

Much like the boomers' parents—members of The Greatest Generation—targeted Florida, a greater number of baby boomers will look beyond the U.S. borders because of the different experience, the attraction to perceived risk and the thrill of the exotic. In many cases, it's simply the lure of a different culture and a step outside the predictable second-home box.

"Baby boomers are famous for believing one thing and then behaving totally different from what they think they do," says Eric Snider, who has a doctorate in social psychology and serves as a consultant to upscale active adult communities. "They are after exclusivity, amenities and personal experiences. Boomers are all about personal experiences."

Of the number of U.S. citizens who own property abroad, nearly one-third of them do so in Mexico, our neighbor to the South. A December 2012 move that has gone a long way toward easing buyers' fears about safety in Mexico's popular resort areas occurred when Seattle-based Windermere Real Estate, the largest real estate company in the western United States with more than 300 offices and 7,000 agents in nine states, opened its first international franchise office in Mexico. Located in Cabo San Lucas, the office was the first opened by a major U.S. real estate chain into Mexico since the downturn in the U.S. economy and the border-based violence fueled by Mexican drug cartels.

"We simply didn't have the infrastructure in place to support an office in Mexico in 2005," said Geoff Wood, Windermere CEO. "Fast forward seven years, and we now have 300-plus offices in nine Western U.S. states, most of which have a natural migration of residents to Mexico. Add to this the 79 million baby boomers who will reach retirement age over the next 18 years and studies show that many of them will purchase a second home in resort areas, such as Mexico."

And the studies also show that a majority of boomers have not saved for retirement and will need to spend fewer dollars in their future years. According to a report by Washington, D.C.-based Center for Economic and Policy Research (CEPR), baby boomers have not saved and they will be forced to work longer and/or move to less expensive places than they anticipated. Property taxes, health care, and cost of living increases will force boomers to more than thinking about moving to other countries, especially if they plan on living at the same level of comfort as they do now.

While the negativity surrounding the country peaked at a time when more and more Americans could have used a less expensive place to live, the Windermere decision has eased the fear factor because of the clientele and geographical areas it represents. The company tends to attract sophisticated, upper-end buyers who have done research on their targeted area.

According to Wood, despite what Americans may have heard, read and seen, the country is not under siege. News reports—including a segment on 60 Minutes—have depicted the entire country of Mexico as being an absolute mess, awash in blood and guns on every street corner. Ironically, people living there have a dramatically different perspective, especially in the "fly-in" destinations that continue to hold their value.

"The media has done a great job of playing up the fear factor in Mexico," Wood said. "But there are those who own property and do business in the area that are gradually dispelling those stories. Like any country, there are unsafe areas, but our experience is that Los Cabos is very safe and offers great real estate opportunities for both U.S. and Mexican homebuyers."

Sales to Americans abroad slowed between 2005–2012—mirroring a pattern in the States—yet many regions have since experienced steady sales, thanks mostly to the international boomer profile. And, the search for appealing property works both ways. Foreigners continue to look to the U.S. for leisure and retirement living.

"Remember that World War II ended at the same time in Europe as it did in the United States," said Lawrence Yun, the National Association of Realtors' chief economist. "Many of the Europeans had bought in Spain but the Spanish market is undergoing a transition now. Some of them see the lower cost of U.S. real estate and consider it a good investment."

The group with the most "in flow" potential is members of the rising middle class in Brazil, Russia, India and China (the "BRIC" countries) who are expected to buy vacation homes in California, Arizona, Florida and Nevada.

"I expect to see 80 million people rising to the middle class every year in the BRIC countries," Yun said. "Approximately one percent of them will move to the bracket of super rich and the biggest status symbol they can have is a home in an international city on the West Coast or Las Vegas or Florida. Many of these are cash buyers who don't have to worry about the mortgage markets."

Canadian property has provided an attractive alternative for U.S. buyers. Retirees, aging baby boomers and youthful investors "from the states" are drawn to Canada for its wonderful skiing, health care, bargain medicine, terrific sailing and clean air. Europeans have long coveted summer homes in East Coast waterfront regions of Nova Scotia and New Brunswick.

So, why even undertake the chore or researching and possibly buying a second home? Owning a residence has long been the way in which Americans create personal net worth. Houses have historically accounted for the largest and single most important acquisition one makes. If our disposability of income reaches a threshold where we can make prudent investments, real estate has long been a lucrative avenue.

"The Greatest Generation" took pride in being debt free. Owning the roof over their heads was a lifelong goal, and it took a lot of persuading to get Mom and Dad to even consider the concept of tapping into the equity of a home they already had paid off. Members of this group often were reluctant to spend money on themselves in order to make their lives more comfortable.

Conversely, baby boomers never met a loan they didn't like. The bottom line is that they will continue to be creative with financing, and they love having the status—and the actual experience—of a second home. Owning a property in a place as mysterious as Honduras or Tuscany will further push their fun and romance buttons.

And, they will introduce international getaways to their children. If you think the baby boomer group was immense and steered the housing market plus every element of the retail industry, the throng that contains many of their consumer-crazy children—the proud members of Generation Y could prove just as powerful because of their flair for adventure. These youngsters, born in 1979 or later, will have 74 million members (an estimated 3 million more than the boomers) and make up 34 percent of the population by 2015. They will prefer homes that will be useful rather than prestigious, and they will be willing to trade size for lifestyle and convenience factors.

Doesn't that sound like a small bungalow close to the beach or a casita with a view of the mountains?

Looking Abroad post September 11, 2001

The events of 9/11 made the world stop, gaze horrified at the senseless tragedy, reflect on the fragility of life and question its everyday uncertainty. As human beings living together on this planet, we became globally united in a common spirit and one unwavering belief.

Terrorism is not acceptable, it will not be tolerated and people cannot live in fear. We will go on with our lives, though a little more skeptical and certainly more cautiously.

The residue of 9/11 has made our eyes clearer and our ears keener. We ask more questions and seek more explanations—not just concerning safety and travel but also about major issues and challenges we face every day. The aftermath of 9/11 is one of the reasons potential buyers better understand the issues concerning ownership of foreign land. Buyers are more willing to learn and to be armed with the right questions. These buyers are simply savvier and know if their questions cannot be answered by an individual, they will turn to information provided on the internet. In addition, real estate developers and agents have increasingly become more aware that purchasers do understand the issues. Buyers are concerned with title matters, use of an escrow agreement, subdivision authorizations, recorded deeds and condominium regimes, capital gains tax implications and property conveyance procedures.

CHAPTER

9

Why Self-Management Makes Sense

Well, congratulations. You own it! You finally made the big decision to follow your dream and buy that vacation home. So . . . now what? You want the property to start generating cash right away, but you want to be careful to do everything right. Let's start with the basics. You have three choices.

1. You can hire a management company to handle everything.
2. You can use a management partnership program.
3. You can self-manage . . . as in "rent by owner."

Option number three, rent by owner, is the only way to maximize your income on your vacation property. In other words, it's your best bet. Of course, this depends on how much work you are willing to do. But I'm not talking about backbreaking work, or even a huge commitment of time. Remember the adage, it's not how *hard* you work, it's how *smart* you work. That is certainly solid advice when it comes to renting your property on your own. So don't be scared into thinking it's a Herculean task. It's not.

I know what you're thinking at this point: is it really worth it to do it myself? Yes! Here's why.

Two Main Reasons to Rent By Owner

The first is the most obvious reason. You guessed it—money. You can make more money simply by not paying management company commissions, which may be significantly higher than you realize. Then, there are savings on the other costs associated with hiring a property manager such as linen pools, maintenance fees, and cleaning fees (when you rent by owner, you can charge the cleaning fee on top of the regular rental rate and taxes).

The second reason to rent by owner will surprise you because it seems to be everyone's biggest worry: having complete control of who rents your home. When you hand your keys over to a property manager, there's no telling who they will rent to. When you rent yourself, you are in complete control of who rents.

I like to talk to each renter on the phone. This is my chance to get to know these folks. I am friendly and personable and let the renters know that they are renting my second home. This is a great way to build a rapport. And, by establishing this relationship, the renters now change from customers to friends. Friends will take care of your home. If you stay in a hotel and spill coffee on the carpet, what do you do? Probably nothing. But if you rent a friend's home, how differently would you handle that spilled coffee? My renters take care of my home, and so will yours.

This really goes further than the obvious. Let's face it. There are certain categories of people you will no doubt *not* want to rent to. I'm not by any means talking about racial, ethnic, or religious distinctions. But a bunch of rowdy, hard-drinking college spring breakers are almost sure to do some damage. They are all but guaranteed to be partying and carousing. Just imagine how many things could be broken. What a hassle they might cause for the neighbors. Who wants to negotiate with college students about recovering damages? You can almost guess how that's going to turn out (and it's not a pretty picture for you). You, as the owner, have the ability (and a duty to yourself) to speak with each renter. Proper screening will help you weed out these types of renters. Refer to Chapter 16 for tips on how to weed out less desirable renters.

Another major fear for owners managing their properties themselves is maintenance. You are probably asking questions like, what do I do if the air conditioning goes out? What if the toilet stops up? What if the renters lose their keys? The simple truth is . . . these things rarely happen. Don't let these issues make you run into the arms of a management company! These are all things that we will discuss in detail later in the book. One thing to keep in mind is that when a renter calls the management company, the management company most likely has to contract a repairman. You can just as easily call the repairman from your home 600 miles away. So don't make your decision based on this alone.

Another good reason to rent by owner is you *will control the vacancies*. No matter what management companies say, *your* best interests are not their only concern. Remember, they may have hundreds of customers (owners) to worry about. You only have one—yourself. For example, management companies will sometimes sell a midweek rental leaving very valuable, easy-to-rent days open. What the company is doing is taking the easy way out. But the easy way is not always the best way (at least not for you). However, if you make yourself dependent on these middlemen, you will have no choice. You see, a management company looks at it this way: let's say the company has 100 rental homes that it manages. What does the company do if it gets 100 qualified renters? Does the company try to match the renters' needs to the right properties for the right dates, regardless of which properties get the most bookings? Actually, for many property managers, the answer is no. If the company did it that way, certain owners would end up with a disproportionate amount of bookings, and the management company would have a few very happy owners and many unhappy owners. And, of course, unhappy owners will not renew their contracts and the management company will lose money. So the company spreads the qualified renters around, making sure all of the owners receive at least some rentals. You can bet that company will try its hardest to make sure each home gets one week booked ... it's all about keeping volume and revenue going. From the company's perspective, it's better to have 100 semi-happy owners rather than a bunch that are fuming mad when they end up with zero bookings. What you need to realize, of course, is that what is in the company's best interest, in many cases, is diametrically opposed to what is in your best interest.

Renting by owner allows you to break free from this far from ideal situation. Here is an example of an owner who, without a management company, took advantage of filling his vacancies to the fullest:

Fred owned a property on Cape Cod for 20 years. When he retired from his job, he did a little research and decided to take on the task of renting by owner. He thought it would be fun to do. Fred's cottage always rented very well during the peak season. On the Cape, that is June through August. But he never had any off-season rentals. Then, he advertised his property on the internet. He not only filled up the peak season, he also rented many off weeks and long weekends during the fall, winter, and spring. He nearly doubled his rental occupancy from 8–10 weeks when using the management company, to

16–18 weeks on his own. He is now helping out a couple of other owners by booking their properties for them.

Another benefit of self-management is that you can better control your personal use of the property. Many times management companies make you sign a contract stating you will allow the company to rent a certain number of weeks. The company may even dictate when you can use your own property, for instance, the company may not want you to occupy the property during Christmas, spring break, or the Fourth of July. These are often the highest revenue weeks, and the company does not want owners using those weeks themselves. As a self-manager, you set aside the time you want for vacation or some special event. After all, what good is owning the home if you don't retain control over when you get to enjoy your own property?

Renting by owner is the best way to achieve a positive cash flow. Remember how we talked about break-even point back in Chapter 3? Remember, if your monthly mortgage payment is equal to or less than one peak week rental rate, then you should be able to achieve positive cash flow. Let's plug in some real numbers and look at this formula as a rent by owner. Here's how: take a property that rents for $2,000 a week during peak season with a monthly mortgage payment of $2,000. There are 12 peak weeks (Memorial Day to the third week in August), most if not all of which are generally going to be occupied. If you rent these 12 peak weeks, then you have just made enough money to pay one whole year's mortgage payments. Then you'll need to rent five more weeks to pay for incidentals like power, phone, association dues, minor maintenance, etc. Rent by owner and have 17 weeks booked (33% occupancy), and you have break-even cash flow. Rent more and you have positive cash flow.

And while we're talking about money, when you rent yourself, you are accepting all the payments yourself. So guess *where* the renters are sending those payments? Right to you! You get all *your* money up front. Management companies don't send you your money until

30 days after month end. Some companies don't send out the money until it has cleared the credit card companies, which can take up to 90 days.

> Carol, a client of mine, called me to thank me for the seminar that she attended a few months prior. Carol was especially excited to report that she had booked her whole summer already. She had 15 weeks booked at $1,000 per week. She required her renters to send a $200 deposit and the full rent up front. She had $18,000 worth of rental money in her bank account already. She brought up a good point that I had not thought about before: Think about this . . . the management company that she used prior to "renting by owner" managed over 100 properties (a relatively small management company). If the company rented out all 100 properties then they would have $1.8 million in the bank earning interest for four to six months. When was the last time you received an interest check on *your* money that the management company is holding?

Using a Management Company

Because they offer convenience, there is, of course, a strong appeal to using a management company. But for most of us, it's not worth it. And don't let a real estate agent try to convince you otherwise. Many real estate agents in vacation property areas are also property managers, so when they make their case they are doing much more than trying to help you. They are going to try to convince you that they can rent your property better than you can. I'm betting that they can't.

Now, let's look at our break-even formula when using a management company. For the sake of argument, let's just say you rent the same number of weeks, 12 peak and 5 other weeks, and your rental rate is the same. For every week you rent, management companies take 30% for commissions (usually more, but I'll be conservative). So now your $2,000 becomes $1400. Then the management company charges you a cleaning fee of $100 ("by owners" charge the renter). Now your $1400 becomes $1300. If your renters use a credit card you get charged a 3% fee. American Express is even more. So your $650 becomes $630. With these charges alone, you have just given away 37% of your money. Therefore, you would need to book 27 weeks (52% occupancy) to equal the same amount of net cash in your pocket as the person who rents by owner. What I'm saying here is that you will need to rent 10 more weeks with a management company to come up with the same money. Math doesn't lie.

Truly, the example above is a very conservative figure. If you currently use a management company, you are probably shaking your head and saying, "No way." Besides the commissions, add the other incidental charges and fees then you'll see that the figure that the management companies' keep becomes more like 50%–60% of your gross profit.

All of this begs the question, why, would anyone use a management company? I can only think of two reasons: first because they don't have the time to devote to taking reservations and self-managing. Or secondly, which is the more likely scenario, because they're afraid of what they perceive as the risks of renting by owner. For example, my biggest fear, the phone call I fervently hate to receive, is that a renter has arrived, and the home has not been cleaned. My cleaning service is definitely my lifeline. Using a reliable service is crucial. I wish I had a magical solution to this problem, but it is by far the most difficult part of renting by owner. (It is not insurmountable, however, and we'll talk about how this can be avoided in a later chapter.)

I get the feeling that some of you are still not convinced. You're thinking, I have a family and work full-time. How much time will doing it myself take on a daily basis? This is a realistic question. You *must* have some extra time, because there is indeed work involved. Here's how my time is spent. Throughout the year, I usually spend

5–30 minutes per day responding to email and voice inquiries. My busiest time (for Florida rentals) is from January to March 31, when I may spend an hour or so emailing and calling. This is when I make 80% of the bookings for the whole season. After I'm booked (which is generally by April 1), I spend approximately one to two hours per week sending directions, communicating with my housekeepers, charging credit cards and general accounting. Four times a year I spend 30 minutes filling out my sales tax forms, and I do have to visit at least twice a year. Oh, I almost forgot, you also have to factor in one to two trips per week to cash the rental checks. But that's a happy chore.

And don't ever fool yourself into thinking that everything will be coming up roses if you just sit back and let the management company do all of the work. After all, you say, how much money could it cost me? Here's a horror story of one woman who purchased her dream vacation home and rented through a management company:

Karen bought her dream vacation property in Destin, Florida. She is a very business savvy individual and really did her research. Her objective was to purchase a property that she could use herself and rent out when she was not there. When researching properties, she not only factored in the price of the property, she also took into consideration the cost of ownership. Karen used her computer; she opened a spreadsheet, and went through all the numbers. She factored in 30%–40% for management company commissions as a cost of ownership, and surmised that she could afford to purchase the property, even with those commissions. She accepted the fact that it would cost her some money out-of-pocket on an annual basis and was quite happy with the numbers.

Well, even though Karen did her homework, that's not exactly how it worked out. Here's what really happened. Karen bought her dream home and contracted a management company to rent and manage the property for her. She went through the main rental season and did not receive her moneys in a timely fashion from her management company. So from day one, they were taking money out of her pocket. When she finally received her first invoice and rental check, she was astonished to find out that the management company took 83% of her rental revenue! No, your eyes didn't deceive you—83%!

Don't believe it? Neither did I. Karen showed me her invoice. Here's how she got gypped out of her money. The management company rented her home for two- and three-night rentals. (Even though it was peak season when they very easily could have filled full weeks.) So, in a given month where her rental revenue was $4,000, she received a check for $680. Here's how the management company broke it down: in the month there were 31 days, the company had every night occupied at $130 per night. There were nine two-night rentals, three three-night rentals, and one four-night rental. The home had to be cleaned 14 times. The management company required that the owner pay for cleanings, so 14 cleanings multiplied by $75 is $1,050. Then, the management company assessed a linen refresh fee of $350 (the company said this was a standard fee to all owners mid-season). There was a $120 charge for credit card fees and an $80 fee for beach chair rental (the management company ran a special for "free" beach service on the four-day rental, and charged the owner for the expense!) Then the company charged her $25 for the furnace filter to be changed, and $8 for each of three light bulbs changed. $500 to replace a TV that was missing (why wasn't the renter charged?), $150 for carpet cleaning, $75 for pest control (even though the complex did it regularly as part of the association dues), $75 for an after hours call for a lost key, and $71 for a maintenance call on a clogged garbage disposal. Finally, adding insult to injury, was the most ridiculous fee I had ever heard of . . . they kept $800 of the rental income in an escrow account. For what? Karen never did get an answer to this one.

In the end, Karen faced having to sell her property at a loss—even though it had appreciated 20% in the last year. Now, don't be discouraged. Her comeback story is truly amazing. She consulted with me, fired her management company, and after nine months of self-management she earned $28,000 in rental income, all of which she kept. Three years later Karen has purchased three more properties and is self-managing all of them!

Partnership Programs

For those of you who were wondering, there *is* a compromise between hiring a management company and doing all of the work yourself. It is called a partnership program. This is when you agree to have a management company manage your property . . . but only part of the time. How do you find out about these programs? Seize the initiative by going directly to the management company and offering them a deal . . . if I book, then I'll give you X, and if *you* book, I'll pay you X. But what's a reasonable commission? Usually what you should offer is 10%–15% off the company's regular commission rates. This is business that they would not get otherwise. While it's not ideal, you'll be surprised by how open they will be to your suggestions. And, there is a lot of room to negotiate, such as which weeks they will handle management issues, just the weeks they have the home booked or all of the time? These finer points of the partnership can usually be hammered out fairly easily.

I do caution you, though, whatever you do, be sure to handle the bookings yourself. This is the best way to keep them honest. Here's the scenario . . . you advertise and take inquiries for your property. You speak with a renter, and they say, "I want to book it," you give them the number, and say, "Call this number tell them you want the Karpinski unit #1234." The renter calls that number, engages in conversation with the management company and just makes one comment about something that they were looking for like, "Well, we really wanted a home with two fireplaces, but we spoke with Christine, and we have decided her home will be better." Now, the management company takes this opportunity and says, "Well, we have so-and-so home down the road and that has two fireplaces . . ." Guess what, my friend? You just lost out on that valuable rental!

Finally, what should you do if you already have a management company, but now you've decided you want to get rid of them? When is the best time to fire your management company? I would try to avoid ending a contract with your management company in the middle of peak rental season. I would be leery of that scenario because most of the vacationers have already booked their accommodations. Since many of the bookings are made 30 to 90 days before the peak season, I suggest that you get yourself through the peak season, then, start advertising your property on the internet in your off-season and transition into self-management for next year's peak rental season. Or, as an alternative, you may want to call your management company and talk to them about partnership programs.

In 2012, I purchased a new property at the end of April. This is the "latest" in the booking season I had ever purchased a property. I was a bit nervous about getting my summer booked in such a "last minute" fashion.

On top of buying so late in the season, there were a considerable amount of cosmetic upgrades that needed to be done to the property before it was rental ready, Therefore, I didn't even have any decent photos to post for advertising purposes. Much to my surprise, I was able to get the entire season booked up.

As it turns out, while many travelers book in advance, there are a good number of people who book at the last minute.

So the moral of the story is if you are having a very difficult time with your property manager, even if it's the middle of the busy season, and need to make an immediate change, just do it! There are plenty of travelers out there.

By now, I think you get the point. Cut out the middleman and you win. Yes, there will be a little more work involved, but in the long run it will be well worth it. And as one season melts into the next, you will become more and more proficient at managing your own property. You may even want to give yourself the commission you save, and go take a vacation.

10

Effective Advertising

Advertising is powerful. Think about it. How else could you convince people that smoking is fun and that light beer really tastes good? Madison Avenue spends billions every year to get its messages across, and succeeds with often alarmingly effective results. Jack Simpson, a seasoned real estate columnist, once wrote, "Advertising is a powerful tool ... without it, your business is dead. If you ever run out of money, cut your pay, cut your staff, quit paying your bills, but DON'T ever stop advertising. Because if you do, it's all over!"

Another wise businessman said, "Eighty percent of all advertising is wasted. The trick is to find out what draws the other twenty percent in."

Indeed, one of the keys to being successful in the vacation rental business is the effective use of advertising. Ideally, you want renters to look for you. You don't want to have to look for them. So, how exactly do you do that? Well, even in this Information Age, newspapers still have a role to play, but not the ones in major metropolitan areas. Advertising prices in metropolitan newspapers are outrageous! And, let's face it, very few people these days spend the time and effort to scour big city newspapers looking for vacation rentals. Your print advertising dollar would be better spent on an ad sheet in your office, in a church bulletin, or in a small community newspaper. These forms of advertising have proven to be quite effective and not too expensive. In fact, sometimes the local newspaper can be the *only* way to find certain rental properties. One summer when we visited upstate New York, I couldn't find a single rental online. So what did I do? I dug out the local newspaper and started looking. Sure enough, we eventually found a place.

Still, in my experience, I have found that the internet is the first place that a potential renter will look when researching vacation spots. These days, when people want to buy concert tickets, real estate, flowers, gifts, you name it, the internet will have it. And the good news is that websites can be 100% effective in renting vacation properties as long as they are utilized to their fullest. Plus, the cost is remarkably low.

It gets even better—you don't have to be a computer whiz. You only have to know how to email and surf the Web. Of course, if you don't own a computer, it's nearly impossible to successfully rent by owner.

Internet Advertising

So now I've convinced you that the internet is the way to go. Great, welcome aboard! But the World Wide Web is incredibly huge. How in the world are you going to get your message out there amongst all that clutter? Won't it get lost? No, it won't. That is, not if you do it the right way. New York City is a big, crowded place too, but with a good map or, even better, a competent tour guide, you can get exactly where you want to go. Let me be your internet tour guide.

We're now at the point where you need to become familiar with four different kinds of websites. They are:

1. Vacation Property Listing Services (Portal Sites)
2. Specialized Websites
3. Universal Websites
4. Personal Websites

Let's examine each of them.

Vacation Property Listing Services (portal sites)

Vacation property listing services are websites that advertise vacation property for "rent by owners". The main purpose of these sites is to put renters seeking accommodations in touch with vacation property owners. I call these types of sites "portal sites." Most portal sites charge a fee ranging from $300 to $1000 per year (some are free), others charge on a three to six month basis, and a few charge a three to five percent of bookings. On portal sites you can enter information about your property such as a description, the number of bedrooms, amenities, etc. You can even upload photos of your property. Some portal sites will allow you to add a link to a personal website (described later). The portal sites will then do all the necessary marketing (such as search engine ranking) to help renters find you and help you find renters.

What is important about portal sites is that they help the renters see, feel, touch, and imagine your property. It makes them want more. A portal site is basically a gateway. Think of it as the classified section of your newspaper. Let's say you are looking to buy a new Toyota. You pick up your local paper and turn to the automobile classified section. Now, why did you go to that section and not to the sports pages? Because you had a purpose in mind . . . to find a car. It's the same with portal sites. They are like the classified section of the internet. You bought the entire newspaper, but you were only interested in one specific section. It's the same with the internet — all of it is available to you, but you're looking for something very specific. Yes, it is like finding a needle in a haystack, but with modern search engines, it is actually quite easy to find exactly what you are looking for. The portal sites will do search engine linking for you, so that's one less thing you have to worry about. When a person is looking for a vacation rental, in all likelihood they will end up at one of the major portal sites that are designed precisely for that purpose. There are hundreds, possibly thousands of such sites online.

That being said, all portal sites are not created equal. You as the owner want to make sure you use a portal site that is effective and easy to use. A portal site should be easy for you to use and more importantly, easy for the renter to use. Attributes that make a portal site effective and easy to use are:

For The Owner

Basic features that all portal websites should have:
- The ability to easily create initial listing in a comprehensive manner, including detailed property descriptors, photos and pricing information.
- The ability to update and change your rates, photos and other listing information on a regular basis.
- Optimized search listings at popular search engines, meaning the site should be listed within the top 10 for search engines in your category. After all, this is how your renters will find you in the first place.

Advanced features that are nice to have but not always available:

+ Property availability calendars and reservation request forms.
+ Foreign language and currency conversion to expand potential renter audience.

For the Renter

+ It provides multiple ways to find rentals by browsing listings or searching.
+ The ability to browse or sort listings by meaningful categories i.e., area, number of bedrooms, rates.
+ Search by available dates.
+ The ability to easily view availability through a calendar.
+ Telephone number for the portal site to assist renters or take complaints about properties.

Just as the classified section of the newspaper limits the size of your ad, portal websites generally have limited space or fields available for you to fully describe your property. In addition, some specialized websites will not allow you to link to a portal website page. So for this reason, I advocate that you also build a personal website.

Specialized Websites

In addition to portal sites, there are a number of specialized websites that you can utilize for advertising your property. These are websites that cater to the particular needs, desires, or interests of certain groups of people. Some of these sites are devoted to listing vacation properties and others are not. Some will have a designated area where you can add your property, but on others you may have to do a little digging to find an area for you to add your link (your personal website address).

The best example of a specialized site that is devoted to vacation property listings is www.PetFriendlyTravel.com. The main objective of the site is to connect a targeted group of renters (pet owners) with a specific group of property owners (those who accept pets). Most specialized sites work much like portals, allowing owners to enter property descriptions for a yearly fee.

But don't restrict yourself to specialized sites designed specifically for renters. A good example would be www.flyshop.com, which does not have travel as its primary purpose. It is *Fly Fisherman Magazine*'s website. The main purpose of this website is to sell the magazine. You'll find all sorts of information, of course, about fly-fishing. However, as you look more deeply into the website, you will see a section called "Travel Center." Go there and you can add your link to your cabin or home located in a fly-fishing area.

There is also a third type of specialized website that does a little of both, draws in the vacationers looking for accommodations, as well as people visiting the site for a special purpose. Examples of these would be chamber of commerce or local area websites. Let's look at a chamber of commerce site, for example. It will have all sorts of area information including shopping, restaurants, local festivals, activities, and accommodations in that particular area. So this website may draw people to it for many reasons, not just to look for accommodations. Most chambers will allow you to advertise your property on their website—most often for free to members. How do you become a member? Most only require you to be a sales tax collector, which most of you will be. So be sure to take advantage of this valuable perk that is available to you.

Universal Service Websites

Universal service websites offer a particular service related to vacation travel. Most often, these will be included on your personal website (some portal sites will also allow links to these).

Mapping websites. The most well-known of mapping website is Google Maps (maps.google.com). You can add a link from the map to your website. Adding a property location map is very helpful for the prospective renter. Many would like to know where your property is located and how to get there.

Note: To protect your property and your guest, do not put the map link to the exact street address. For instance if your property is located at 123 Sand Street, link to only to "Sand Street," or a nearby intersection, "Sand Street and Beach Road."

Payment options websites. If you accept electronic payments of any kind, then most often you will be able to provide a link to that site. PayPal (www.paypal.com) is a good example of a payment options site.

Personal Websites

A personal website is a site that you (or someone you hire) build and maintain. The main objective is to have a site where you can give detailed information about your property. You will link your personal website to many specialized sites (and some portal sites). But do *not* think that your personal website will be your main form of advertising. That's not the goal. Understand that your personal website is only a selling tool to help describe your particular property and your rules, policies, and rates. Its basic purpose is to "wow" the potential renter with more details, photos, and in-depth information regarding your property's unique features. You don't need to spend time or money to understand how to draw vacationers to your particular site. In other words, don't try to figure out search engines. (That would be like to trying to deliver newspapers to each person you thought might be looking for your classified ad in the newspaper.) Search engine ranking is a complicated task best left to professionals, portal sites, and specialized sites.

Now, here's something to keep in mind. If you think of the portal site as your online *classified* section, then your personal website (to continue the automotive analogy from earlier) is more like the car dealership, where the customer can come in, see the product for him or herself, and begin making a decision. You should think of your personal website as a place where renters can find all of the information they need to know about your vacation property (including lots of specifics that the portal websites don't allow). Providing all of this detailed information is your personal website's major purpose. And it should be designed and presented in such a way that most of the questions a renter might ask are already answered. That way, when the renters decide to go ahead and contact you, the point of their phone call or email message will not be to ask a bunch of routine questions—it will be because they are seriously interested in renting your property and are probably, at that point, very close to making a booking.

When building a personal website you have two main choices:

1. You can use the website space you receive through your Internet Service Provider (ISP).
2. Obtain your own domain name and find a place to host your site.

While using space you already have (through your ISP account) seems attractive, there are many benefits to having your own domain. The pros and cons of each will be discussed below. First, let's explain what each is and how to use it.

Personal Space from Your ISP

When you sign up for internet service, along with your email address and dial-up, cable modem, or DSL service, you typically are given a small amount of website space that you can use to host a personal site. Check with your ISP; you probably have free space available to you. To view a personal website hosted by an ISP, internet users will have to enter a website address that follows a pattern similar to the following: home.emailaddress.earthlink.com.

Note: Sometimes you can purchase a domain name and redirect the address to your ISP. If you do so, be sure to cloak, or hide, the address forwarding so that your chosen domain name remains displayed.

Registering Your Own Domain Name

Your second choice, and the one I recommend for developing your personal website, is to register your own domain name or internet address and an associated email address. Example: www.howtorentbyowner.com and christine@howtorentbyowner.com. Domains can be purchased for a year-long period with an annual renewal option. The cost to register a domain can vary significantly; however, most are $35 or less per year. I recommend www.godaddy.com.

Once you have registered your domain name, you need to find a place to host your site. Hosting companies also vary greatly in price and in degree of service. I suggest you look for basic service only. After all, you only have one property to list, not a whole store full of products.

Why Choose a Domain Name Instead of ISP-Provided Web Space?

You may ask, why should I go to the trouble and cost of registering a domain when I may have personal web space already at my fingertips? A domain name is permanent (so long as you renew yearly). How many times have you changed internet companies? Each time you do so, you have to notify all your friends that your email address has changed. Well, with ISP-provided web space, you'll have to move and/ or rebuild your website too. What a pain in the neck! This also means that anyone who has bookmarked your site will now have an address that no longer works. And, what about all of your previous renters? How will they contact you again?

So you see, building a personal website with your own domain name can help you build a brand name, or a name everyone will remember for your rental property. For example, HowToRentByOwner.com is much easier to remember and gives more of an air of professionalism than http://home.christinekarpinski.aol.com (try saying that one three times fast).

Another major advantage of having your own domain name is for your property value. Yes! When you go to sell your property, think of the advantage of saying, property with a great rental history *and* complete website is included. Now you're selling an established business rather than just another property.

Building Your Personal Website

There are several ways to build your own website. You can hire an individual, (college students can typically do it for $100 or so), or you can hire a web design company (they can be very expensive). Or, you can do it yourself. "What?" you say, "I have no idea how to do it. I have trouble even programming the DVR! How am I ever going to design my own website?"

Relax; it really is easier than you think. If you can navigate your way through a program such as Microsoft Word, then you can build your own website. I did. You can even take a class through your local library or through the continuing education classes at universities.

I suggest you try one of the many online programs where you can purchase the domain name, as well as develop and maintain your website. These all-in-one sites are inexpensive (between $5–$15 per month). And, they tend to be very user friendly. One such site is www.godaddy.com.

Now, what should you call your website, and what should you use for an email address? Try to tie the name of your personal website to your vacation property so it's easy to remember. For example: HuntingCabin.com or FlyFishing.com. Then devise an email address that easily attaches to the website, such as hunt@huntingcabin.com or dan@flyfishing.com.

Which Are the Best Websites for Advertising Property?

People often ask me, "What is the best website to advertise on?" There's no one answer. Each property is unique and what will draw one type of vacationer will not interest the next group. You have to find websites that are directly related to your renters' needs and interests. In today's landscape there are certainly a few websites that are known to be the best producers of inquiries and bookings.

In my opinion, in order to be successful, you will need to put your property on at least two of these six sites: AirBnB.com, Flipkey.com, HomeAway.com, PerfectPlaces.com, VacationRentals.com and VRBO.com.

In order to find the right websites to be listed on, there are considerations only you can determine. Are you near a marina, skiing, scuba diving, or casinos? Do you accommodate pets, handicapped vacationers, or senior citizens? There are specialty sites for all these types of properties and more. Get the picture? So you have to think like the renter. Is he or she a skier, a scuba diver, a nightlife devotee, or a big kid? Renters are going to decide based on their interests and their families' interests.

Decide what unique features your property has to offer and advertise accordingly. Imagine for a moment that you are not the owner. You are the renter looking for *your* property. Where would you begin? To find the best websites to advertise your property, you must think this way. Go to any search engine and type in the words you think the renter would search for to find your property. Look at the first few sites in the search results. Ask questions like, are there other properties on this site in the same area as my property?

It's generally better to be listed on sites that have many other properties in your area. Renters like to have choices, and if you are the only property listed in your area, chances are that the renters will move on to the next website that has more choices. Don't be shy either. Email the owners of a few properties and ask, "How well is this site working for you?" You may think of this as asking the competitors for advice, and it may seem odd, but this is a field where most people are not business people in the ordinary sense. Not in the cutthroat sense of big business where this may be considered privileged information. Many owners are happy to share their positive experiences.

It is important to list on multiple websites, at least three to five of them, for maximum exposure. It's still quite cost effective. Even listing on three sites will cost less than $1500 per year (though for maximum exposure it'll likely cost closer to $2000 per year). Rent your home for one or two weeks, and you've made your money back. How many sites you need to list with is a simple matter of supply and demand. If you're listing a property in a very popular destination, you might be able to get away with listing on just two to three sites. However, if your vacation property is in a somewhat obscure area, it would probably be wise to list it on five websites.

In some situations, cross advertising off the internet might make a good deal of sense. For example, in Colorado, I know that many vacationers check both in internet and ski magazines. The owners, quite logically, advertise in both.

Proper Exposure

More travelers than ever are choosing to rent vacation homes over staying in hotels. The number of homes available for rent has also grown. But the number of travelers seeking homes to rent still far exceeds the number of vacation properties available. Simply put, the demand exceeds inventory.

At a recent seminar for vacation rental owners, I heard this common refrain: "I have rented my vacation home for X number of years and have always been booked; but over the past year or two I'm getting fewer weeks booked." How can this be true if demand exceeds inventory?

The most revealing piece of the puzzle may be the answer to this question: "How many websites do you advertise on?"

Gone are the days of listing your property on only one website. For many years I listed my properties on one website. But with the increasing popularity of many websites, I have found cross advertising is the only way to get the maximum occupancy booked.

Here's the proof: I'll get an inquiry from "Jeff Smith" via my advertisement on one website, then minutes later Jeff Smith will also send me an inquiry from my ad on a different website. He found my property on two different websites—he may not even realize that it's the same property. Something about my home obviously piqued his interest when he saw it on each website.

What that tells me is Jeff Smith is shopping around from one site to the next, maybe comparing prices or to see if more properties are available that fit his needs. Jeff is what I would consider a savvy vacation rental shopper—he's looking on many sites and sending inquiries to multiple owners. But what if Jeff were a bit more timid about hitting that "inquire" button? The probability that he'll email me an inquiry is directly related to whether my property is on the website when he decides to send an inquiry. As long as I am listing my homes on all the major vacation rental websites, there's a good chance I will get a lot of bookings.

Over the past few years, my bookings grew incrementally as I added my properties to more websites. The benefits of listing on more than one website include:

- **Attracting different audiences**—There are obvious differences in the look, feel and navigation of various vacation rental websites. Some vacationers love a certain website while others might find the same site difficult to navigate.

+ **Additional exposure for your property**—Each website attracts different types of website users. Advertising your property on various websites will maximize your exposure and increase the opportunity for more bookings.

+ **Regional exposure**—While here in the U.S. we automatically think that U.S. travelers are our largest target group of renters, but—advertising on websites that are popular outside the U.S. can bring added exposure and more bookings. Europeans have been using vacation rentals (they call them Holiday Rentals) as their primary travel accommodations for even longer than the U.S. While the average U.S. worker gets fifteen days of paid time off, in Europe, depending on the country, they get four to six weeks paid time off. If you advertise on websites in Europe, you'll be doubling your exposure to travelers.

+ **Different inventories**—Inventories also make sites unique. While one site may list thousands of properties in a particular geographical region, another site may only have a few homes in that area. While some vacationers migrate toward the websites that offer more choices; others may get overwhelmed and prefer fewer choices.

+ **Different features**—No two websites are exactly alike. Different websites offer different features beneficial to both the owners and vacationers. For example, while one website may have the functionality for the travelers to drill down according to their desired criterion, another site may require them to scroll through many listings to find their perfect property to rent.

+ **Balance seasonality**—Most sites deliver scores of inquiries during the busy booking months of January, February and March. But when you're looking for renters during the shoulder or off-seasons, certain sites may work better during different times of the year. For instance, I have found that every year my winter renters always book from one particular site.

+ **Cost vs. return**—In the vacation rental business, advertising is cheap; the average vacation rental property owner spends only 2–10% of her gross rental revenues on advertising. In many other industries, 10–20% of the gross revenues are spent on advertising. The additional bookings you'll receive when you list your property on more websites usually outweigh the costs.

The main drawback to listing on multiple websites is the extra work of managing and updating each listing. When you change your rates, photos, descriptions, etc., it can become cumbersome to edit each website. To mitigate this work, utilize services that are compatible with multiple websites. For example, if you list your property on Airbnb you can link to your VRBO.com calendars.

On Your Websites

On your websites, you will need to include some pertinent information about your property. The portal websites will vary a bit from one another. But most will have fields where they want you to enter relevant data about your property. If they do not have specific fields, be sure include all your information in your description. Here is the standard information you should provide:

One-Line Description

They usually first ask for a brief, one-line description of the property. Here's an example of a one-line description: "Immaculate 3 BR, 3 BA condo, ocean front, great for families." Notice that the abbreviations are the very same kind you would use in a newspaper classified ad. This will be the attention grabbing line that captures your renter's interest—the line that makes them click on your ad out of hundreds of choices.

More Detailed Description

Then you will need to write a second, more detailed description (however, even these will sometimes have a limitation on how many total characters you can use). My recommendation is that you write three to five clear, concise paragraphs. Don't write too much, however, because you might lose the readers' attention. This is where you will give full detailed information about your property. This is your sales pitch. Refer to the next chapter on how to write a good description.

Photos

You will want to post some really eye-catching photographs too. We all know that old cliché about a picture being worth a thousand words. Well, it's true! Read Chapter 12 to learn how to take good photographs, or consider hiring a professional photographer for the interior and exterior scenes.

Note: Remember, website content and photos have copyrights. If you see an ad you like, do NOT copy it! That's plagiarism and illegal. And if you're using a photo you did not take yourself, be sure to get proper permission from the photographer and/or publication where you found the photo. If your photos have any recognizable faces, it's best to get written permission prior to publishing them on your website.

Contact Phone Numbers

It is an absolute must that you include your phone number, both on the portal website and on your personal website. I know there are some of you who are a bit squeamish about your privacy and are uncomfortable with the idea of posting your phone number out there for the whole world to see. Well, just keep in mind that this is a business. Would you want to do business with a company that had no phone number? Probably not, so you have to provide a number where the renters can easily reach you.

In addition to the numbers themselves, be sure to include your time zone (for example, Eastern Standard Time or EST). Remember, not everyone will be calling from the same time zone. This is important because when you put yourself in the renter's shoes, you have to realize that they may be working their way through dozens of listings. When they reach yours, it would be best if they call at the right time when you will be there to actually take the call. Otherwise you might miss out on impulse buyers. Consider cell phones too. But no need to purchase a toll-free number for reservations, with bundled rate plans and cell phones, people don't worry about long-distance calling anymore. Otherwise, they look too much like business numbers and renters may not hesitate to call you at 3 A.M.!

Email Address

Be sure to post your email address. Most portal websites will have a field where you can enter it. Some portals may hide your address and require the renters to inquire through the portal. This is for your protection. It helps to keep the spam down.

Rates

Quote all rates—nightly, weekly and seasonal rates. This information should go both on the portal site and on your personal website. Don't think you can leave the rates somewhat ambiguous, perhaps drawing in the curious with the intention of hooking them on your property before hitting them with the price. Give an example of a specific seasonal rate. A list format works best for rates because it's easiest to read. Use dashes to set off each item and asterisks for special notations.

Ellipses are great to draw the eye across the page and prevent a cluttered look. Be very clear and detailed to make it easy to understand your rates. Read Chapter 14 for specific pricing information and examples.

Additional Charges and Restrictions

You should also quote any fees, taxes, or additional charges. It's always a good policy to be as up front and honest as possible. Some portal websites will have a field for these, others will not, so you will have to input the information manually. In either case, make sure that you include this information not only on your personal website but on the portal site as well. Additional charges may include pets, deposits, cleaning fees, and more.

Restrictions would be things that you do not allow. The "don't even call me if . . ." items. The most common restrictions are: no rentals to anyone under age 25, no pets, no smoking, and minimum length of stay.

Amenities for Your Property

Many websites have check boxes for things that you have on your property, and some require you to just type them in. Don't overlook anything here; many renters want the conveniences of home and more. This is where you spell out everything you have. These would be things like a pool, tennis courts, hot tub, full kitchen, etc. There may be specifics such as linens provided, coffee maker, toaster, etc. If you have it, list it.

Local Attractions

Don't forget local attractions. People want to know what there is to do in your area. For example, many people might consider the Myrtle

Beach, South Carolina, area as strictly beach. Renters might not realize that there are several attractions that would appeal as much as the beach, such as a nearby battleship, an impressive aquarium, a golfer's haven, and many other not-so-well-known local attractions.

Calendar

Most portal websites have calendars available or allow links to universal calendars. They save both you and your renters a lot of time.

The importance of keeping your calendars up to date cannot be over emphasized, however, it's been a bit of a sore subject with many vacation rental owners. I have heard all the arguments against them but I stand behind my statement: It's imperative that you keep your calendars up to date. And here's why: You'll receive more qualified inquiries and more bookings.

Contrary to popular belief the listing sites are here to serve the vacationers, *not* the owners. (Don't bash me on this statement . . . yeah, yeah, I know the owners *pay* the money to list our properties, but we're paying these sites to bring vacationers to *book* our properties.) Let's face it, there could be a million properties available to rent, but if there are no *renters*, we make no money.

Think about the process of booking a vacation rental versus booking a hotel. When booking a vacation rental is a long, arduous process. In a snap, however, travelers can book a suitable hotel in any city, at any price range, and with any criteria. Conversely, booking a vacation rental takes much longer! We need to give the vacationers all the available information to simplify the process of finding a vacation home to rent. Keeping your calendar up to date is one way you can simplify the process for the renters.

An interesting observation, which solidified my stance, came during usability testing conducted by HomeAway, Inc. back in 2005. I was able to sit behind a one-way mirror and observe would-be travelers navigating through various Websites. The testing found that although many of the travelers had particular dates in mind (some set in stone, like their children's spring break, for example), they didn't go in and search by availability. Initially, participants went window-shopping to browse various properties with many different price ranges, amenities, etc.

When they got a feel for the market and what they were looking for, they either revised the search using specific criteria (number of bedrooms, number of baths, dates, prices, etc.) or they immediately drilled into calendars.

- When they arrived on a property listing with no calendar, they couldn't be bothered to inquire about availability. Instead they continued to search until they found a suitable property with the dates they needed visibly available.
- When they arrived on a calendar that displayed everything as available, they said, "Hmmm . . . Must be something wrong with it, no one wants to book this one."
- When they arrived on a property with their dates booked, participants with "set dates" continued looking for other properties.
- When they arrived on a property with their desired dates booked, participants with "flexible dates" said, "Well, I think we could go an additional week."
- When they arrived on a property with their desired dates available (but a lot of other dates booked), it gave them a sense of urgency. "All the good homes are going fast. . . . I better hurry up and call right away!" Some of the participants were so affixed on that property that we had to excuse them from the usability testing.

As you can see, the behaviors of our customers tell us that we should provide up-to-date calendars.

Now—go and update your calendar!

Reviews

The best way to "sell" your home is have someone else do it for you—this is best done by reviews from travelers who have stayed in your property. But what if you just started and have none yet? Do you have friends or family who has stayed in your home? If so, ask them to write some reviews for you!

Another thing you can do to boost the number of reviews is buy a guestbook and place it in your property (I sell my favorite one on my website www.howtorentbyowner.com). When your guests stay in your home, they will likely write in your guestbook (because they are relaxed and on vacation) and as soon as they get home, while they might have the best intentions to write an online review, life just gets in the way.

Many owners are concerned about getting a "bad review". Yes a bad review can significantly impact your credibility and your rentals. The best offense is to be proactive. Make sure to get as many positive, good reviews as you possibly can. Statistically speaking, it's inevitable that someday you will get a not-so-favorable review.

For fifteen years, I boasted that every review I received for my properties were always glowing and wonderful compliments—not one bad review! During my sixteenth year of renting, the inevitable happened! Here is exactly (including her spelling and grammar errors) what a traveler wrote on my VRBO.com advertisement:

"Upon entering the cabin, I quickly noticed it was not as represented in the photos on their website. There is no fireplace in the master and there is not a view from the hot tub—in fact, the hot tub in not where it is in the pictures. Here are just a FEW of the issues we had. There is no wifi, even after multiple attempts to hook up with the owners assuring us there was. I found it ironic that even those they kept saying it should be working upon reading the guest book, I found multiple entries stating they had problems and could not connect. The view is completely blocked by overgrown trees. The grill does not work. The sheets in the master are stained. (I've provided photos of both stained sheets & obstructed view to owner, There is no hot water hook up to the washer. The windowsills are covered with dead bugs. The fire alarm went off every time we heated the stove. Boards on the balcony are loose and need attention — as you can imagine, loose boards, a beeping fire alarm, and no wifi make major inconveniences on a family vacation with a husband who needs to connect to work & kids. The shower downstairs makes a LOUD shrieking noise for the duration of the shower & the paint around the shower head is peeling & rotting. Needless to say THIS CABIN NEEDS A LOT OF ATTENTION and a new cleaning crew. It is not super clean and stained sheets are disgusting. Another annoyance, where they've moved the hot tub to (not where it is in pics w view) is on the parking lot that you share with another cabin and there is virtually no privacy. It's pinned between the parking lot & a cabinet. We spent most of our time in Gatlinberg which was nice, but an overall major upset on accommodations. I've rented on vrbo for years and never had an experience like this. I would not recommend this cabin unless they come out there, make needed repairs, replace the bedding (the top quilts look like they've not been cleaned in years) and give it the much needed TLC."

When I read this review my blood boiled! The traveler never contacted me to complain about anything while she was there (except she could not get onto the internet, which was user error).

I tried to dispute it through VRBO.com but they would not allow the review to be taken down).

Not only was most of this false, I had just completed $20,000 worth of work on this particular cabin. Of course I took this very personally!

My only saving grace was the other reviews that were written. Thankfully the guests who stayed the week before had posted a really nice 5-star review touting all the new stuff in my cabin. And the guests who stayed after them had also done the same (the reviews show the dates the traveler stayed as well as the date that the review was posted). Basically my guests who stayed before and after had refuted the travelers "false claims".

On most websites that allow guests to review your property, the owner can post a response to the review. I of course took the opportunity to write my own rebuttal. Here's the response that I wrote:

Read the rest of the reviews for this property and you can clearly read between the lines and see that this person was just trying to get a free vacation from us. All of these claims are unsubstantiated and preposterous! Allow us to elaborate and you will see the ridiculousness of their "claims": First they claim that the BBQ grill does not work; it's a charcoal grill (a very high-end cast iron grill)—ummm ... how is it supposed to "work"? Secondly, they claim there's no fireplace in the bedroom. That's correct! There is no fireplace in the bedroom nor do we advertise one! They say that the quilts are old—that cannot be further from the truth—we just totally redecorated, got all new furniture and quilts (see the previous review). As for the internet not working—these people contacted me (numerous times) but they kept typing in the wrong access code. They did finally get it right after about the 20th attempt. I can go on and on but do not appreciate having to defend ourselves against false claims. Again—please read the other reviews for this property! Please disregard these people who just wanted to get a free vacation on us.

I was on "high alert" afterwards and asked my guests who booked what they thought when they read that "bad" review. Everyone said they read the one bad review and it prompted them to read my response as well as the other reviews. They all said it helped shape their decision to rent my cabin. Some said they especially liked my response—they could see the human side of me as well as my sense of humor. In the end, little did I know but that one negative review sandwiched between bunches of glowing reviews actually helped my bookings. I took the lemons and made some very sweet lemonade!

11

Writing a Good Description (Ad Copy)

The importance of writing a good advertisement description cannot be taken lightly. Just as your photos will help your renters see, feel and imagine your property, the goal of your written description should be the same—help your renters see, feel and imagine your home.

What we have to realize is there are three basic types of information gatherers. The first type might gather most of their information from your photos. The next type might be more comfortable with a phone call (having you describe your home). And the last group might read your description in full detail. To make sure that you don't miss out on any renters, it's important for you to target all of these different types of prospective renters.

Here are some helpful tips from Amy Ashcroft Greener for writing better descriptions of your property. Amy is a vacation property owner, but makes her living as a voice talent. Her work credits include several years as a copywriter, as well as radio and television news reporting. Since Amy has written and recorded hundreds of TV and radio commercials, she's excellent at "selling" a product in the shortest amount of time. This is the exact approach vacation rental owners need to take when wring their ads for their homes—you only have a short moment of opportunity to catch the reader's attention.

Painting Pictures with Words

By Amy Ashcroft Greener

I'll be blunt. Either you're a good writer or you're not. Most people fall into the "not" group, and that's okay. You can always hire a professional to write great copy for your webpages. Trouble is, very few owners do and opt to do it themselves.

Just be aware that if you aren't the best speller or grammarian, you need to move forward with care. Incorrect spelling, typos, and poor sentence structure are common place in vacation property descriptions. You don't want to be the listing that stands out to people because it is full of mistakes.

Truth be told, many owners are capable of writing good, basic copy. Your work may not have the flourishes and flow of an experienced copywriter, but you can do it. The process is not overly difficult, but it requires some extra effort and thinking beyond your personal perspective.

Think of your webpage as a sales brochure. If you picked up some literature from a business, and it had less-than-professional photographs, copy, and layout, you'd think twice before spending your money there. The same thing goes for a vacation property, only more so. Remember, people don't know you—or your rental—and your copy can say a lot about how you manage your property. Here are the elements of a great vacation property webpage:

- Easy to scan or read for key points
- Clear and concise
- Not too much information; not too little
- Top-notch photographs
- Extra features that site visitors appreciate, i.e., availability calendar, location map, guestbook, local weather, and rental agreement
- Simple rate structure and clearly outlined fees and taxes
- Multiple ways to contact you

If you present your property using all the above elements, your site will stand out among the crowd. Of course, this assumes you have a property that is well maintained, regularly improved, and is a desirable rental! A great webpage is one half of the equation.

The copy is the nuts and bolts of your sales presentation. Most owners labor over this, yet it doesn't have to be that way. Like any task, if you break it down into smaller chunks it's easier to accomplish and less daunting. Here are the steps

1. Interview yourself
2. Make a road map for the copy
3. First sentence: 17-word maximum
4. One paragraph, three sentences
5. Use key words that sell
6. Proofread before you post

Interview Yourself

All good copy begins with a few good questions. Even though an owner may think he knows everything possible about his rental, writers have a different perspective. A writer can be much more objective and you need to write from that same position.

Here's a list of questions to get you started. Some of the questions are meant to be thought-provoking, not necessarily factual. These are designed to help you see beyond the "2 bed/2 bath/sleeps 4" way of thinking. Good copy is based on substance, but it also has feeling and imagery.

If you're not physically at the rental, use photographs to help jog your memory. Pull up your images on the computer, grab a notepad, and jot down some quick answers. Remember, you're not trying to write copy here; just go with your first impressions to develop a basis for your property description.

- What three words best describe your rental?
- What are the three best features of your rental?
- When you are inside the rental, how does it make you feel?
- When you are standing outside your rental property, what is it like? Are there noticeable changes with each season?
- Describe your location and view. What do you see and hear around you?
- Describe your location in terms of distance to prime destinations near you. (For example: a two-minute walk to the ocean; five miles from Disney World; or seven blocks from the Theater District.) Write down several answers if possible.
- What draws people to the area?
- Why would someone want to stay at your property?
- What advantages do you offer compared to similar properties?
- What types of renters would you expect your property to appeal to and why?
- Walk into each room of your rental. For each room, do the following:
    1. List three things or qualities about this room that you enjoy most.
    2. Describe the furnishings and decor; how do they make you feel?
- What improvements have I made to this property?

Make a Road Map

Remember learning how to write a letter in school? First there was the date, then the salutation, then the introduction, followed by the body and the closing. Well, you're going to do the same thing for your rental copy, by breaking it down into smaller segments. That gives your writing a road map and makes the job much easier.

Here are the segments you'll want to include. Think of each one as a separate unit or paragraph. The introduction must come first, but all the other units can be ordered in whatever way works best for your property.

Introduction: Just a Taste

Start out strong and make people want to read more with short sentences and words that create images. Think of an introduction as a welcome mat that brings them inside.

Location: Specifics and Advantages

"Where are you located?" is a question owners hear over and over. Location is everything, so be specific, but also use key words like "convenient," "private," and "close to town" to convey the advantages your location provides.

Sleeping Accommodations: Bed Sizes

Tell people exactly what to expect so there are no surprises. If you have a multi-level condo, describe where the bedrooms are located, what size bed is in each room, and whether you provide additional blankets, pillows, sofa beds, air mattresses, etc. Rentals often accommodate groups of people, so renters appreciate knowing more details.

Features: Make a List

Big paragraphs that are loaded to the gills with features make for challenging reading. Frequently, people glance across large blocks of copy and may miss important items. Lists are much easier to read, have better retention rates, and are a snap to write.

Benefits: Sell Me on Your Rental

Features are important, but benefits are what the customer wants. Tell them why your property is ideal for them. Will a week at your rental be a perfect getaway for their family? Will honeymooners enjoy romantic views from the hot tub? Will sun-lovers thrill to being able to walk out of the condo right onto the beach? Put pictures in their heads, and they'll envision themselves at your vacation home.

Wrap It Up

Two or three sentences are all it takes to close your sales pitch. Very few rental owners do this on their pages, and it's an opportunity missed. Keep it simple and brief, but warm and inviting. Remember, you want people to see you as a friend and gracious rental property owner, not a corporate hotelier.

Shorter Sentences

If I remember one thing from my first news writing class in college, it was that a lead sentence for a news story should be no longer than 17 words. Honestly, I can't remember the research my professor quoted, but I do know that long-winded sentences don't work for readers. Shorter sentences get to the point, and they stand out. An occasional longer sentence is fine; just don't make it the rule.

Three Sentences per Paragraph

This is my personal formula for keeping paragraphs from becoming huge blocks of copy. People in a hurry often glance over the big paragraphs and may miss good information. To counter this, I recommend that you keep paragraphs to three sentences. Sometimes you may need to have a larger paragraph and that's fine. Just balance it by making the other paragraphs shorter in length.

Use Key Words that Sell

Mention the word "free," and everyone listens. Use that word on your webpage, and people won't miss it. (I use it in our low-season rate specials. Guests, who rent three nights in the dead of winter, get one night free. It works.) There are several other words that scientists have proven as good attention grabbers, including:

discover	love	save
easy	money	secret
fast	safety	yes

Now, for my personal favorite vacation property descriptors:

activities	extras	retreat
centrally located	fun	romantic
classic	inviting	rustic
clean	largest	secure/security
convenient	peaceful	spacious
cozy	perfect	warm
easy access	private	well-appointed
easy to find	quiet	well-equipped
exceptional	relaxing	wonderful

You'll notice that beautiful, nice, spectacular, and magnificent were not on my list. These words are so overused—especially in titles—that they just don't have impact. Use them sparingly.

Using key words will help people imagine themselves in your rental. If you sprinkle the words "peaceful," "escape," "romantic," "quiet," and "couples" into your copy, you'll immediately draw the attention of empty nesters or busy young couples.

Proofread Before You Post

Use a spell-checking program to look for spelling and typographical errors. After you're done, ask three people to look over your property description. Choose people with good communication and writing skills and who will give you an honest appraisal. Ask them to review your writing for sentence construction, grammar, content, and effectiveness (would they be enticed to rent your property based solely on what they've read?). Don't publish your copy until you have three sets of eyes look it over and receive positive feedback. By having others review your copy, you can feel confident that you've written an accurate property description with real selling power.

12

Picture Perfect Rental Photos

By Amy Ashcroft Greener

"One picture is worth 10,000 words."
—Chinese proverb.

Photographs are the most powerful tool you have on your vacation rental listing. Nothing else draws you into a web page and holds your attention more than images. We all know what we like in a good photograph, but capturing that quality in our vacation rental images is more elusive.

Put yourself in the shoes of someone searching the internet for the perfect vacation rental. Welcome to the world of comparison-shopping on the internet. Today's search engines bring up countless vacation rental websites from around the world in seconds. And, as an owner, all you want is just a little piece of the action to fill your calendar.

It all starts with your thumbnail photo, that postage stamp-sized picture next to your property's headline or title in many vacation rental listings. It's the first glimpse into your property's listing and can heavily influence whether or not someone clicks through to your page. Many owners choose to show the exterior of their property or the view. But you can show any image that you feel is a good draw for visitors to the site.

The best thumbnails are usually different than those of other listings. So if the vacation rental listings that fall around yours are full of light beige condo balconies or golden brown log cabins, find an image that sets yours apart. It can be a deck with an orange market umbrella or a red-heart shaped jetted tub. Vivid blue skies or green ocean waters are great visual draws, too. Interior photographs that are simple and uncluttered also translate well into thumbnails.

Today's consumer grade cameras have improved by leaps and bounds in just the past few years. Higher megapixels and resolution in newer point-and-shoot cameras means you have the ability to upload pretty decent quality images to your listing. But having better equipment doesn't guarantee great photographs. While it helps to have a good camera, you need to also have the eye for a good shot and a bit of skill for the best results.

I'd like to mention that when I first wrote this chapter for Christine several years ago, I was a typical vacation rental owner who took my own photographs. Since that time, I've taken my passion for photography to the professional level. I now have a different perspective and would encourage anyone who can afford to hire a photographer, to do so. It's an investment that will pay returns almost immediately because your listing will undergo an immediate visual transformation and as travelers are comparing properties, yours will be a stand out. I recommend looking for a photographer who specializes in real estate photography because they will have the vision and skill necessary to make your rental property look its very best.

So if you have your heart set on taking your own photographs, don't let me dissuade you because there's the heart of a photographer in all of us! To start down that path, I want you to know that taking beautiful images of your home is not going to take an hour. Plan on a full day to do the job right.

OK, so you're still wondering how could you possibly spend all that time on one room for just a single picture? Here are a few reasons why:

- The camera flash reflected in the window and made a huge white glare spot.
- You moved the camera oh-so-slightly while shooting, and the image is blurry.
- Someone left a plastic trash bag or stepladder in the background. (Don't laugh, both happened to me.)
- You thought you had everything in the picture, but did not.
- The time of day that you took the picture washed everything out.
- The shade on a lamp appears crooked.
- The picture just doesn't look right; it lacks a focal point.
- The room is too dark and photographed poorly.
- The picture was horizontal, and it would have been better vertical.
- The picture was vertical, and it would have been better horizontal.
- Yikes, you're in the photograph because you stood across from a mirror.

Every single one of those examples has happened to me at one time or another. That's why taking a couple dozen shots is to your advantage. Another benefit is that you will take more time to do the job right. After taking one shot three or four times, you'll eventually move to another spot and try something different. It forces you to look for new ways to approach the room and photograph it. Sometimes the picture you took just for the fun of it turns out to be the best of the bunch.

Where's the Ladder?

Next to my camera, this is the one item you can't be without when taking pictures. Every photography studio I've ever been in has a step ladder and you should too. By bringing the vantage point up a foot or two (or three if you're feeling bold), you can capture much more of the room. Very large rooms or those with open floor plans are ideal for ladder shots. But there's a caveat to using a ladder: use it sparingly and only where appropriate. I always shoot a large room or space at waist level for a more intimate feel and then I will select a good vantage point and use the ladder to slightly to change the feel of the image. Where I really prefer to use a step ladder is outside the property where I need to bring myself up several feet. The last thing you want to do is angle your camera upwards to the subject because it is unflattering and can distort the vertical lines of the building or house. Also, just by the nature of a ladder, you want to always have someone with you to secure the ladder so you are safe while looking through the lens at your subject.

The Secret is Staging

Staging is referred to in the real estate industry as the artful presentation of a house to potential buyers. This is most often seen at an open house, where you'll find soft music in the background, candles lit, attractive place settings on the dining table, posh pillows scattered on the sofa, the fireplace ablaze, or the smell of apple-cinnamon simmering scents. The whole idea is to entice visitors with a feeling of comfort and warmth and present a home in its best possible light.

Though we can't enjoy the olfactory sensation of simmering scents or feel the heat generated by the fire, a photograph can convey whatever we want it to. That's where you have creative license to design a photograph that best represents your property. The best thing is that staging doesn't cost much. Let's go room by room and look at possible staging techniques.

The Bedroom

The focal point is usually the bed, so an attractive bedspread or quilt along with pillow shams is paramount. Make sure the bed is impeccably made—no wrinkles or bumps in the bedding. Toss a trio of pillows on the bed and you've got "instant posh," as I like to call it. Use a silk tree or plant nearby to bring the outdoors in. Sometimes you may need to pull it into the picture to just frame the edge of the photograph (one of my favorite tricks). You certainly wouldn't leave a silk tree right next to the bed, but in a photograph it appears perfectly fine. Try using a lower wattage bulb in the lamps; it's softer and more appealing. Take pictures with the lights on and then with them off. Also, take photos with the curtains or drapes open, as well as closed. Be aware that horizontal mini-blinds will sometimes make wild "zebra stripes" if they let too much bright light through. Place a nice book or two on the nightstand, as though someone's been enjoying a good read. Chenille throws can also look nice draped across the edge of the bed or footboard. Again, take pictures with and without the throw so you've got choices if it doesn't look right.

The Kitchen

Kitchen photographs tend to look the most cluttered of all pictures posted on webpages. Blenders, toasters, coffee makers, microwave ovens, paper towel holders, radios, canister sets, towels—you name it—give instant clutter to a picture. Sure, that's stuff people need when they're at your rental, but do you want it to give the impression of a cluttered kitchen?

First, clear off all counters except for the necessities—the microwave, the coffee maker, and maybe a utensil caddie. Everything else goes in the cabinets (at least for the time being). Actually, I keep our blender, crock-pot, and even the toaster in our Lazy Susan—kind of a makeshift appliance garage! This is especially helpful if you have a small kitchen, as many rental homes do.

Next, get rid of knick-knacks if you have them. You know, those cute craft-show doo-dads that hang on the wall under the wall cabinets. Another potential clutter source is the top of wall cabinets. For years, people have strung silk ivy and displayed dollar store baskets in this space. Less is more in this case, and if you don't have a good decorator's eye, it's best to clear off the cabinet tops.

If you have an island or eat-in kitchen counter, it's nice to show off that area with appropriate flourishes. A wooden bowl of plastic fruit can look like a still life in the center of the island, while three simple place settings at the counter can look inviting to guests. Keep towels, potholders and oven mitts tucked away for the photograph session. And no magnets or sticky notes on the refrigerator; it will look neat and clean with nothing at all.

And finally, avoid bright, overhead lighting to keep the picture more intimate. I like to use the vent hood light or light over the sink to bring illumination in small amounts into the picture. If you have recessed or track lighting, you'll be in great shape because these disperse small amounts of light without overpowering the photo.

The Family or Living Room

This is one area you can have a lot of fun with. First, it's usually a larger room and gives you more opportunities for different angles and shots. Second, you can set the tone with the decor. And third, you can play with accessories here more than with any other room. For example:

- Toss coordinating pillows on the easy chair or sofa.
- Drape a cotton or chenille throw over the edge of the sofa.
- If you have a fireplace, make a fire.

- Angle an area rug on the floor to make the area more intimate.
- If you allow candles in your home, light an arrangement on the coffee table.
- Bring a silk tree into the picture to add vertical line and color to the picture.
- Use low-wattage bulbs for added intimacy.
- Put a wooden checkerboard on the coffee table to imply that a game is in progress.
- If you choose to turn the TV on, be sure to select a channel like Food Network or The Travel Channel for attractive images.
- Make sure the pillows are arranged perfectly and the sofa cushions are smooth.
- Angle furniture so that it fits the picture, not the room (an industry trick by photographers who shoot editorial layouts for magazines).

The Bathroom

By far, the bathroom is the most difficult room to photograph due to its size. Whether it's long and narrow or just small and average, unless you have a master bath suite, you've got a challenge. First of all, ask yourself whether this room *needs* to be photographed. If your bathrooms are pretty basic, no one will find those photographs very interesting. On the other hand, if you have a beautiful step-in Jacuzzi tub with a view of the mountains, you've got a winner.

- Be careful of cluttering up the bathroom. Too many candles, towels, dishes of potpourri, decorative glass bottles, and cherubs can ruin a good thing. Pull back and keep it simple. Two fluffy towels placed next to the tub, along with an attractive bottle or two of liquid soap or lotion give the impression of a high-end spa.
- It's hard to take pictures around mirrors, so keep in mind where you are and where the camera is pointing. In some instances,

you may have to step outside the bathroom and shoot the photograph from the doorway.

+ Bathrooms are typically brighter; so don't worry about dimming the lights here.

+ Please don't take a picture where the toilet is front and center. It's just bad.

The Deck, Hot Tub, Porch, Etc.

Believe it or not, a bright sunny day isn't always the best for shooting outdoors. The sun washes out colors and casts strong shadows (especially on covered decks and porches) so ideally a day with some clouds to soften the light is better. Besides lighting issues, outdoor photography has a few additional concerns. First, the season and weather you're experiencing and second, the background. If you have a beautiful home on the beach, then by all means you want a sunny day with blue or green water and lots of colorful beach towels and umbrellas. If you shoot during the off-season (even if it is sunny), you won't get the same feel as the beach in full swing. I have one picture that I took during fall that shows the lake around the corner from our chalet. The colors are breathtaking and give the viewer a look at another season at our chalet. When taking photographs outdoors, you're at the mercy of Mother Nature and her schedule. So be prepared when the conditions are right to get out there and take a lot of pictures.

+ Be aware of the background. If there's something odd or not very attractive behind your subject, move and see if you can frame it differently.

+ No people in the hot tub or the swimming pool. Your guests want to imagine themselves there; it's just best to leave it to the imagination.

+ Stage the hot tub. Take two towels, two wine glasses on a tray with a bottle of wine and you've got an instantly romantic setting.

+ Turn on the tub. Put the jets on high for maximum effect. Another trick: stand on a small ladder and take the picture from an angle off to the side for a professional look.

+ If you have Adirondack chairs or beach chairs, stage them with towels, beach balls, a glass of lemonade, a hardcover novel, or any other appropriate item.

+ Set the table. Use attractive place settings to envision al fresco dining on the deck, porch, or balcony

+ If you have a porch swing, you can stage it with a book and small pillow.

Shooting 101—Good Composition

As an amateur photographer, I've been fortunate to work around professionals all my life. Here are some of the things I've learned from them along the way:

Vertical and Horizontal Shots

As a photographer I like to take a lot of portrait, or vertically-oriented photographs. But unfortunately the vacation rental web sites aren't really optimized for vertical photographs. If you have a room like a small bathroom and you have no choice but to photograph it vertical, then that's what you have to do. But whenever possible, shoot all your images horizontally so you get the best orientation for vacation rental sites.

Find a Focal Point

Just as each of us has our good and not-so-good features, so do rental properties. Walk around a room and decide what its best features are. It may have several, and if it does, you'll need to take more pictures. For example, if you have a beautiful stone fireplace, it only makes sense to make that a focal point in a picture. But what if you have a big entertainment center just across the room—out of sight of the fireplace shot? You can try to take a picture that would include both, but it may not be possible without a wide-angle lens. If you can't include both, move across the room to another angle and see if you can get another shot—equally good—that highlights the entertainment center. When you review your pictures, you can decide which one works best.

Go Off-Center

Nothing in nature is perfect; so don't try to be precise and centered with every photograph. Off-center is good—it looks more realistic and is more pleasing to the eye. How many times have you seen a picture of a bed in a bedroom shot straight over the middle of the bed? Is it original? Is it interesting? Now take that same bedroom photo and stand as far back as you can from the corner and shoot across it diagonally. Now it's more artistic and makes the room appear larger because you're showing other features of the room—not just a big old bed.

Rule of Thirds

Think of your viewfinder as a blank piece of paper. Now mentally draw a tic-tac-toe graphic on it—two lines vertical and two lines horizontal. This is how artists and photographers use the Rule of Thirds to find pleasing placements for their compositions. The idea is that you center your focal point or key subject on one of the areas where the lines intersect. What you're trying to avoid is aiming your camera right at something and having the focal point fall dead center. The Rule of Thirds will help you place the focal point off-center but in such a way that it looks natural and just feels right to the viewer. Of course, any artist or photographer will tell you that rules are made to be broken, so don't use this as a steadfast rule. It's just a guideline to help remind you to keep your subject's focal point in the most visually pleasing position. I like to start by using the Rule of Thirds when I begin a session but then I look for more ways photograph the same room but with a different perspective.

Lighting

Each hour of the day, the sun moves overhead and makes very perceptible changes in the way a room looks and feels. For example, our chalet's living and dining room areas appear cold in the morning when the sun is on the opposite side of the house. Later, the exact opposite happens: between 2 P.M. and 4 P.M., the sun is so bright and strong coming through the high windows that it washes out the colors of the room. The golden hour for taking pictures in that area is late afternoon, usually between 4 P.M. and 6 P.M. This is an important factor often overlooked by amateur photographers. Take your time and watch how the sun affects your subject, be it the exterior of the cabin, the hot tub on the deck or the master bedroom. Determine the best time of day to shoot, and you'll be rewarded with photographs that are eye candy to vacationers.

As far as artificial lighting is concerned, take pictures with both lights on and off. Sometimes the warm glow of a bedside lamp will make a better photograph. Other times, a light may cause glare or may be too bright. Again give yourself choices—take shots with both lights on and lights off. If you have recessed lighting in your property, it really looks good in photos. These focused areas of light from the ceiling add ambiance without washing a room out. Overhead lights, especially big kitchen fluorescents, are usually best left off. Fluorescent light bulbs cast a cool hue on a room and are rarely flattering. Small lighting sources, however, can be nice touches in a photo. Illuminate the area over the kitchen range, by turning on the range hood light. Or a single light over the sink can brighten up the area.

Uploading Your Images

After you've edited your images, you'll need to upload them to the vacation rental sites your property is listed on. Before uploading, check the image guidelines with that particular site so you know the maximum file size and recommended pixels. You want the best possible look for your photographs and this will help you achieve that. This way, when you save your photographs, you'll have them at the size for best results. For example, most vacation rental websites will let you upload an image up to 2 megabyes (mb). A larger file size contains more digital information and will take longer to load, but once it's uploaded the photograph should appear much clearer and possibly larger than your original one. For vacation rental web sites, you'll want to set your pixels at 1024 x 768 for the best resolution. However, if you have photographs with a lot of lines or detail in them—like fine tree branches, shingles, siding, railings—you may want to change the pixel settings to 800 x 600 to avoid moiré, the jagged lines and crispy look that can happen with these types of images.

The Bottom Line

After all this you may say to yourself, "That's an awful lot of work just to get a few nice pictures of my rental." And you're absolutely right. But when you get compliments from people saying how much they liked your pictures or how nice your home looks—you'll be glad you took the extra time. Think of good pictures as an investment in your investment, corny as it may sound. With better-than-average photographs, your property will present a polished, professional image and give people a reason to email or call about your rental.

Note: Remember, photos have copyrights. If you're using a photo you did not take yourself, be sure to get proper permission from the photographer and/or publication where you found the photo. If your photos have any recognizable faces, it's best to get written permission prior to publishing them on your website.

CHAPTER

13

Virtual Tours

The newest advertising technology available to vacation rental owners is virtual tours. You can optimize your advertisements by adding a virtual tour to your personal website and asking the portal websites to link to it.

Virtual tours bring a new level to the ability for potential guests to see, feel and imagine being in your property. Just as with taking photographs, virtual tours involve some planning, staging and technology expertise. As always, you can choose to do it yourself or hire a professional to do it for you.

Since I am not an expert in virtual tours, I have turned to an expert in this field—Ed Reese who has written this section on virtual tours. Ed Reese is a vacation property owner who has extensive knowledge of creating virtual tours.

Increase Renter Confidence With Virtual Tours

by Ed Reese

Last summer I was planning my honeymoon and really wanted to book a vacation home on Vancouver Island, British Columbia. However, after looking at properties for several weeks I was still unable to find a property for this very special vacation. Why? I just wasn't 100% convinced that these properties were exactly what they were advertised. Many of the properties had amazing photos, well-crafted descriptions, and guest testimonials. But, because of the importance of this trip, I still had some doubts. Many of my questions were still unanswered. How close are the neighbors? Is it really walking distance to the beach? How spacious is the living room? Sometimes photos are limited in their ability to accurately highlight a vacation home. However, my questions could've been easily answered (and my doubts erased) by including virtual tours. That extra assurance would've probably been enough for me to make that reservation last summer.

There's an added bonus. In addition to instilling confidence in the quality of your property, it also cuts down on the number of questions from prospective guests. Because virtual tours show every inch of the property, many questions and concerns are answered without a phone call or an email. In fact, when I receive questions about one of my properties, I'll often reply with the link to my virtual tours and a brief response rather than a lengthy description. It saves time and the guests love the perspective. It's especially useful in showing unique properties. For example, one of my vacation properties is a European style cabin with no walled bedrooms and a 15 foot vaulted ceiling. This type of lodge is common in Europe, but relatively rare in the United States. Guests have a difficult time understanding how it could comfortably sleep five adults. That is, until they see the virtual tours. Then they see exactly how the sleeping areas are divided and understand how spacious a home with no "official" bedrooms can be.

It's part of an increasing trend as well. Our online culture is becoming more and more interactive. Virtual tours allow your guests to virtually roam through your home, grounds, and area. They'll forward these links to family and friends who will start to feel like they really know your property (and can't wait to go there). I frequently hear from guests how my virtual tours help them view the properties, make a more informed vacation rental decision, and have fun during the process. My virtual tour page is consistently one of the most popular areas on the website. More importantly, it's the second most popular entry page on my website (behind the home page), meaning that many people are forwarding the links on my virtual tour page to family and friends.

Getting Started

First, you have to make a choice. Is this something you can do yourself or does it make sense to hire a professional? While you might be able to use your iPhone or iPad to create a virtual tour, taking the photos is only half of the battle. But here are a few quick and easy questions to ask yourself to determine if this is for you:

- Would you enjoy staging, lighting, and photographing your vacation home?
- Do you already have a high quality digital camera, tripod, and lighting kit or wouldn't mind purchasing new equipment?
- Would you enjoy taking the time to learn a new technology?

If you answered yes to all these questions, then producing your own virtual tours is an option to consider. Virtual tours consist of three main components: taking the photos, stitching the photos together, and publishing the photos/interface.

Taking Your First Photos

Good photographers constantly battle light conditions. This is amplified when shooting 360 degrees. Try to shoot in lighting conditions that are as even as possible and to use as much interior light as possible to balance exterior light. Also remember to look everywhere for unsightly items. Virtual tours capture everything! Look for garbage cans, socks, food, and anything else that might be lying around. Another early mistake is not checking the level frequently. You must make sure that your camera and tripod is level. The last major tip regarding taking the photos is the use of bracketing. Take one photo at the recommended light level and then manually shoot the same exact photo one stop higher and one stop lower. By compositing these photos together, you'll be able to see the inside of your home as well as the beauty outside. Here is a list of steps and tips:

Clean Up Steps: Most Important Areas

- Clean windows, doors, screens, and large reflective surfaces
- Fix all non-functioning lights
- Clear off kitchen counters
- Remove magnets or personal knick knacks from fridge, doors, etc
- Organize or hide books and magazines that may "clutter" a piece of furniture
- Toys or other play areas should be organized or hidden entirely
- Dust and polish all furniture and counters
- Hide brooms and cleaning products
- Stand back and look for anything out of place or that may adversely "date" the photos (holiday decorations)
- Sweep or pressure wash walkways, consider leaving "wet" for a different look for concrete patios

Taking The Photographs: Tips to Obtain Quality Results

+ Lots of windows and natural light? Shoot at dawn or dusk when light is less powerful

+ Draw curtains if exterior lighting is too powerful or if you want to hide the homes location

+ Hide the sun behind trees in outdoor shots to avoid lens flare

+ Turn on all interior lights or use light kit to increase visibility in the room

+ Take a photo every 90 degrees. It's easier to piece together right angles.

+ Make sure the camera and tripod are level and horizontal

+ Setup the tripod in the center of large rooms and where the tripod footprint is not hiding details

+ Keep hands, feet, and pets behind camera

+ Always use the camera's timer

+ Bracket your photos manually if possible

Helpful Additions To Consider

+ Fresh Flowers

+ Bowls of Fruit

+ Plants and Lighting

+ Run a sudsy bath, add flower petals, candles, etc. for romantic effect

+ Stage a romantic dinner table setting with candles and quality flatware

What Not To Do

+ Don't rush the staging portion. It's very important.

+ Don't limit yourself to one take. You may need several to get the right look

+ Don't assume that your tripod will stay level after the first shot. Keep checking.

Stitching Software and Publishing

To convert your series of photographs into a 360 degree virtual tour and post them on the internet you'll need stitching software. Some companies to consider when looking for stitching software are 3Cim, PanaVue, PanoTek, iPix, and Easypano to name a few. There is quite a range in price. Entry level stitching software can be found for as little as $30 while professional versions can easily cost more than a thousand dollars. Fortunately, most packages include publishing software that helps create your web interface and enables you to post to your website. Still, it's best to make sure the software you select is a good fit for your project as well as your budget.

The Professional Services Approach

If all of this information sounds too technical, time consuming, or costly, there is another approach—professional services. There is a growing number of vendors who specialize in producing high quality virtual tours for the vacation rental market. Expect the overall cost to be as low as $250 for three virtual tours and as high as $2000. The typical range is $500–$1,000 for 3–5 virtual tours with a $20–$50 per year hosting fee after the first year. A few companies to consider for virtual tour vendor are 3Cim or Imagemaker 360 to name a few. Be sure to take a look at their portfolio and ask them a lot of questions until you're certain you've found the right vendor for the job.

Summary

Whether you're producing the virtual tours yourself or outsourcing to a vendor, the difference on your website will be immediate. Online viewers will know exactly what your home offers and see every square inch. While that might sound frightening to some, it's reassuring to most guests of vacation properties. Much like high quality photos, exceptional copy writing, and keeping an updated calendar, incorporating virtual tours is another way to increase your occupancy and improve your guest's on-line experience.

14

Pricing—Be Right on the Money

The subject of pricing *anything* can seem a bit subjective. After all, what is a fair price for an airline ticket? A new car? A steak dinner? A vacation home rental? The standard answer is, whatever price the rest of the market dictates. So when it comes to pricing your property, it is important to be right on the money. Literally! Price will directly affect the amount of response you get from your ads. To get just the right price, you will have to do research (I told you that work would be involved) on other properties in your area and find out what these other owners are charging. The best way to do this is (yet again) to think and act like a renter. Shop around for rates. Log on to the internet and start searching. Make sure you are checking out similar properties. It's helpful to compare apples with apples not oranges. You can also check with management companies that rent properties in your area. Do whatever it takes to make an informed decision on what you should charge.

One mistake that many owners make is pricing their property much lower than their competition. I caution you that while it's certainly acceptable to charge a little less, maybe $10–$50 per week (to give you a competitive edge), pricing much lower may give the potential renter the wrong impression. They may think that your home is somehow inferior to the others. When I first started renting by owner, I was worried that I would have to give away the farm in order to get renters. I thought I would need to price my place significantly lower just to get the business. Fortunately, a phone call from a renter made me rethink this philosophy. He asked, "What's wrong with your home?" Shocked, I replied, "What's wrong? Why?" His response was, "Well, your home is so much cheaper, there must be something wrong with it!" That was a real eye opener for me. After that, I raised my price to be exactly the same as the other units in my building, and the rentals flowed in at a steady pace.

OK, let's look at the opposite end of this issue: what about charging more? It may well be that your home has granite countertops, the most expensive furnishings, or other advantages that people may be willing to pay more for. And if you own a single family dwelling, you have much more flexibility with regard to rates because these homes can differ significantly from one another. So if your home is much nicer than the next guy's, you can indeed charge more. But, if you are a condominium owner, unless you own the penthouse, most likely your unit is laid out exactly like the rest of the units, and therefore, you have to price your property within a similar range as the others. There's really no way around it. Yes, your expensive furnishings and fixtures can be used as a selling point and perhaps command a little higher price however you cannot charge twice as much as everyone else. While it may be true that your home *is* nicer than the rest of them, in all likelihood this means that you will probably book faster and quite possibly more often than your competition. If you're going to charge significantly more than your competition, then your home needs to be significantly better.

Pricing structures

Next, let's discuss the different pricing structures. By this I mean rates for specific seasons. Typically there are four to eight pricing seasons. There are the typical seasons—spring, summer, fall, and winter. But, you might also have other "hot" times within those seasons, such as spring break or fall foliage times, or maybe there's an event in the area that draws in many vacationers, like a festival or sporting event. These weeks you would probably want to price higher since demand is higher. But let me add a caution: don't make your prices too complicated.

Here's a typical listing of rates:

Season	Start	End	Per Night	Per Week	Per Month
Spring	Mar 01	Mar 15	$185	$ 925	N/A
Spring Break	Mar 15	May 01	N/A	$1,150	N/A
Late Spring	May 01	May 24	$185	$ 925	N/A
Summer	May 25	Aug 11	N/A	$1,350	N/A
Late Summer	Aug 12	Sept 08	$215	$1,075	N/A
Fall	Sept 08	Oct 31	$150	$ 700	$1,800
Winter	Nov 01	Mar 01	N/A	N/A	$1,100

Rates do not include X% Sales Tax and $X Cleaning Fee. Pets OK with owner's permission ($25 fee nightly/ $150 weekly), $XXX Security Deposit is required. Note: Until confirmed, rates are subject to change without notice.

As you can see from this example, the rates for each season have corresponding dates and prices for each time period. First, let's take a look at the corresponding dates. We all know that the seasons change in March, June, September, and December. But this owner's corresponding dates do not follow the calendar exactly. Did you notice that the summer rates start in May? This is because May is the highest demand. Your highest demand will be during the high or peak season. So if you have a ski home, the winter is peak season. If you have a beach home, it's the summer. You get the idea. This is the time when you can charge the most amount of money.

Looking more closely, you will notice that some time periods have nightly, weekly, and monthly rates, and some do not. This is for the same reason . . . it is based on demand. There is no need to quote rates for things that you wouldn't consider selling. This owner obviously will not rent on a nightly basis during the summer. Weekly rentals only. This is because the owner's quite sure that he or she will rent full weeks during this period. Why cut yourself short and allow someone to rent for three or four nights when you can have more income from the full week rental? And, on the same note, the owner does not show monthly rates either. That's not to say that he or she will not rent all four weeks of the month to one person, it's just that there is no discounted rate for that time period. After all, why give a discount on something that you can sell at full price? As always, it's all about thinking like a smart businessperson.

Let's look at the nightly rates. As you can see, they are not just the weekly rate divided by seven. There's a good reason for this. Nightly rates typically are 1/5 to 1/6 of the weekly rate. This owner can even advertise a special in the spring: "Rent 5 nights, get 2 nights free." Or how about this one: "Spring special: 33% off regular rates (summer rates)."

Now take a look at the owner's fall rates: $150 per night or $700 per week. "But," you say, "why would this owner offer such a low weekly rate?" In this owner's area, the fall has a high demand for two- or three-night rentals, and virtually no demand for weekly rentals. Therefore, the owner can charge a higher nightly fee and by lowering the weekly rate, he'll raise his chances of getting an otherwise empty week booked.

We also need to talk about monthly rates. Typically the monthly rates are quoted only during the slowest season. From this example, you can see the slowest seasons are fall and winter. Monthly rates are generally equivalent to a two- or three-week rental during that time period.

And be sure to clearly state all extra fees. Notice the footnote below the rates.

Rates do not include X% Sales Tax and Cleaning Fee. Pets OK with owner's permission ($25 fee nightly/ $150 weekly), $XXX Security Deposit is required. Note: Until confirmed, rates are subject to change without notice.

It's not a good idea to add the state sales tax figure to your price. The average consumer expects to pay sales tax. (Besides, the sales tax department likes to see taxes listed separately.) Also, let every renter know up front any other fees that will be assessed.

Lastly, don't overlook the last line about rates are subject to change. This is for your protection. Your quoted rates can catch you off-guard sometimes especially if your rates change right near a particular holiday. For example, Thanksgiving was November 22, in 2012, making Thanksgiving weekend from November 21st through November 25th. So your rate changed to your low season rates on November 26th (after Thanksgiving week). Let's say you had someone call on November 30, 2012 looking to rent next November 27th through December 1, 2013. If you did not have the disclaimer, you would have to rent it to them for the posted rates. But guess what? Thanksgiving in 2013 is on November 28th! You'd be giving away a peak holiday weekend for much less than you should.

Pet Fees

For those of you who will accept pets (I think it's a good idea), it is absolutely appropriate to charge a daily pet fee. Think about it. Pet owners know and accept the fact that when they go away they have to pay for boarding for their pets. I, as an owner, do not want to *encourage* guests to bring their pets (pets can cause damage, but the risk is not as great as you imagine). If you do not charge extra for the pet, it could open up the door for this scenario . . . "We want to board Fido because he's such a pain. It would be nice to have a vacation without him, but it's way cheaper if we just take him with us."

Still, I would accept pets as a convenience for my guests. Just as the convenience items in the grocery store cost more per ounce, you too should charge more. My recommended pet fee is at least $20–$30 per night. I personally charge $25 per night and have never had anyone complain.

Charge By Night Or Per Person?

The rental market where your property is located usually determines whether you charge by the guest or by the night. What works well for one rental area may not work for the next.

Let's look at two dynamically different rental markets, Tennessee and Florida.

In Tennessee, the first question a potential renter asks is "What is the extra person charge?" This is because in Tennessee the rental rates are typically published based on double occupancy with extra person charges. It's common for owners and property management companies to charge "extra person fees" and the guests are accustomed to paying this way.

There are two schools of thought for conforming to the market or doing something different. If you conform, the guests will easily be able to compare and contrast properties based on price. If you choose to be different, it could give you an advantage or it could play against you.

Take a two-bedroom, two-bathroom cabin that sleeps six. Here are two ways you could price it:

$99 per night based on double occupancy.
Each extra person is $10 per night.
The total for six people would be $139 per night.

Or

$139 per night. No extra person charges.
The total for six people would be $139 per night.

The $99 rate looks very attractive for anyone who is budget conscious. One person who looks at two exact cabins priced both ways might go for what seems to be the bargain-priced cabin. But another person might be inclined to shy away from the less expensive property because she thinks, "There must be something wrong." The main thing that worries me about this pricing strategy is it sets a temptation for renters to "not tell the whole truth," as in this scenario: Do I tell about the baby (or worse yet, 5 kids) and pay $10 extra per night per child?

Now look at the other pricing, $139 per night flat rate. On the upside, you will get the full rate each night your property is booked, regardless of whether there are two people or six people. Some renters hate the "nickel and dime" add-on charges, and would rather pay a flat fee. But the big disadvantage to the flat-rate pricing is your property can get passed up because the other one "seems" less expensive to the renters who are scanning for price.

Now let's look at Florida. The rental rates there are typically published based on a flat rate with maximum occupancy charges included. If I even thought of adding an "extra person charge," I think guests would tell me to hit the road. I do have a "maximum occupancy" and "extra person charge" clause in my contract, which the guests sign. But how many times have I charged an extra person charge? Let me think. . . . Zero! Don't count on extra person charges boosting your bookings or revenue in Florida.

Minimum Stays

Many people ask me, should I require a minimum stay? As you can see from the example above, yes, it is advantageous to require minimum stays. The owner in the example requires a minimum stay of a week in the summer and a month in the winter. A lot of owners will not rent anything less than three nights, period. Others will do nightly rentals all year long. It's all a matter of preference and what your market dictates. The people who require three-night minimums mainly do this as a quality-of-life issue. It's a lot of work to coordinate daily check-ins and checkouts, not to mention the increased number of checks coming in as well as deposits returned for nightly rentals.

Discounts

Here's another one I hear a lot, "Will you give a discount?" Sometimes I will and other times I will not. It all depends on the situation. For peak weeks, I never give discounts. When there are times that are not easily rented, then sure, we can negotiate. Knock off 15%, the cleaning fee, or whatever you feel comfortable doing (but *never* knock off the sales tax).

It's your home, and it's your call, but I will not give my home away. Remember, though, each time you allow a renter into your home you are taking a chance that things could happen. Some offers just are not worth it. Use discretion. You may get someone who wants to rent your home for 75% off. Think about it. Is it worth it? This is not some deep discount hotel. If you are doing everything right and renting all of your peak season and achieving positive cash flow, you shouldn't need to take that risk.

Be careful not to give discounts too early. I make a general rule that I will not give a discount until three weeks prior to the rental date. Learn from Duke's example:

Duke got a call from a renter 11 months prior to the rental date. They wanted to rent the last two weeks in April and asked if he could receive a discount if he rents for two weeks. Duke looked back at his past three years and had never rented those two weeks. So he agreed. He was generous and gave them 30% off his normal April price. Now the time passed and in January, Duke started getting a lot of calls for the week of April 19–26. He soon found out that this year Easter was very late, creating a high demand week that he easily could have rented for full price. Don't let this happen to you!

All that being said, there is one time that I will always give a discount—and that's to active members of our military (no not police or firefighters, just to the military). But I do require proof—they must send me an email from their military email address or send a copy of their military ID. Whether it's peak season or off-peak, I always offer a ten percent off the base rate as a "thanks for your service" discount.

Raising Your Rates

The real beauty of vacation property ownership is that you call the shots for your business. If you feel your rental demand or property improvements warrant a price increase, then go for it and raise your rates. Your main considerations in raising your rates are when to do it and by how much.

Timing. The best time to increase your rates is before you start booking for the following year. I know it sounds rather simple, but if you wait, you may end up booking now for next year and you'll lose out on the rate increase.

At bare minimum you'll want to evaluate and raise your rates prior to January, which is the start of the busy booking months. But if you would like to get a head start on next year, a good rule of thumb would be to increase your rates after 95% of your current busy season is booked. For example: Say you have booked the entire summer, with the exception of August 19–26. You could raise your rates before you book that week and simply advertise a special, "$X off August 19–26" and X would be equal to the amount you raised your rates.

How much? Many owners increase their rates 10 to 20 percent each year, which seems to be standard for the industry. Before you simply raise the rates, make sure to compare your rates with other properties in your area (properties rented by owner and through management companies) to make sure your property is competitively priced. Also, don't forget to evaluate all your expenses before quoting new rates:

- Cleaning fees;
- Charges for amenities: golf, work-out facilities, parking fees, ferry charges, firewood, and any other fees that may apply;
- Local and state sales tax.

Regardless of how or where you advertise your property advertisement, you should have some sort of rate disclaimer, like "Until confirmed, rates are subject to change without notice." I feel it's unprofessional, however, to change a rate after the property has been booked, confirmed and paid.

Friend Rates

A question that never fails to come up at my seminars is: "My friends always ask if they can use my home. What, if anything, should I charge my friends?" Let me preface the discussion with: the IRS looks closely at investment properties that are rented primarily for deeply discounted weeks. Does that mean you should not give discounts to your friends? No, the IRS mainly looks for investors who are using their properties mostly for their family and friends, but then use it as a tax shelter. This does not pertain to the average owner; we want to make money! So everyone knows you have a home in Hawaii, and now everyone's your best friend. Here is how I suggest you handle these folks. If your friend wants a peak week and wishes to book ahead of time, then by all means, let them. Just charge the full price. What? Won't they think I'm stingy, and not a true friend? Here's what I tell my friends. "This is an investment. And a business. If I give you a week for free, that's like taking $1,350 (the rental rate for the requested week) out of my pocket and handing it right to you. If you would like a week for less (or free), then I will let you know when/if I have a last minute week open. If it's not booked, you are welcome to use it."

That may sound cold, but it's true. I am happy to let my friends use my home, but not if it takes money out of my hands. You may, of course, want to consider having a "friend rate." After all, they will be using the power, water, etc., and that will cost you money. A fair friend rate is between $25–$50 a night. And as a note of caution, I would not allow your friends to clean the home themselves before leaving (unless you require all renters to do so). This can be a friendship-breaker. It's best to have them pay the cleaning fee.

Donations, Trades, and Exchanges

Owning a vacation home can offer you some nice perks. You can exchange your home for other vacation homes, services, or even tax deductions. If you need maintenance, repairs, or work done, consider offering the contractor a week at your home instead of paying money. This can work well for many types of services that you need at either your vacation or personal home. Just be careful not to short-change yourself. Don't give away a $1,000 week in exchange for a service that you would only pay a couple hundred dollars for.

Note: Bartered services are taxable, so you must charge and pay sales tax on the bartered cash value.

Trades are fun and easy to do. One of the main sales pitches for timeshares is that you can trade your week and travel the world. Well, you can do this with your vacation investment property too. There are websites that charge a nominal fee for direct and indirect exchanges with owners throughout the world. iTravex.com offers exchange services to owners through their site. You might also consider just contacting an owner directly from any of the various listing sites. It can't hurt to ask.

Donations are a nifty way to help out a good cause, and sometimes they can even be tax deductible* (check with your accountant). Think about donating a week that doesn't normally rent very well. Most charities would be happy to accept a week for an auction or raffle. Again, be sure to write in a clause that the winner must comply with all rental rules and policies. Be sure to also require a damage deposit.

By now you should have a solid understanding of the fundamentals of pricing. Become a market watcher and pay close attention to the rates your competitors charge. Make sure that you know all that you need to about the significance of the changing seasons, upcoming holidays, and special events. Don't be afraid to be creative when it comes to bartering your vacation home for services or other useful purposes. And, by all means, never forget that this is a business. After you drum that concept into your head, the whole issue of pricing becomes so much clearer.

* Be sure to speak with your accountant or tax attorney regarding tax deductions. Blanket statements cannot be made concerning taxes. Depending on how the business is set up, how it's claimed on your taxes and the type and terms of the donation, your donation may or may not be deductible as advertising expense. This is a gray area, and you should have your tax professional make a determination on how it is applicable to your situation.

15

Organizational Techniques

Organization is a difficult task for many people. With the fast pace of twenty-first century life, it is so easy to get snowed under an avalanche of paperwork. Computers are supposed to make everything much easier, but sometimes they only add to the confusion. Mass marketers recognize this modern dilemma. Why do you think there are so many ads in the newspapers on New Year's Day for organizational items? From Home Depot to Office Max, Wal-Mart to Walgreen's, everyone seems to be hawking all sorts of things that can organize your life.

Owning a vacation property and renting it out yourself can be very challenging to organize. You'll be taking multiple inquiries from different vacationers, often for the same week. This one's name is Mark Daniels and that one's name is Daniel Marks, how will you keep track of who wanted which week? Or, how about this one: "Oh no! I booked the same week to two different people!" Then there's the paperwork involved, did you send out the rental rules for Mark or for Dan? Then the payments start coming in. Who paid? Who is due to pay? And who is due for a deposit refund?

Then (yes, there's more) there's the property itself, did I service the air conditioner last time I was there or was it two-times ago? How about supplies? Was I out of dishwasher detergent or dish soap? Or was it trash bags I needed to buy?

Thankfully, I have some good news. There's no reason to get overwhelmed. Organizing your rental property business does *not* have to be a big headache. In fact, if you learn the right organizational techniques, it can run as smoothly as a well-oiled machine. But it is imperative that you get yourself organized right from day one. I want to share with you all the things that you need to consider. Exactly how you choose to do them is up to you. Just like some people prefer their pants be hung neatly in a closet and others choose to neatly fold them in a drawer. Neither way is right, and neither way is wrong, as long as the pants are not crumpled in a pile on the floor. The same is true for your vacation property. You can choose to use an organizer book, or you can choose to do everything on your computer. Whichever you are more comfortable doing is fine . . . so long as you decide on a certain system and stick with it religiously! Otherwise, it will not work at all.

For starters, set up your email program so that incoming rental emails go into a separate folder. Refer to the help section in your email program to set up "folders and rules." Be careful using any sort of email filters or spam blockers because most, if not all, of your rental inquiries will come from unknown email addresses. You may very well miss out on valuable rentals if you use these filters. Unfortunately, you will just have to deal with the spam (I know it's a pain in the neck, but just laugh at it, and delete it). This is precisely why you want a separate email folder. If you come in and have only two minutes to check your email, you can easily scan your folder to see if you have any new email inquiries. If you do, be sure to respond immediately.

Organizing on Your Computer

Welcome to the Information Age. A lot of organizational tasks can easily be done on your computer. If you are one of those people who does all their personal accounting on the computer, and you have a system that works well for you, then most likely you *can* do everything you need to do on your computer. If you are not currently 100% familiar with the programs associated with online accounting, however, now might *not* the best time to learn.

I am one of those people who have been hesitant about computerizing all of my banking and business activities for my vacation rentals. Here's why. When are a lot of your rental calls going to come in? Not when you are sitting at your computer. More often, they'll come in the evening, when you're cooking dinner, or as Murphy's Law dictates, *while* you're eating dinner. When that phone rings and it's a renter, if you have to go into your office, wait until your computer boots up, and then open up the program where you have all your info, how much time will that take? I think it's easier to quickly flip the pages of a calendar and reply with a simple "Yes, I have it available," or "Sorry, that week is booked." By looking at your calendar you can figure out the answer in a matter of seconds. You could even respond when checking your voice mail from the road—just have that calendar with you, no computer required.

Now, here's something else you'll need to do to keep yourself well organized (I think you'll like this one) . . . keeping track of all the checks that come in. Yes, you can put them into Quicken or some other computer program, but you will have many checks coming in that should be deposited right away (you want checks to clear the bank *before* you send out directions). If you rent the 17 weeks necessary for the break-even cash flow formula, and use the deposit + 2 payments method, then the minimum number of checks you'll have coming in is 51. That's not 51 checks over 52 weeks; it's 51 checks over 12–16 weeks. Because of this, I prefer an organizer book.

If you are one of those people who would like to organize on your computer, listen to what Bart, vacation property owner and vacation rental software developer has to say about organizing on your computer:

We own vacation properties in Hawaii that we rent by owner. We started of course with just one property. Back then we used the paper calendar method to organize our rentals. Then growing from a single home to half a dozen properties, we found ourselves dealing with increasing inquiries, snowballing reservation information and a lot of paperwork, including inquiry information, reservation and accounting data, receipts, contracts, etc. Without a computer system, it became unwieldy.

Additionally, we like to spend time at our vacation home. So we needed to be able to bring our 'business' with us when we traveled. We had to have a system that was mobile, accessible at all times, from anywhere, so that we would not miss out on valuable inquiries or reservations while we were away.

It is important to us that we organize our vacation rental by owner business like any real business. What we needed was a good set of tools to manage all aspects of the business from advertising to reporting at the year's end. When selecting a management program, be sure to look for these key elements:

- Accurate Calendaring and Scheduling
- Reservation Data and Payment Data Management
- Month End Accounting
- Year End Reporting
- Web Based System

Calendaring

To avoid errors in double booking and other scheduling disasters, you'll need to organize a calendar of reservations. It's beneficial when these calendars can be accessible to a group of people from remote locations. This is especially helpfully if you are using a partnership program with a management company. You can also have your calendar available to your housekeepers and maintenance staff. One click of the mouse should convert a reservation inquiry email into a reservation on the calendar.

Reservation Management

You must be able to track the life cycle of each reservation and all of the reservation details created along the way. Old reservations need to be archived, and inquiries that do not become reservations need to be deleted to clean up.

Accounting

You must be able to account for the income and expenses that make up the entire operation. Therefore, accounting organization is an important aspect of a home vacation rental business."

One note of caution when using systems that are specifically integrated with vacation rental advertising websites—many such sites will *not* allow you access to the booking and reservation information if you don't have an active advertisement with them.

Let's just say you utilize their booking tools and you keep all of your reservation information on their website. What happens if you are no longer happy with their website? If you do not renew your listing, you lose access to all of your booking and reservation data. For this reason, I would be very careful about putting all of your eggs in one basket.

Organizing in a Book

I joke about it and call it my "Rental Bible." I do not leave home without it. Don't try to use a wall calendar, you will find those tiny little boxes run out of space too fast. Simply purchase an appointment book at your local office store, and customize it to fit your needs. Or, you can purchase the one specifically designed (by me) for vacation property rentals, *The Vacation Rental Organizer*.

If you purchase *The Vacation Rental Organizer*, all of the information is self-explanatory. Just fill in all the blanks and you are good to go.

If you choose to make your own book, then be sure it has some pages for vital information pertaining to your property, such as lock box codes, financial information, and home owner's association information. You'll also want a few pages dedicated to contact information for housekeepers, maintenance people, and networking (other owners in your area). Don't forget to also have property inventory pages such as appliance makes, models, and serial numbers (in case you have to make a service call from home). And leave some pages for a ledger of income, expenses, and sales tax.

Determine how most of your bookings will be reserved and set up your book accordingly—either nightly, weekly, or monthly. Next, you will need to decide whether to rent Friday to Friday, Saturday to Saturday, or Sunday to Sunday. The norm for rentals is generally from Saturday to Saturday. This works well for most renters because they can leave their homes on a day off from work and come home and have a day to unpack, unload, and unwind before starting the workweek. There are some owners who rent their property from Sunday to Sunday successfully. The advantage is that if you have a week open, you can easily rent the weekend (Friday and Saturday) and checkout Sunday, and still have a weekly renter follow, checking in on Sunday. Also, for destinations that most renters will fly to, sometimes it's less expensive and easier to get flights on Sundays. Fridays on the other hand, tend to be very busy and expensive travel days. The disadvantage to renting any period other than Saturday to Saturday is that people are creatures of habit. Most renters look for Saturday to Saturday, but you would rarely lose a rental over it.

In your organizer you will want to keep track of all inquiries and bookings you get from renters. Develop a system (in your book) of jotting down notes about each person you speak with so that you can refer back to who they are when you have further conversations (either email or phone). Don't forget to keep track of where the renters found you. When it comes to portal renewal time (payment due to the listing sites), you will want to know how many qualified inquiries came from that site. By qualified, I mean how many inquiries actually resulted in a booking. Don't just count your emails. From one of my listing sites, I got 30–40 rental inquiries a week, but I never had one booking, so I did not renew my membership to that site. In other words, make sure you are getting enough bang for your buck.

Another thing you should make a habit of is photocopying each check you receive from renters. If you do not have a copier at home, most banks will photocopy them for free when you are depositing. Take that copy of the check and staple it right into your book. This will make it very easy to see if you have received a payment or not, as well as give you all the renter's information (name, address, etc.) from his or her check. Also, this is a good practice for income tax purposes. At year-end, or God forbid during an audit, you will have all the information available at your fingertips.

As for signed and returned rental rules and payment agreements, no need to staple these into your rental book. They will make your book too bulky. Just make note that you have received them then file them away. The only time you will need these is if you have problem renters, which (thankfully) is not often. If you do have a problem renter, and you have to keep a portion of the security deposit, then you'll want to staple that correspondence into the book.

You will also want to keep good track of the various services you pay for. Keeping up with the housekeeper's payments, lawn maintenance, and other weekly or per-rental maintenance bills can easily get confusing (it's happened to me), especially if you are working with an individual who does not have a formal billing system established. Be sure to write in your book the check number that you paid with and its corresponding billing date.

Another major advantage of keeping all this information in a book is when you go to sell your property, you can easily show the buyer the past records proving your rental history. Yes, you can print the documents off a computer program, but computer printouts are easily manipulated and sometimes are viewed as less credible.

In case I still haven't convinced you how important this rental book is, let me share a story with you. Perhaps my personal experience will get the point across. It happened a few years ago:

A week before one of my seminars, I got a call. My dear great aunt in Tampa had a stroke. I hopped on a plane to be there for her, and I took my rental book along (of course, I don't leave home without it). I had only expected to stay two days. While I was there, she passed away. Naturally, I stayed for the funeral. Now I had to fly from Tampa to Destin for my seminar. The problem was, all my seminar materials were at home.

Thankfully, the flight from Tampa to Destin makes a stopover in Atlanta (my home town at the time). So my husband agreed to meet me at the airport and give me all the necessary stuff for my seminar, but I had to have no carry on luggage. I was faced with a dilemma. No carry-on luggage would mean that I would have to check my luggage, and my rental book would have to go inside ... out of my hands ... and risk getting lost. I had no choice, so I did it.

Now, for all the traveling I have done in my life, I have never lost luggage. Well, I am not sure what I ever did to offend Murphy, but his Law followed. You guessed it, my luggage got lost! I did not care about any item in my suitcase more than that rental book. A lost wallet would have been easier to live with. As it worked out, my luggage did end up back in my hands, but the mental anguish I went through was not fun. The moral of this story: don't let this book out of your hands!

By now, I think you can see the importance of organization. Your vacation rental business will never work if you have little scraps of paper with scribbling scrawled across them. No, that's for your kid's lemonade stand. This is serious business. You need a well thought out system that works for you. Life can be hectic enough, so when you're offered a chance to organize things (which leads to *simplifying* things), I have three little words of advice . . . go for it!

16

Choosing Renters

Who should you target, who you don't want to stay, who are the ones you are inadvertently turning away . . .

Wouldn't it be great if everyone in the world were honest and trustworthy? If that were so, you'd never have to worry about renting out your vacation property. But, we live in the real world, and (though this may not sound very nice) there are going to be some people you simply don't want to rent to. Don't go on a guilt trip over it. It's your property, and you have the right to use discretion. For example, I have found it quite useful to require a minimum age. I will not rent to anyone under 25 or to college students. Ever been to a beachfront hotel during spring break? I once visited a hotel manager surveying the damage left in the wake of one of these raucous annual events. Broken and empty beer bottles in the elevators, mayhem in the rooms, half-finished fast food containers rotting on the beds, and more trash than I care to remember strewn all over the place. The manager shook his head, sighed, and said, "Hey, we're just happy to survive spring break."

Well, this ghastly scene does *not* have to happen to you. After all, you own the place, and it can only happen if you let it happen. An open door policy may sound fair, but this isn't about being fair.

Like the manager said, it's about survival. And while this policy of no college kids has its obvious disadvantages (lost potential customers), it has some major advantages also. You are only a small businessperson and, unlike the George V Hotel in Paris, you can't afford to cover the repairs that a rock-and-roll band might do to the property. A bunch of college kids can sometimes trash a place even worse than Led Zeppelin in the group's heyday!

At this point, you may ask, is it legal to have these kinds of restrictions? What about all of those fair housing laws the state and federal governments have enacted? Will I end up with some ACLU lawyer after me? Relax. Here is what the law says:

Fair Housing Act

"Title VIII of the Civil Rights Act of 1968 (Fair Housing Act), as amended, prohibits discrimination in the sale, rental, and financing of dwellings, and in other housing-related transactions, based on race, color, national origin, religion, sex, familial status (including children under the age of 18 living with parents of legal custodians, pregnant women, and people securing custody of children under the age of 18), and handicap (disability)."

Did you notice that *age* is not written into the Fair Housing Act? Take full advantage of that. You are indeed allowed to have a policy stating age exclusion (i.e., no students, or no one under 25, only 55 years and older, etc.). Check with your local city and state for exclusions in your state to these laws regarding transient rentals.

Screening Your Guests

Properly screening your guests is your most important duty as an owner. You *must* screen each guest. *Never take a booking without speaking to your potential renter on the phone.* If you do not have time for this very important step, then maybe this is not the right business for you. I'm dead serious about that. To omit this step in the process could be disastrous.

Often, you will have many email conversations with your potential renters, which may give you a certain amount of comfort. But you never know who is really behind that computer in cyberspace. You have invested too much time and money to give the keys to someone you don't know. You may say, "Well, I don't know them when I talk with them on the phone either." Your goal during your telephone conversation is indeed get to know them (at least a little bit).

The phone screening process does not have to be a dreaded chore. We're not planning a funeral. We're planning a vacation! That's fun. In fact, it's a very satisfying task, especially when you get all the nice compliments and thank you notes from your renters after they leave. The screening process is a skill you already have ... even though you may not realize it. Simply be yourself.

> When I'm speaking with renters on the phone, I am friendly and personable. My main objective that I want to get across is that they are renting my second home. I make it a point to convey that I am not some big management company or businessperson. I am a real and genuine person, just like them.

When screening guests, it's important to use your instincts. When a renter calls, I never say I have anything available until after I have done a bit of screening. (Even if I have had previous email conversations with the renter and told them it was available. . . . I could have booked it ten minutes ago.) If you keep your availability in question, you always have an "out" ("Sorry, I'm booked.") that you can use at any stage of the screening process. Disclosing your availability to the renter right from the start may back you into a corner. Instead, when they ask for a week, I say, "I think it's open, but I'm not sure, let me check." Then while I'm "checking" we engage in conversation, and I get to know them.

First thing I ask is, how many adults *and* how many children? I may even ask the ages of their children. I engage in conversation and get personal. A lot of times your renters will share all sorts of information about themselves, and you will find yourself doing the same. I also use this time to be sure that my property is truly the right home for them. I look at this as being a travel agent. I am trying to match the renters' needs with the property. If they want a place in the hustle and bustle of the town and my home is secluded, I advise them to continue searching. What, you say? Turn down a renter? Sure. Think about it. Do you want someone to stay at your home if they are not going to be happy there? Do you want them to curse you out when they pull up and find out it's not what they expected? Think about the ramifications. If they are not happy, are they going to take care of your home? Will they call and demand a refund? Or worse, sue you for false advertising? Best not to go there! Just be honest. I have tried to talk many people *out of* renting my home. Some choose to rent it anyway, but at least they know what they are getting into, and they will respect you (and your property) for it.

In my experience, families with small children make the best renters. Now, I realize that some of you may be thinking, wait a minute, rent to people with small kids? They can be worse than college kids! What if they scribble crayon on the walls or spill grape juice on the rugs? In reality, this rarely happens. The risks are not as high as you might think. Also, in addition to cutting yourself off from at least 50% of your prospective renters, you may be violating the law. As I said earlier, you are allowed age restrictions, *but* you cannot discriminate against families with children under 18, unless your property is located in a place, such as a 55 and older community, that has obtained the licensing exclusions to do so. Even if you are still certain that you don't want kids, if I were you, I would not say so in my advertising.

Now, back to the conversation with my renters. Remember the first question: How many adults and how many children? If I hear "all adults," then my antenna goes up, and I adopt a different mindset, or I use my "out" . . . "Sorry I'm booked." (Just as in any game, it's best to hold onto your out until the very end, only use it as your last resort.) You don't want to rule out *all* people with no children, you only want to rule out those under 25.

So, your next question is, how will I know if they are under 25? Again, the answer is the obvious one . . . just ask. Believe it or not, most will answer honestly. If they answer honestly and are under 25, this is a good time to use your out. If they are truly over 25, then most often they'll be flattered and tell you all about themselves, making it that much easier to engage in conversation and get to know them.

Well, what if I ask and they lie? Sure, there are things that you could require as proof such as a copy of his or her driver's license. But really? Come on. If they lie to your face (over the phone) then chances are they'll lie to you in writing too. Kids have fake IDs. This would only provide a false sense of security on your part. How would you verify that the IDs they send are really their own?

Instead, when you are speaking with them if you feel that their voices or demeanors are that of people under 25, you can use your "out" right at this point. Or consider another tactic . . . how about something like this: "Well, I just have to ask and make sure that you are really over 25. Because, you see, I am not allowed to rent to anyone under 25. It's not my rule; it's the association's rule. Our home is in an association, and our by-laws state that we are not allowed to rent to anyone under 25. They're pretty strict about it too. If the association finds out, they will evict you, and I have absolutely no say in the matter. And, if you are evicted, then you lose all your rent and your deposit. I feel pretty bad for people under 25 years old these days. I was there once myself. I was very responsible. But it's always those few bad apples that spoil it for the rest of us." That usually scares them off, and if it doesn't I can always use my last out!

Sometimes you can get a lot of the preliminary screening work completed before even speaking to a potential renter on the phone. When you receive email inquiries, you can do a little detective work. Look for clues. Take a look at the email address. If it's something like big-bad-boy@college.edu, what's your first clue? Is it the Big Bad Boy? Possibly. But even the college.edu can be a clue. I would still reply to this email as I would every other. It could very well be a professor or an employee of the university, or perhaps a young person doing the search for his or her parents. You would not want to discount any renter just because of his or her email address; however, have your antenna up for screening.

Don't Get Scammed

The good news is the vacation rental industry has become increasingly popular, making it much easier to rent your vacation home. The bad news is the vacation rental industry has become increasingly popular, creating a fertile field for scammers. These scammers are sometimes difficult to detect—even I have been stumped by a few of the inquiries. Be sure to keep potential scammers in the back of your mind as you receive and respond to all email inquiries or phone inquiries.

The Classic "Nigerian Scam"

The Nigerian Scam is one that has been around for a long time, and today this scam is not isolated to Nigeria, it has originated in many countries. The basic scam involves the "renter" who will pay you with a cashier's check that is many times in excess of the actual rent. The scammer sends you a cashier's check that is virtually undetectable as counterfeit until, of course, you deposit it and it goes through the banking system. During the time it takes your bank to realize that the check is counterfeit, the renter will most assuredly have some desperate need to cancel and get his money back. If you send him a refund, you have just been scammed.

I have seen copies of these checks and they are very good-looking counterfeits. They'll often have watermarks, holograms and everything else that makes them appear authentic.

If you get an email inquiry that looks like this, what should you do?

The following is an actual inquiry that I received:

Name: Tajudeen olatunji
E-mail: tajudeen_olatunji@yahoo.com
Tel: + 234 08058042348
Arrival date: 10/2/2006
Departure date: 1/3/2007
Total no in party: 4 (including children)
No of children: 2
Further info:
Hello, i here here by use the medium to negotiate your advertised apartment which will serve a temporary residence for a little while i will spend in you domain am a business man and i already have a contract which i will have to execute lessurely. my company have issued a cheque to me in agreement that i will be booking hotel,but since i will be coming over with my wife and my 2 kids i will need a spacios apartment just like the very advertised one. i want you to get back to me fast so we can negotiate on payment.i wouldn't mind to pay now so i can be rest minded thet i have a place ready.

Clues that tell me this is a scam:
  + The spelling and grammar are poor;
  + The name is obviously a foreign name, and the phone number is outside the U.S.;

* The email address is from a free email service;
* He uses words like "apartment" even though this inquiry was for a log cabin;
* He needs a temporary residence for business, even though this property is in a remote location;
* He wants to pay in full now even though his rental dates are more than 90 days from the time he sent his inquiry.

Here's another actual email inquiry, though this one is not so obvious:

Name: Juliette Ginn
E-mail: julietteginn@yahoo.com
Tel: + 1 80372760XX
Arrival date: 23 Sep 2006
Departure date: 4 Oct 2006
Total no in party: 2 (including children)
No of children: 1
Further info:
    hello, I am intereted in this rent and will like to know if it can be made available for 23rd sep thanks

Clues that tell me this could be a scam:

* The phone number, though it has a U.S. area code (South Carolina); when I called it, no one by the name of Juliette lived there (I removed the full phone number because it was an actual working number);
* The email address is again from a free email service;
* The rental dates are in international format (day, month, year).

This inquiry is much more difficult to detect as a scam. The rental dates were for two weeks away from the time of the email (many are for distant dates). The name seems real, the phone number has a U.S. area code, and the wording, though not perfect spelling, could be indicative of someone who doesn't type or use the computer much. I engaged with this person just to see what they would come back with. Sure enough, when I emailed her and asked for her correct phone number, she said, "I'm sorry I must have typed in the wrong phone number, my phone number is +447040110705," (note the number doesn't even come close to the original number she emailed me). OK, I thought, she could be traveling from the United Kingdom (44 is a U.K. country code). But as soon as we started speaking about the money, I told her I only accept credit cards. When she said she didn't have a credit card (many Europeans don't), I offered for her to pay via the next safest way to get money from foreign travelers: PayPal or an international bank wire transfer—neither of which she was amenable to. Any legitimate foreign travelers would have been able to pay via one of the first three payment options. She only wanted to send a cashier's check—a bogus one for sure. Needless to say, I didn't rent to Ms. Juliette Ginn.

What To Do If You Get Scam Inquiries

The first thing you should do is forward it to whichever website it came from and ask them to block the sender so no other owners fall prey to the scam.

The next thing you should do is report it to "Nigeria—The 419 Coalition Website" http://home.rica.net/alphae/419coal/.

If the scam is obvious, like the first example, do not reply! (Once you reply, they have your email address and they will continue sending you more). If you are suspicious about an inquiry, like I was with the second example, proceed with extreme caution.

- NEVER send refunds for cancellations until two weeks after their checks have cleared your bank;

- NEVER send money back for overpayment;
- DON'T ever accept more than the amount due.

The modus operandi for the classic "Nigerian Scammer": They book your property, send you a cashier's check for an amount above the rental rate and then ask you to cash it and send the balance back to them. The problem is—the check, though it looks authentic, is fake!

Please note: While poor spelling and grammar used to be the main Nigerian scam indicator, these scammers are getting slicker—figuring out proper English. Furthermore, if you commonly rent to travelers from non-English speaking countries, if you base your decisions strictly on spelling and grammar you could be turning away some legitimated travelers. You should always evaluate a potential scam based on the context of the inquiry, not simply the wording.

Here is a story from an owner who almost mistook a bona fide inquiry for a scam:

I got an inquiry from a man from Africa.

I have to say my initial thought was, "this is a scam." However, there was something, though I can't put my finger on it, which made me think it could be legitimate; so I decided to do a little research.

The inquiry was pretty simple. The person provided his job title and company address, asked for a two-week time-frame, whether we provide airport transfers, and bank information for a wire transfer of payment. That was it.

Thankfully, one of my best friends had lived in Africa. So I forwarded her the inquiry and asked if she could help me evaluate it.

After my friend looked at the inquiry, she told me that the organization that he worked for sounded familiar. And the surname was a common African name. My friend told me that while she could not tell if this was 100% legit, she didn't see any red flags.

With this information, I decided to answer the inquiry. I was looking for the one telltale sign of a scam—the inquirer will send "extra funds". Thankfully there was never a mention of sending "extra funds."

As an added measure, while emailing back and forth, I noticed that the renter provided additional information about himself in his signature (including 2 company/organization websites and his cell phone number). This allowed me to do further research on him.

I went to the websites that were attached to his signature and I found his profile on the company's executive profiles, which provided his job title and educational background.

With all of this information, I decided to take the booking. I have to say I still was on pins and needles until they came and went. And, guess what? They were a lovely couple, had a fantastic trip, wrote us a wonderful review about how they had such an enjoyable stay, and mentioned that they would like to return next year with friends.

Who would have guessed that an inquiry that I almost deleted would have turned out to be a smooth transaction and possibly repeat renters for years to come? However, having said all this, while this is an exception, I am sad to say, most of the African inquiries are indeed scams.

Note: The recipient of this inquiry owns a property in St. Maarten, a very popular destination for international travelers. If you own a property in an area that is less likely to have foreign travelers, take extra precautions.

And if all of this does not scare you enough, here are three stories where people have fallen victim to a scam.

One owner who received an inquiry from a scammer had a gut feeling all along that something was "just not right" about the inquiry. But she took the booking anyways. When she got the certified funds in the mail from the "renter" it was of course for an amount in excess of the rental amount. Having worked in a bank before she looked at the certified check and thought something didn't look right. She took it to her bank and after a few people studying the check; they determined that it was indeed counterfeit. This owner narrowly escaped this scam.

A second owner received a "scam" certified check and deposited it into his account.

It took the bank a few days to realize that the check was counterfeit. Once they realized it was counterfeit, they contacted the FBI and froze all of his assets. During the whole time all of his assets were frozen. The investigation took nearly six months! What a nightmare it was for him.

The third person, didn't own a vacation home but the story is the ultimate in extreme ramifications of being scammed.

A man posted two bicycles for sale on Cragislist.com. You guessed it—he received a check for more than the cost of the bicycles. He was suspicious so he went into the bank that the check was drawn on to verify funds in the account and make sure the check was legitimate. The teller told him it was a valid account, so he cashed the check. At that point, the bank employees called police and man was arrested on fraud charges because the check was actually fraudulent.

The man was taken to jail, spent the night and was charged with three felonies. He had to spend tens of thousands of dollars and over a year to clear his name . . . all over one bad check. Now don't let this happen to you!

The 809 Area Code Scam

We receive rental inquiries from everywhere so we see a lot of different phone numbers. If you are in a rush to book a rental, however, you may want to double-check the number you are calling. The 809 Area Code Scam is one of the most effective phone scams. Initially, the 809 area code looks and dials like a domestic number (no country code needed to dial), but it is a "pay-per-call" number in the Dominican Republic. These phone numbers work much like the 900 phone numbers, where the caller is charged an exorbitant sum per minute. The longer the scammers can keep you on a call, the more they can charge you (up to $25 a minute).

Since the Caribbean has many area codes, this scam is not confined to 809 area code phone numbers. You need to take extra precautions with this type of scam. When in doubt, have the renter call you. As another precautionary measure, you can perform a reverse number look-up by going to one of the free services like this one: http://www.anywho.com/rl.html. And, finally, bookmark this area code listing website, http://www.bennetyee.org/ucsd-pages/area.html, and look up every unfamiliar area code before you call a potential renter.

Checking Account Fraud

On the few occasions that you may have to keep a portion of the damage deposit you might want to consider sending bank-certified funds, a money order or charging it to the renter's credit card. If you couldn't trust these renters with your home, why should you trust them with your personal checking account information?

Checking account scams are on the rise, and some scammers use technology to print checks with your checking account numbers. They also use your checking account number to pay for bills, goods or services over the phone. The likelihood of this happening to you might be slim, but why take chances?

Phishing Scams

The new way scam that vacation rental owners are now plagued with is called "Phishing".

According to Dictionary.com, Phishing is defined as: "to try to obtain financial or other confidential information from Internet users, typically by sending an e-mail that looks as if it is from a legitimate organization, usually a financial institution, but contains a link to a fake Web site that replicates the real one."

There are two ways vacation rentals owners can become victims of a phishing scam—through a vacation rental portal website or through their email accounts.

The scammers try to harvest your username and password. After they have access to your account information (either your email account or your listing information), they intercept your rental inquiries. They "sell" your property to travelers and collect the funds from them. The travelers paid the scammer for what they "thought" was your property.

I got an email that looked exactly like a HomeAway.com inquiry. I say exactly, but there were a couple of very slight differences (likely not visible to most people). Anyhow I hovered my mouse over the links and they did NOT link to HomeAway.com but rather a different website [phishing site]. This website was trying to get me to "log into" their website [which could have easily fooled me because it looked almost exactly like HomeAway's site]. If I had not been diligent, then the scammers would have my login and password information.

The bad guys are out there and vacation rental owners seem to be their next targets. Be very careful with your email passwords and your rental website passwords! Do NOT click on links in any emails until you hover over and look at the URL you will be going to. BEFORE putting your User Name and Password into ANY website, double check the URL of the page you are on to be sure you are logging into the right site. When in doubt, don't click links in an email but rather go and type the URL into a Google search and find the site that way. Always stay on your toes!

There Are More Good People Than Bad

After reading a chapter like this, it's pretty depressing to think about all the risks you face with renting out your vacation home. But to be quite honest, I have responded to more than 30,000 email inquiries and have taken more than 5000 reservations. I have never once fallen prey to any of these scams. As in all other aspects of life and business, use your judgment, be cautious and you too will be safe from the scammers.

CHAPTER 17

Increase Bookings

Beyond advertising on more websites, how can you attract more travelers to rent your property? The first thing you must realize is, the more restrictive you are, the fewer renters you will have. While it's certainly acceptable to have any policies and restrictions that you want (inside the law), you must also acknowledge that this decision could result in fewer rentals.

If your goal is to have maximum occupancy, you're going to have to learn the importance of flexibility. By adding or making minor adjustments to your furnishings and advertisements, you may find that you'll increase your bookings.

The following suggestions are ordered from simple, low-cost adjustments to policy changes

229

and exceptions to more substantial expenditures and changes to your property.

Sell what you have. Finding good renters is not as hard as you may think. You will likely get lots of inquiries and there's often no need for a hard sell from you (after all, they called you . . . not the other way around!). If there is something that comes up in the conversation that seems like a drawback to the potential renter (i.e., they were hoping for a great view of the beach, and your home does not have that) there are ways that you can turn that to your advantage. Here's Cody's story:

Cody owns a home near the beach. You can see the water just a bit from her home, but nothing that could really be called a view. Every time someone calls his or her first question is, "What kind of view do you have?" Cody used to say, "Sorry, I have no view." The renters would say, "That's too bad. I'm really looking for a view," and that was the end of the conversation. Cody got pretty tired of having all those renters slip right out of her hand simply because she had no view. She had two options: the first was to sell her home and buy another. This was not a good option. Homes with a view were $100,000 more; she couldn't afford it.

The second option made a lot more sense. She could change her tactics. Cody diligently searched the internet for all properties that were on the ocean with a good view. She found out that they not only cost more to buy, but they also cost more to rent. She realized she had an opportunity here, and she seized it. This is how she has changed her way of answering that same question—and how she now gets bookings.

Renter: "Do you have a view?"

Cody: "Sorry, when we bought the home, I really wanted that view too, but we just couldn't afford it. Then I started thinking, how much time am I really going to spend in the home anyway? I'm really going to be on the beach every day. So we bought this home. I love it. My home is great."

Renter: "Sorry, I really wanted the view."

Cody: "That's OK, I understand. Let me see, I do know of some other owners who have properties with a great view . . . let's see, OK, here's the same type of home as mine, two bedroom, two bath, great view. Do you want their name and number?"

Renter: "Sure, please!"

Cody: "OK, it's #24AB5 on website.com, John Smith #234–123–4567 . . . wow, his home is really nice, nice price too."

Renter: "Really? How much?"

Cody: "Well, it looks like it's $800 more per week than mine, but it's nice."

Renter: "Oh, I really can't afford that . . . can you tell me a little more about your home, maybe it wouldn't be so bad not to have the view."

Cody is not selling the renter something he or she doesn't want; remember the renter contacted her first. At first, renters want everything—the view, the large size, the location, the most for their money, etc. Then, when they narrow it down, they realize that they have to make compromises . . . and the only selling that you need to do is to help them with those compromises.

Don't forget the babies. Families will represent the largest percentage of renters. Many of them will have young children, so think of things that will make families choose your home over someone else's. I cannot tell you how many times renters have called me and said my home was not exactly what they were looking for, but they compromised other criterion because I have two things that will make their travel much easier and their stay much more enjoyable—a high chair and porta-crib. Those two items cost a mere $150 to purchase and I have made my money back a hundred times over.

The next two suggestions are more substantial changes to standard rental policies. But if handled well, you will be rewarded for your flexibility.

Alter your age restrictions. You may want to consider bending the rules on your under 25 years old restriction. If you own in a region where limiting your prospective guests to those over 25 could limit the number of rentals, you may want to consider making an exception to your rule.

Ski areas are good examples, since many skiers are college students. Remember, there are plenty of responsible college kids … not all are bad! Just require a larger deposit, a midweek cleaning at an extra charge (the housekeeper can assess the property while she's there), and make it clear that you will not tolerate any "hell-raising." Tell them if you get a call from neighbors or from the police, they will be evicted and they will forfeit the deposit (write this specifically into your rules).

Perhaps your property isn't in a ski area but it just isn't renting well. I have known some owners who have actually written on their ads, "Under 25 welcome with restrictions." Again, there are plenty of responsible young adults. But I cannot emphasize this enough; realize there is a risk when renting to younger people. Sometimes it's well worth it to take a chance.

Here's a story that drives this point perfectly:

The first year I owned my property in Destin, Florida, I was nervous about whether I would get renters. One of the first calls I got was from a mother looking for a home where her teenage daughter and four of her friends could go on a senior trip. "Mom coming too?" I asked. Her response was "No." Of course, my initial reaction was "No way!" I explained to the mom my age restriction policy and my need to be very strict.

She pretty much begged me and offered a huge deposit, reassuring me that these girls were very well behaved young adults. They don't drink, smoke, etc. This mother seemed so genuine and she put money (large deposit) behind her words. I did let the girls rent my home, and while I was biting my nails all week long, when my housekeeper called to confirm that the home was left in perfect condition, I had no regrets.

But the story didn't end there. Six years later, I got a phone call from this same mom. She said, "Christine, do you remember me?" "Of course," I said, "Your daughter and her friends were some of my first renters." She explained that her daughter had now graduated from college and was getting married (she was still under 25), and she loved our home so much that she wanted to spend her honeymoon there. Naturally, I gladly said, "Yes." I can't tell you how good that made me feel about my decision six years earlier. So sometimes it is indeed OK to use your heart when screening potential guests. And who knows, you may just be securing potential renters for years to come.

Consider accepting pets. I know what you're thinking . . . I don't want pets in my vacation home! But before you make any rash decisions that could affect your bottom line (money!), read on.

Who Travels During the Off-Season?

The Answer: Travelers whose travel dates are not constrained to their children's school schedules. Or people with the other type of children—their beloved dogs.

According to American Pet Products Association (APPA) *2011–2012 National Pet Owners Survey*, thirty nine percent of US households (or 46.3 million) own at least one dog. They also noted that twenty three percent of the pet owners have taken their pet on a trip in the past twelve months.

Most property owners are reluctant to accept pets because they worry about the pet damaging their homes. But those fears are often unfounded. Remember, your guests who are renting your home are going on vacation for taking in the sights, rest and relaxation. If their dog does not travel well, they're going leave it at home. If they have a little "Fifi," "Pepe," or "Princess" who gets her nails and hair done every week, however, they wouldn't consider leaving her at home. Ninety-nine percent of the time, the pets that travel are going to be perfect houseguests. And here's the icing on the cake: Vacation property owners who accept pets increase their occupancy by 10 to 50 percent!

I always booked up my beach property for spring and summer, but rarely had fall or winter bookings (my property has three bedrooms, and after the kids are in school, couples without children are the only people who travel to my area. These couples are only looking for one-bedroom homes). So I decided to accept pets in the fall and winter only, and I went from one or two weeks booked in the fall to having all of September and October booked! Needless to say, I've kept that new policy in place ever since.

Furthermore, when you accept pets, you'll be able to charge an additional fee associated with the pet. The fee will often translate into enough money to get the carpet cleaned more often or replace the carpeting! Pet owners expect to pay this extra fee in lieu of the boarding costs they would have to pay otherwise. The bottom line is that you will make more money. If you have strong reservations against accepting pets, you can ask for an additional deposit for the pet, so if the pet damages anything, you will be covered.

If you choose to accept pets in your vacation rental, don't overlook the necessity of establishing clear rules and pet fees. Here's a suggested guideline:

It is appropriate (and I advocate) charging a daily or weekly pet fee. If you don't charge a pet fee, you open the door to this scenario: "We want to board Spot because he's such a pain, but it's much cheaper if we just take him with us."

When setting your pet rates, think of accepting pets as a convenience for your guests. And just as the convenience-size items in the store cost more, you too should charge more. My recommended pet fee is $10–$20 per day or a flat rate fee of $50–$200, depending on the length of their stay.

Here's a suggested clause that you can add to your rental agreement for renters looking to bring along their four-legged friends:

PETS: Pets are permitted in rental home only with prior approval. $X per pet fee applies.

1. All pets must be on leashes at all times.
2. Pet owners are responsible for cleaning up any/all pet refuse.
3. Pets are not allowed on furniture at any time. Any evidence of pets on furniture may incur extra cleaning fees.
4. All pets must be up to date on rabies vaccinations and all other vaccinations. Heartworm preventative is highly recommended.
5. All pets are to be treated with Advantage or similar topical flea and tick repellent three (3) days prior to arrival. Fleas and ticks are very rampant in this area and can cause harmful or fatal illness to humans and pets. All items above are the sole responsibility of the pet owner.
6. The homeowners assume no responsibility for illness or injury that may incur to pets while on the premises.
7. "Vicious or Dangerous Dogs" trained for dog fighting or with any tendency or disposition to attack any dog other domestic animals or humans without provocation, are not permitted at any time.

And if I haven't convinced you yet, here's another story that shows how accepting pets can increase your rentals:

A woman who owned a nice cabin in the mountains of Colorado called me for advice because she was only booking her cabin two to three weeks per year with an occasional weekend booking. Her cabin was within driving distance of three ski resorts, but wasn't really close enough to advertise that her home was associated with any of them.

I advised her to start accepting pets. The minute she did, her bookings started flowing in. Two years later, she books the whole ski season, rents to hikers three or four weeks during the summer, and she rents 10 to 12 long weekends throughout the year. She has never been happier! She said that she has to clean the carpet more often, but it has been well worth it . . . and she now owns the cabin right next door too.

The remaining suggestions involve physical changes to your vacation home, from purchasing beds and amenities to overhauling your property to make it more accessible. These run the range of cost and complexity, but making any of these changes should help increase your bookings throughout the year.

Look at your bed sizes. If you were to call any hotel and ask which of their rooms fill up first, I can assure you the answer would be the rooms with king-sized beds. If prospective renters are accustomed to sleeping on a king-sized bed at home, it may be out of the question for them to "downsize" while on vacation. If you have room for a king-sized bed, I recommend buying one the next time you need to replace your mattresses.

Assess the configuration of your beds. Evaluate your home's bedrooms while thinking about the specific group of renters you intend to target. For example, if you have a two bedroom with a king in one bedroom and two twin beds in the second bedroom your target group would likely be a couple with two children. If you put a full or queen size bed in place of the two twins, however, your target group of renters will expand, opening up your home for two couples traveling together, as well as the family with the two children.

Add some extra sleeping space. Sometimes it's not your policies that detract renters, but something about the property itself. There are many ways that you can add things to your property (some less expensive than others) that will increase occupancy. Don't overlook the number of people your property will accommodate. I am not a person who likes to pack them in like barracks, but by adding a pull-out sofa bed, futon, trundle or Murphy bed you can allow room for two extra guests. This can very well be the difference between renting or not.

+ A one-bedroom property can be transformed from a home that accommodates one couple into a home for a small family: mom, dad, and one or two children

+ A three-bedroom house can now accommodate sleeping space for eight people, as opposed to six people. This arrangement enables two families to share the rental together: two couples and four children

Add amenities. As always, a little comparison shopping can be helpful. Look at other properties in your area. What do they have that you do not? I know if you are in Colorado, don't even consider trying to rent a home without a hot tub because skiers look for properties with hot tubs. In Minnesota, a sauna is a must. In Tennessee a pool table is the amenity of desire. You may be thinking that these are rather pricey additions, but the additions will pay for themselves with the resulting number of extra bookings.

Make it handicapped accessible. You may also consider making your home handicapped accessible, though this is a much larger investment, you have to look at the bigger picture. The number of baby boomers reaching retirement age is growing every day. So by making your property handicapped accessible, you could be ensuring rentals for the long haul. If your bathroom or kitchen or deck is due for a remodel, you would definitely want to consider this.

You may not realize that handicapped people (not just older people) have a very hard time finding vacation properties to rent. They often have to stay in hotels simply because they have no other choices. While it's always best to purchase properties that were built as handicapped accessible, for a few thousand dollars you can fairly easily update a home to make it handicapped accessible. Be sure, however, to refer to government guidelines when updating your property for handicap accessibility or advertising it as such. Note that there are different types of special needs accessibility: for example, wheelchair accessible requires a bedroom with 36" doorways and a roll-in shower. The bathroom, kitchen, and bedroom must have enough floor clearance for a wheelchair to turn 360 degrees. Another category might require 36" doors, bars in the bathroom, an elevator, etc. So be sure to carefully check out these requirements beforehand.

So, you see, finding ideal renters involves much more than simply screening out a few bad apples. You need to be creative and give some thought to all of those people who might make great renters, if you gave them a chance. Yes, by all means, exercise discretion, and don't just rent out your home to every person who comes your way. But don't be close-minded either. And make exceptions to your general rules whenever you deem it wise.

Special Offers and Discounts

Selling vacation rental "inventory" should be looked at similarly to any other product that is sold with a shelf-life and expiration dates. Let's compare it to selling eggs—they have a specific date which they are no longer available to sell. As the expiration date for the eggs draws closer, the store might run a sale to get rid of them before they go bad. The same is true with "open nights" in your vacation rental—once the date passes you have no chance to ever sell that night again. If your goal is to maximize the income on your property, it's best to employ some tactics and run a "sale" on your inventory before it expires.

Utilize your advertisements. Though your goal certainly should be to book your property well in advance, realistically, it's not always possible. Many of the websites you advertise on have an option to post specials (sometimes for a minimal extra charge). You can use them to advertise reduced rates, offer last-minute discounts or just use them to make your listing stand out. Remember a special offer doesn't have to be a deeply discounted rate. It can be a complimentary dinner at a local restaurant, free attraction tickets or even something you offer to every guest. Advertise whatever makes your property unique. Be creative!

Special offers coupled with a fast and easy change to your one-line description could lure the renters looking for last-minute accommodations. In the example below I changed the title from "Great 3 BR condo on the beach" to one that starts with "Aug 12–19 open!" There's an excellent chance that this one little change will make the phone ring.

Alter your minimum night stays. Let's say it's a few days before a week that your property is wide open. You get an inquiry for a three-night stay. This is when it might be time to consider an exception to your "weekly rentals only" rule. While I don't make exceptions to this rule very often during the busy season (because as soon as I do, I'll get an inquiry for the full week); during the off-season all exceptions are fair game.

Make an offer to current or past guests. Another thing you can do to boost your bookings and sell last-minute inventory is make an offer to your current or past guests.

If you have some last-minute open dates, email your past guests and offer it to them for a discounted rates. After all, these guests have already "proven themselves" to be good guests who will care for your home. This works very well in areas where your guests primarily drive from three to five hours away.

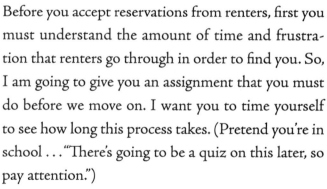

CHAPTER

18

Taking Reservations

Before you accept reservations from renters, first you must understand the amount of time and frustration that renters go through in order to find you. So, I am going to give you an assignment that you must do before we move on. I want you to time yourself to see how long this process takes. (Pretend you're in school . . . "There's going to be a quiz on this later, so pay attention.")

First, look at the clock and make a note of what time it is. Then, think of a location where you would like to spend your vacation. Let's say Colorado (you can pick anywhere). Now figure out where in Colorado you wish to go. We'll pick Breckenridge. Next, think of the budget you want to spend, for example, $1,500 for a week. Then choose the dates you will want to arrive and depart. And don't forget that you have to find a property that suits your size and particular needs, say, two bedrooms within walking distance to the ski trails or on the bus or trolley route to the slopes.

After you've made these initial decisions, go to the internet, and start searching for three comparable properties that fit those criteria. Visit a variety of websites. Do whatever it takes to find them. Once you find three properties, look at the clock again. How long did that take? Can you find those three properties again? Did you bookmark them or write them down?

Most likely it will have taken an hour, two hours, or maybe even more. Since you did not follow through and actually contact the owners, you don't even know if the properties you picked are actually available. Maybe the owner didn't update his or her calendar, or the property may have been booked earlier today. What if none of them are available? Then, you have to start over again.

The point of this exercise is to let you experience what inquiring renters have to go through in order to find *your* property. I want you to realize that once the renter finally finds a property that he or she sends an email about, he or she is already at the point of frustration. They are eager to finally secure a booking. And if that renter hears back from all the owners saying they are booked, the frustration grows. They will have to go through the searching process all over again and will be even more eager to book the first home that is available.

View this as if you were buying any other product, a Honda Civic for example. Now, if you are buying a new Civic, you have plenty of options; after all, there are many dealers that have hundreds of them lined up in their lots. Well, let's say you don't want a new Civic, you want a used one. That's going to be slightly more difficult. If you are looking for one particular color or year, you may scour through the paper each week and visit many dealers. Once you finally find that one perfect car that suits your needs, are you going to think about it for a long time? Probably not. Most people would buy it right away.

The same is true with vacation property rentals. If the renter wanted a hotel room, then he or she would have thousands to choose from. But a two-bedroom, two-bath home in Breckenridge might be a bit more difficult to come by. When they finally do find exactly what they are looking for, they will want to reserve it right away.

By all means, when they contact you, don't blow a potential rental by not calling back in a timely manner! It doesn't matter what your circumstances are or what is going on in your life. Make this a priority. Even if you (the owner) plan on being away, especially during the busy booking times, be sure to have someone you can trust check your email and/or phone messages so you don't lose out on valuable bookings. Let the following story serve as an example:

> Shirley and her husband own a vacation property in northern Minnesota. Shirley handles all the booking when they rent it out. In August, she delivered their new baby boy. The last thing on her mind when she first got home was her rental property. After about a week, she finally logged on to her computer and found about 25 rental inquiries for fall weekends. Now, since all these inquiries were a week old, she decided instead of emailing back, she would call. She was amazed to find out that every one of these people had already found and booked another home. The renters were not just browsing, or whimsically searching, they were actually looking to book. She would not have traded her new baby for any amount of bookings but now, if she's going to be away from her computer, she has her husband or a family member check her email.

The bottom line is this: when you get an inquiry, either by phone or email, please understand and respect the fact that your renter has worked very hard to find you. Contact them right away! Even if you have it booked. More often than not, the first owner who picks up the phone and quickly returns the renter's call, or dashes off an email response, will be the owner who gets the booking. (Tip: When emailing a response, be sure to write something in your subject line so that the renter does not mistake your email for junk mail.) There are thousands of salespeople who would kill for the direct target marketing capability that we are so fortunate to have in the vacation rental business. Take full advantage of the marvelous opportunity opened up for you by modern technology. The internet will make that phone ring. But it can't do the follow-up (returning calls and emails promptly, being well organized and professional, etc.). These important tasks are up to you. The key to being well organized is to write down the information for all inquiries and bookings in your rental book.

Telephone Communications

I never book a rental without speaking to the renter on the phone. Via email you never really know who is on the other side of the computer screen. Even if I have had numerous email conversations, I always require the renter to call me (or I call them). This gives me one last chance to screen the guest a little more closely (it's always better to be safe than sorry).

Don't take the phone for granted. It's a simple to use tool, but you still need a well-organized system. By doing business on the internet, you have to remember that you will get calls from all over the country, maybe even outside the country. Therefore, you need to know the various time zones, and which state belongs with what area code. You'll need an up-to-date list because area codes change a lot these days. So if you live on the East coast don't hurry to return a call to the 310 area code at 9 A.M. That's California, and it will only be 6 A.M.! Here is a good area code website: www.bennetyee.org/ucsd-pages/area.html

There is no need to install a separate phone line in your home for taking reservations. This is not like owning traditional investment property where you don't want your renters to have your home number, know where you live, etc. This is quite the opposite. You want the renter to know that this is your second home, and that you are just a regular person, not some big company. You want them to feel privileged to stay in your home.

For this same reason, I don't suggest posting toll-free numbers, nor do you need a separate phone line for your renters to call you with questions, problems, etc. There are a couple of reasons. First the cost, and second, when they know it is your home they are calling and not some management company, they are less inclined to call you all hours of the day and night. And with cell phones today, people don't worry about making "long-distance calls" like we used to.

At home I have one of those one-price, bundled packages for my telephone, cable and internet. The telephone is what they refer to as "digital phone service", also known as VOIP (voice over IP). I recently discovered my voice mail has the capability to send me (via email) a digital version of my voice mail messages. With my phone provider there was an extra charge of $2.95/month.

When I travel, I generally have my phone forwarded to my cell phone so I don't miss out on any bookings. When I am in town but otherwise just out of the house (running errands, shopping, walking the dog, etc.), I don't forward my phone calls. In the vacation rental business, timing is everything, especially with last-minute bookings. When someone is looking for a place to rent at the last minute, they don't have the time to wait for you to call back. Generally speaking, if they don't get you on the phone when they call you, they'll just move onto the next owner. I can't tell you how many times over the past 15 years working in the industry I have lost a booking just because I called the person back a few minutes too late.

Now when someone calls my home phone and leaves a message, I get an email sent to me with an attachment I can open and listen to on my cell phone!

To remain successful in the vacation rental industry, we all have to step up our games especially as it becomes more competitive and saturated with properties.

Call your telephone service provider and see if this service is available to you. If not, you may want to look into changing providers so you don't miss out on any bookings!

When it comes to voicemail, I find it advantageous to have an voicemail with separate mailboxes. The ones that say, "If you're calling for Mr. or Mrs. Paradise, press 1. If you're calling Judy, press 2. If you're calling John, Press 3, etc." A system like this works really well for your rentals. You can say, "Thanks for calling. If you're calling about the rental in Destin, Florida, please press 1." When they get to voice mailbox 1, your message should assure them that you will call right back. And then really do it! This way you won't lose any bookings.

You can also use your separate mailbox to say something like, "I'm sorry, I'm totally booked until August 21. If you're looking for a rental after that time, please leave your name, number, and the dates you are inquiring about, and I will get back to you."

Here's a helpful tip. When you get into renting, you will begin to realize that there are patterns in certain days and times of the year that see more inquiries than others. You'll notice that on the first really nice sunny day in the winter, you will receive a lot of calls. Right after the first snow there typically is a spike in calls from renters who want to go skiing. During the Super Bowl women will be searching and sending inquiries. Another very busy time is the week right before Christmas (This makes me crazy. I'm not even ready for the holidays and already people are planning their summer vacations!). Right after the New Year and around tax refund times, you will also see an influx of rental calls and inquiries. Be sure to check your voice and emails even more frequently during these critical time periods.

Put It in Writing

OK, so let's say you have done everything up to this point. The renter contacted you. You have spoken with them. You screened them, agreed on dates, and the renter wants to book it. Now what?

As a way to protect both you and your renter, you will want to put everything down in writing. You will want to send them a copy of your rental rules and billing confirmation (see Appendix 1). These documents are critical. You do not need to mail them; it's perfectly acceptable to email these documents to the renter. Have your renter print and sign these documents and send them back with their deposit check. DO NOT ACCEPT DEPOSITS WITHOUT SIGNED COPIES OF THESE DOCUMENTS (I know that's obnoxious to write in all capital letters but you get my drift, right? It's pretty important). You may want to write something like this:

Enclosed is our rental contract and rules. Please print, read, sign, and send it along with your deposit to the address below. Thanks so much, and if you have any questions, feel free to contact me.

Thanks again, Christine

Now we're ready to get to the good part . . . collecting the money.

Payments

When you think about it, this should be a rather pleasant topic, because what we're talking about is making money. People paying you to rent your vacation property. Sounds simple, right? Yes and no. Getting paid doesn't have to be difficult; you just have to put some sensible policies in place right from the beginning. There are, of course, a number of ways you can accept payment. But not all of them are created equal.

Personal Checks

Believe it or not, most common form of payment for many vacation home owners, is still and has always been personal checks. Renters have been sending checks and owners have been cashing them without any problems for many years.

What if the check bounces? I don't think there is much to worry about. I've only had one check bounce in all the time I have been renting. And that was an error. The lady used the wrong account so she apologized and shipped a new check to me overnight. You will just want to make sure the check clears well in advance of their rental dates. This way you are at not at risk of rendering any services before being paid (more on that in a moment when we discuss scheduling).

The downside of accepting checks is you have to wait for the renters to send them to you. Until you have the check in hand there is little guarantee that the booking is solidified and in the meantime you may be turning down other valuable bookings. From the renter's perspective sending a check for thousands of dollars to a complete stranger they found on the internet can be a bit unnerving. Checks don't offer the same safety and security of the transaction that credit cards do.

Cashier's Checks and Money Orders

Money orders and cashier's checks are certainly an acceptable form of payment, but it has the drawback of not being very convenient and could make yourself vulnerable to the scams you read about in chapter 16.

Money orders are inconvenient for the renters because they have to go to a bank or post office and buy the money order (after withdrawing the cash to purchase it), before he or she can send it. For the owner, the delay in the process puts another step between you and the money. Overall a step ultimately you'll be better off avoiding (who knows, maybe he or she will change his or her mind between speaking with me and going to the bank!).

There is one exception to my reluctance to accept money orders or cashier's checks—international guests. These guest (in my case, many of them are Canadian) are using a different currency. In these cases, you'll want to make sure you get paid secured funds in U.S. dollars (or whatever currency you accept). This is when it would be acceptable to ask for a cashier's check or money order. Since the guests are well aware that there is a currency difference, these guests expect a little extra inconvenience and usually have a very easygoing, accepting attitude about it.

But with this exception, comes another caution. In my opinion accepting credit cards is the better solution for international guests.

PayPal

Many vacation rental owners use PayPal for collecting funds. It seems to be a simple and easy solution for collecting funds. Originally started to accommodate eBay and other online auctions, PayPal (www.paypal.com) is a payment method many people like because of its convenience. Essentially, a person can send you your money via the internet. The money comes straight out of their credit card or personal checking account; of course, you have to open up your own PayPal account to receive the money. But the process is relatively simple. The advantage that PayPal has over credit card merchant accounts is the guests will input their own credit card or checking account information, which takes away the liability you would have if you collected their credit card information. Secondly, there are no monthly fees like a regular merchant account would have.

The disadvantages of PayPal are the cost per transaction is higher than a tradition merchant account. Many owners will use PayPal for the initial down payment (so the booking is immediately confirmed), then require the guests to send checks for the subsequent payments—thus minimizing the transaction fees.

Another reason owners are reluctant to use PayPal for their vacation rentals is because if the guest has "an issue", PayPal has been known to side with the consumer (renter) over the merchant (owner). This means if you have a renter who has some absurd complaints and demands their money back, PayPal might just give it to them.

Wire Transfers

One other payment method that people sometimes want to use is a wire transfer. Let me make this one as clear as possible: do not give out your personal account number for the money to be wired to. Instead, call your bank and do a bank-to-bank wire transfer. The bank will have a general account number that you can have the money wired to. Giving somebody you don't know your bank account number is never a good idea. Keep in mind, with wire transfers, the sender and the receiver are both charged a transaction fee. So be sure to consider the fee, and add this charge into your rental fees.

And since so often wire transfers are associated with scams (see chapter 16), again I would recommend using PayPal or credit cards instead. I have never required my guests to pay by a wire transfer.

Credit Cards

We've all become accustomed to using credit cards for just about everything these days, from booking hotel rooms to renting cars to buying things in stores. For many travelers, the deciding factor for which property to rent might just come down to whether they can pay with credit cards.

There are many companies that offer merchant credit card accounts. You can go to your local bank, lending institution, the internet or even Costco.com to find them. The options are about as endless as your mortgage options. Be sure to research and find the one that best suits your needs.

I was late to the game accepting credit cards for my rentals. Initially I thought, why should I pay a portion of the rental monies to the merchant account company when the renters are more than happy to send a check?

The first year that I accepted credit cards (2004) I only took the deposit via credit card. That minimized my cost, but more importantly I felt it was worth the "insurance" that the booking was "good." Surprisingly, I found the renters also looked at me differently, more as a business, trusting that I was more legitimate.

In 2005 I decided to run all my transactions through the credit card merchant account. Accepting credit cards has made my life so much easier by reducing cancellations to near null, eliminating the wait for checks to come in the mail and running to the bank to make deposits. The best part is that I don't have to mail back deposits anymore, thus making the whole process much easier for both me and my renters. To offset the additional costs for the merchant account fees, I raised my rates a smidgen.

Now when a renter asks if they can send a check for the balance, I shy away from that option. I tell them if they have a credit card that's attached to their checking account that would be better for them and me. I explain that it's also safer, and they typically oblige. Accepting credit cards is a win-win for all!

So, should you accept credit cards? I do. I feel the convenience is well worth any costs or risks associated with accepting them. But just as with most other decisions you have to make, you'll need to weigh the advantages and drawbacks for your personal situation.

The drawbacks. The process of obtaining a credit card merchant account can be somewhat cumbersome. You have to fill out an application (quite similar to a loan application), then, based on your credit and the dollar amount per year of transactions, they will assess your situation and assess and assign fees associated with your merchant account.

Then there are the costs. Set-up charges can range between free and $1,000, though the going rate is around $150. (Don't allow a bank to convince you that you must purchase a credit card swiping machine. . . . How can you swipe a card from hundreds of miles away?) Aside from the start-up fees, you will have to pay monthly fees, which range from $4.95 to $19.95 per month. There are also per-transaction fees, which range anywhere from 10 cents to one dollar. Lastly, you'll also have to pay discount rate, which is not a "discount" at all, it's really a fee which is typically 2 to 5 percent of the entire charge. And the kicker is, these fees generally apply to charges *and* refunds.

One stumbling block you might run into could be finding a merchant account company that would allow you to charge vacation rentals on your merchant account. For some crazy reason, some merchant accounts categorize vacation rentals in the same high-risk categories as internet gaming sites, pornography sites, and other not so socially upstanding businesses. Just be sure that you clearly state your intended use for your account. If you skirt the truth it could come to bite you if you ever have a problem with your account.

Moreover, when you accept credit cards from your renters, there is always the danger of charge backs (although they are very rare). A charge back is when someone rents your vacation home, then claims there was some sort of problem (i.e., "the home was smaller than they said it would be," or "the neighbor's barking dog ruined my vacation," "the house was not clean," etc.). They tell the credit card company they are disputing the bill. There is a possibility that you may never get paid if you do not have written and signed documentation of the terms and conditions of the charges. Simple solution: before you charge their credit card, make sure that you have a written agreement with all of your payment and cancellation terms clearly spelled out, signed by the renter.

Liability. Realize that with accepting credit cards also comes some liability on your part. You will be collecting guest's credit card numbers. Having all of this information on hand means that you will have to be especially careful in how you store this information. For instance, if you organize your bookings via an online booking and reservation system, you should not store your guest's credit card information on that system because these systems are not secure. Also never store or send credit card information via your email program.

Furthermore, there are compliance rules and regulations with accepting credit cards, known and PCI compliance www.pcisecuritystandards.org. These are basically rules and regulations that are set up to protect the consumer. Familiarize yourself with the rules and make sure to comply with all of them that apply.

The best way to avoid the liability associated with storing credit card data is use a program such as Quickbooks Credit Cards. With this program, you will be able to send a link to your guests and they will input the credit card data directly into your credit card merchant account—alleviating your liability. If you do this, be sure to charge the deposit as well as the rental rate, as you will not have the guest's information in case of damages or theft.

The advantages. Credit cards offer a safe and secure means of payment for your renters. Suppose you are the renter and you call someone who owns a property you saw on the internet. The owners say, "Yes, I have that available. It will be $1,000 rent plus a $100 cleaning fee plus 10 percent tax. Now, please send me a personal check for $1,210." How can you be sure that person really has a property? Does the condition of the property match the description? Accepting credit cards gives the renters a certain amount of comfort, a feeling that they are protected.

- More bookings—renters feel much more secure paying via credit cards, which means they are more likely to book properties that accept credit cards;
- Instantly confirm the booking—no more waiting for "the check is in the mail" to verify that a booking is solid;
- Receive money instantly—funds available in your own bank account within 24 to 72 hours;
- Easy to use—process rental payments, security deposits and deposit refunds instantly over the internet;
- More last-minute bookings—no more overnight mail for checks, takes away all the hassles when you book a last-minute reservation;
- More international guests—avoid the inconvenience of renters having to obtain and send money abroad;
- Safe and secure—accepting credit cards gives your renters the added comfort that you and your property are legitimate;
- Tax deductible—don't forget, the merchant account fees are tax deductible as a business expense.

Allow me to tell you about something that happened to me. Remember back in Chapter 10 when I said that we rented a vacation home in upstate New York out of the newspaper? Well, as the late Paul Harvey would say, "Here, my friends, is the rest of the story."

My husband and I wanted to rent a house the week of the Fourth of July on a lake in upstate New York. We could not find any homes listed on the internet, so we ended up renting from the newspaper. Since we were late making our reservations, all the less expensive homes were booked. We ended up spending a bit more than we had anticipated. That was OK. We were even a little excited to have a nicer place. We live in Atlanta, however, and the rental house was in New York, so I had no way to see the property. There were no photographs in the paper, and although

I repeatedly asked the owner to send some, he never did. But the owner was a chiropractor, and I trusted him.

We arrived all excited to have a nice, relaxing vacation. We picked up the keys at his office, as instructed. He gave us directions and we were off to spend a week at the lake.

We had certain expectations as we drove up to the house. After all, I spoke with the owner on the phone. I asked all the right questions. I knew exactly what to expect. Sure . . . read on. First of all, we could not find the house. We kept driving back and forth until finally a neighbor came out. When we asked her where Doctor X's house was, she pointed to a dilapidated old shack! Surely she must be mistaken. The home I rented was one of the most expensive homes listed in the paper. The home I rented was supposed to have a deep-water dock for our boat. The home I rented was supposed to have front steps, not a ladder leading up to the door! The house looked and smelled as though it had not been occupied in 25 years. There was no boat dock, no deep water, and I kid you not, there were no stairs up to the 3-feet off-the-ground front door! There was no toaster, coffee maker, barbecue grill, TV, radio, alarm clocks, phone, or picnic table. No, no, no! This could not be! We were scammed!

We ended up turning back around and immediately drove to Doctor X's office. It was not a pretty scene. Doctor X got defensive and belligerent (in front of his patients). We actually feared a bit for our personal safety. We even threatened to call the police. In the end, we did manage to get our rent back but he would not give back our deposit. We were a thousand miles from home, and out $300. It was a holiday weekend, we had no home to stay, and our vacation was ruined!

Now imagine how differently the situation could have been handled if we charged our vacation on a credit card. We wouldn't have worried one bit about Doctor X. We would have walked right out the door the moment we felt uncomfortable, called our credit card company and gotten *all* of our money back.

So, as you can see, accepting credit cards not only gives you the assurance of receiving payments expediently, they also gave your renters a certain amount of comfort, a feeling that they are protected, which is a necessary attribute when you are blindly renting from strangers via the internet. In fact, I am certain that there are some people who limit their search only to properties that accept credit cards because of this fear. You don't want to miss out on these folks' business.

Payment Schedules

Okay, now that we know *how* you will be paid, it's time to move on to a discussion of *when* you will be paid. The key to scheduling payments is to make sure you receive your money (including deposits and fees) well in advance of the date when your guests begin renting your property. Don't worry; there is usually plenty of time to accomplish this. For example, in January, I am taking bookings for July, leaving ample time for the payments to come in.

Payments via credit card. As I said earlier, accepting credit cards is the preferred method of payment for guests and most expedient method for owners. Here is how I handle payments with my guests. I require a down-payment in order to book the property. No exceptions on this one! I will not hold any reservations until I have payment in hand. Mrs. Nicelady has been burned too many times by people who say, "I'd like to book it" only to never hear from them again (meanwhile turning away other prospective guests).

  + Require a flat-rate down payment upon booking, which is generally $200–$500.

+ The next payment would be ½ of the remaining balance due 60 days prior to their arrival date.
+ The final payment would be for the remainder of the balance due 30 days prior to their arrival date.

But here's a marketing tactic that I have used and it's worked quite well in making the renters choose me over the next property—allow monthly payment plans!

Let's say it's January and you are taking a booking for July and the rental comes out to $2000. You can offer the guests a payment plan that allows them to pay monthly. Require a $200 down payment upon booking and $360 per month for 5 months (Feb, Mar, Apr, May and June).

You never know what exactly makes the guest choose you over the next property but sometimes it's the little things that make a big difference.

Payments via checks. While I don't personally like to take checks, I realize that many vacation rental owners still prefer their guests to send checks. If you want your guests to pay by check, then here are some suggested guidelines:

Require a down payment check immediately, (regardless of how far in advance they make the booking—even if it is a year in advance). You should impose a deadline for receiving it (perhaps three to five days).

Meanwhile, until you receive the check—and it clears—keep taking inquiries about booking those same dates. Be honest, tell the callers there is a pending booking, but request their contact information in case there is an opening. Or, perhaps you could interest them in a different date. This happens quite frequently. In fact, in my experience, I have ended up with a large number of bookings through this exact scenario.

For a down payment, require at least $200. I would suggest that as minimum. You will have to determine the actual number yourself, but I wouldn't recommend going over 15% of the total rental amount. Whatever number you choose, this initial deposit is critical. Be sure to cash it as soon as it arrives. If it bounces, that's a sure sign of trouble. This is your first exchange of money, and already there's a problem. Why? Call them, and ask for an explanation. If it is some sort of simple mistake (i.e., maybe they sent a check from the wrong account), you might want to ask them to send another check to cover it (along with any fees your bank charged you for the bounce). If they are cooperative, things might still work out with this renter. If not, find another renter.

Let's move on. Assuming everything works out well with the down payment, you will want to set up a payment schedule for your renters. There are a number of ways you can do this, I will share with you my own method. Here is a typical bill:

Thank you for choosing our condominium for your vacation. We hope that you have a pleasant stay. The unit is located in the XYZ complex at 12345 Scenic Drive, unit #6789, Your City, State, 23456 Phone 234-456-678.

Your confirmation is as follows:
Check-in date: June 16, 2013 after 3 P.M. CST
    (No early check-in please)
Checkout date: June 23, 2013 by 10 A.M. CST

Number of people in party: 6 adults, 2 children

Today's date: _____

After I receive your $200 deposit, your bill is as follows:
Total bill $1,581.75 = $1,350 (rental rate) +
    $75 (cleaning fee) + $156.75 (11% Florida Tax)

1st payment of $790.87 due April 16, 2013 (60 days prior)
2nd payment of $790.88 due May 16, 2013 (30 days prior)

As soon as I receive your final payment, I will send the lock box/key instructions.

Please sign and return 1 copy of this confirmation, and 1 copy of the rules.

Signature_____ Date_____

As you see, I typically break it into at least two equal payments unless it is a last-minute reservation, then I would ask for full payment. You should receive the first payment about 60 days prior to the rental date, this will give you ample time to get another renter if for some reason they change their mind and don't send in the payment. The balance should be paid 14–30 days prior to the rental date. This will provide plenty of time for the check to clear before you send them the key. Remember, the more time you give yourself, the more flexibility you have with payments. With enough time, you could even break it into six payments (which might be preferable for some of your guests).

Before leaving this topic, let me add a few words about long-term and last-minute guests. First, long-term. These are typically "snow-birds," older people escaping the cold, stormy weather of the Northern states who will rent for part or all of the winter months. These could also be people who are taking advantage of the lower prices and will rent for an entire month during the off-season. You should require that people in these situations pay you even earlier in advance, 90 days before the rental date, because if they back out, they will be that much harder to replace.

On the subject of last-minute guests (sometimes a necessity, especially if there has been a last-minute cancellation), please realize that this is a unique circumstance and you will have to adjust your normal procedures to accommodate it. For this situation, credit cards or PayPal are the ideal payment methods because you don't have to wait for payments or for the check to clear.

Security Deposits

In the previous section I spoke about "reservation deposits", it's important to note the difference between security deposits and reservation deposits, especially when communicating with your guests—they need to know which monies are refundable and which are not.

A reservation deposit is money that validates or confirms the booking and is a portion of the total rental bill. A security deposit is an amount of money that is collected above and beyond the total rental fees which is held as insurance in case of theft or damages incurred by the guest during their stay.

Here are some general guidelines to consider when taking security deposits:

- You can charge any amount you choose however a standard practice is around $250 or 10–15% of the total rental rate (whichever is greater). Realize that extremely high security deposits can be a deterrent for prospective guests.
- Include specifics in your rental agreement that would result in partial or full loss of a security deposit. Full disclosure and clear expectation is the best way to avoid problems.
- Security deposits should never be used as a way to nickel and dime your renters. Normal wear and tear should not be used as grounds for withholding security deposits. For example; items such as dishes and glasses are prone to chipping or breakage. You should replace them without charging your renters unless of course they break the entire stack of dishes.

Note: Security deposits cannot not be utilized for as compensation for the pain and suffering you endured because of those "pain-in-the-neck" renters. The basic rule of thumb is: If you don't have a receipt for a replacement item or a repair, you shouldn't charge them for it. Simple as that!

Fines. A second way to let your renters know that you mean business about specific rental rules is to impose fines for specific damaged or missing items. In this case, a fine is a flat fee charged to the renters that is stipulated in the rental contract that your renters must sign. For example, you could charge a $500 fine if there is evidence of smoking inside your home.

More examples of things you can impose fines for:

+ Evidence of pets on the premises (if you have a no pet policy)
+ Lost or missing items (remotes, keys, garage door openers)
+ Service calls for maintenance issues that were caused by guests during their stay (windows left open during rain, overfilling the bathtub causing water damages, improperly flushing things down the toilet)
+ Evidence of smoking inside your home (if you have a no smoking policy)

Note: If you're going to charge fines for specific items/damages, be sure to use the word "FINE" specifically in your rental contract.

Here are a few other things to remember when it comes to deposits. Do not return the deposit until after they have finished renting your property *and* you (or your housekeeper) have had the opportunity to inspect the premises and make sure there are no damages.

Let me add a word of caution here about refunds. If a person calls up, even two days after you receive his deposit check, and says something like, "I've had an illness in my family, we have to cancel. Please refund the deposit money I sent you," tell them, "OK, we'll get it in the mail to you soon." Do *not* send them the refund until their check *clears* your bank. Although I don't want you to get paranoid about scams but they do exist. Don't be a victim. Yes, the guy is probably telling the truth, and there most likely is indeed an illness in his family. But waiting just a few days to get his refund (while their check clears) is not going to hurt him. As I always say, better to be safe than sorry.

Security Deposit Payment Methods

So now that you understand how security deposits work, now you have to figure out how and when the guests will pay you the security deposit. Basically you have three very traditional options: cash, check or credit card.

Cash. If you live near your vacation home, you can meet the guests upon check-in and collect the security deposit in cash. Then you can refund it upon inspection of the home at checkout. Since 99% of us don't live near our vacation homes, this is not a viable option for most of us.

Check. Collecting the security deposit via check is probably the easiest and most common method for collecting security deposits. Even if you have the guests pay for the entire rental via credit card, having them send you a check for the security deposit is the least expensive and most hassle free way to collect the security deposit.

Be sure to actually cash the check and then refund it from your own account after the renters check out. Many owners make the mistake of "holding" the guest's check and only cashing it if there's a problem. While this might seem to be the course of action with the least resistance, it could get precarious if there is indeed a reason to withhold any or all of the security deposit, (especially if the guests are refuting the damage claims). They could very easily call their bank and put a "stop payment" on their check. What if their account has insufficient funds to cover the check? Best way to avoid these issues would be to cash the check upon receipt and refund them later.

Credit card. If you accept credit cards for your rentals, you will have to come up with a separate procedure plan for handling the security deposits. Taking your security deposit via credit card can be expensive and a bit cumbersome. There are two ways to charge deposits via credit card: Charge and Refund or Pre-Authorization of funds.

Charge and refund. The first option is to process the charge for the security deposit just as you would any other payment or "sale." While charging the transaction as a "sale" will achieve the end, it could cost you extra fees that might not be necessary—transaction fees for the charge and for the refund of the security deposit. However, some owners choose to eat the costs because it's simply more convenient to charge the deposit to the guest's credit card. Furthermore, you don't have to worry about timing as you would with a pre-authorization.

Let's say that you take a booking for the week of August 17–24. The total rental including cleaning fees and tax is $2500, and you would like to collect a $500 refundable security deposit.

- At time of booking, charge the renter $500 as a reservation deposit. This will later convert to their refundable security deposit.
- On June 17th, you would charge $1250 (half of the rental rate) 60 days prior to check-in.
- On July 17th, you would charge the remaining balance of $1250, which is 30 days prior to check-in. (making the total amount charged $3000).
- On August 24th, your housekeepers clean and inspect the property. If there are no damages, refund the security deposit (within 30 days of their checkout date).

Pre-authorization of funds. The other option is a pre-authorization of funds, which allows you to hold a given amount of money for a specified length of time. For example, let's say your guests have a $2000 credit limit, and you pre-authorize a $500 security deposit. In the eyes of the credit card company, this renter now has available credit of $1500, because that $500 is on hold for you, the merchant. (These charges often appear as pending transitions in a merchant account.) If there is no damage to your home, you can release the funds. If your home does incur damage, you can charge the necessary amount—also known as a "post-authorization."

Similar to hotels' procedures, a pre-authorization is where you "hold" the security deposit and then release it upon departure. When using a pre-authorization, you'll want to take a "down payment" on your rental instead of converting your reservation deposit to a security deposit. This is because pre-authorization of funds have time limits (generally 14 to 30 days after the charge has been processed). Here are the steps to take if you are taking the security deposit as a pre-authorization using the same booking info from the example above.

+ At time of booking, charge the renter $500 as a reservation deposit.
+ On June 17th, you would charge $1250 (half of the rental rate) 60 days prior to check-in.
+ On July 17th, you would charge the remaining balance of $1250, which is 30 days prior to check-in.
+ On August 17th (check-in day), place the pre-authorization of $500 on the guest's credit card which would serve as the security deposit. Because there may be time limits on holding funds (usually around 14–30 days) you would not want to charge the preauthorization of funds any sooner than 7 days prior to check-in.
+ On August 24th, your housekeepers clean and inspect the property. If there are no damages, release the pre-authorization (although the pre-authorization typically disappears automatically after 30 days for most merchant accounts, you should release the funds as soon as possible as a courtesy to your guests).
+ July 18: After your housekeeper confirms that there was no damage to your property.

Alternatives to Security Deposits

Some owners have stopped taking security deposits altogether and I happen to be one of them! Yes you read that right; around seven or eight years ago I evaluated my processes and I realized that I never had to keep anyone's deposit. I calculated my time vs. the risks and gave up collecting and returning the security deposits altogether. I'm happy to report that I have not had issues.

This is one area where I'd say, "do as I say, not as I do" unless you are confident you can screen your guests properly to avoid issues—I feel that I am an expert at screening guests.

I'm also very good at setting clear expectations in writing and verbally with my guests. After teaching tens of thousands of vacation rental owners over the years, I have found that damages are rarely the reason for withholding security deposits. More often the reason for withholding security deposits is because of some sort of communication breakdown. The guests did not leave the property as "expected"—but the owner didn't specifically spell out what they wanted to the guests to do before they checked out.

Damage waiver fee. Many property managers and some owners choose to charge a damage waiver fee to every guest in lieu of a security deposit. This is what is loosely considered "self-insuring". Basically the theory behind the damage waiver fee is you collect a nominal non-refundable amount from every guest and that money is pooled together to cover all minor damages by all guests. Guests love this option because they don't have to fork out a big security deposit check and in the event of minor damage (amount specifically defined), they would not be responsible for the costs to rectify or replace the damaged item.

Some people charge a percentage of the rental (3–5% of the base rental cost) and others charge a flat rate for example:

Let's say your property rents for $1500 per week and you book 20 weeks per year. If you charge a 3% damage waiver fee that would be

$45 per booking, or $900 over your 20 bookings. If you charge a 5% damage waiver fee, it would be $75 or $1500 over your 20 bookings in a year. So that means you'd have $900 or $1500 per year to cover all minor damages. If you choose to do this, just make sure to put a maximum amount in the contract that the damage waiver insurance would cover, generally one to three times your annual intake so for these examples, it would cover $900 or $3000. Any damages above that and the guest would still be responsible to pay.

Think about it, insurance companies make a lot of money. Damage waivers are a great way to earn some extra money but it does come with some risks.

Damage waiver insurance. There are some companies that offer damage waiver insurance that you can offer to your guests. It's the same idea as a damage waiver fee however it is processed through an insurance company rather than you holding and remitting the money. Most people I know choose to use the damage waiver fee instead because let's face it, insurance companies are in business for a reason—they make a lot of money. Savvy owners opt to put money in their own wallet, not someone else's.

CHAPTER

19

Collect and Pay Sales Tax

I know what you're thinking as soon as you begin reading this chapter: "Wait a minute! I never signed on to be a tax collector!" Well, rest assured, this part of the business is not as ominous as it may sound at first. Let me begin by saying that we are speaking about *sales tax*, not income tax. As a matter of fact, you've probably noticed that I don't speak much about income taxes. That's because I do not know much about them. As I said earlier, I am not an accountant. Once you own an investment property, your income taxes become more complex. Those do-it-yourself tax programs (yes, even the ones that swear they will make everything oh-so-simple) are not the best for your business. Since buying my first property, I have had an accountant file my taxes for me, and I recommend you do the same. It is money well spent.

But you do not need an accountant to help you with collecting and paying sales taxes. Sales tax on vacation rentals is required by most states though not all of them. Be sure to check with your city, county, and state sales tax departments to see if it's required in your area (see Appendix 5 for state sales tax department websites). These taxes can be called a variety of names (sales tax, tourist development tax, transient rental tax, bed tax, chamber's tax, visitors bureau tax, accommodation tax, etc.), but to you the owner, the collector, they all mean the same thing. You must collect and pay sales tax. No sense fussing over it. That's the law, so it's best that you have a solid knowledge of how it works.

For starters, understand that the money does not come from you; it comes from the renters. You are just a middleman for the government. Actually, you should look at it as a duty that ultimately works in your favor. These taxes pay for many things that are directly beneficial to your investment such as roads, sidewalks, beach preservation, and the local chamber of commerce (which is responsible for national tourism advertising campaigns; you know, those colorful, glitzy TV ads that show what a beautiful place your state is). That is why I view these taxes as a good thing.

When I give seminars in Florida, the county departments of revenue attend. I give them a chance to speak with the owners and explain how to file the taxes. They also go into great detail about what the current local taxes are allocated for. The counties *like* the tourists as much as we owners do. For the counties, sales tax brings in revenue, jobs, and growth. For us, the owners, these taxes go toward things that directly impact our property values. How is that? Well, the tax revenues give the counties the funding to make major capital improvements in the area.

For example, in Destin, Florida the county built a five- or six-mile boardwalk right in front of my condo complex which was paid for with bed tax collections. This has made the area safe for walking, jogging, and biking. Moreover, they purchased a trolley to transport renters from off-beach properties to the beach. This cuts down on traffic and congestion in front of my home. And, they purchased dune buggies for the police department to patrol the beaches. All of these things directly impact the tourism in the area and subsequently improve my property values. So if you view the sales tax as a benefit for yourself, maybe that will make it easier to collect and pay. Remember, *somebody* has to pay for all of those things the municipality provides to make a more pleasant environment. It may as well be the renter. Be glad this is a cost you are simply passing on, and not something taken directly out of your own pocket!

If I have not yet convinced you that sales taxes are good for you, let me remind you again—it's the law! There are stiff fines, penalties, and interest penalties if you do not comply. Many states are beginning to come down hard on vacation property owners who are tax avoiders. Please don't be naive and ask, how are they going to find out? The tax departments aren't stupid. They know about the internet. They have people on their staff that regularly and systematically search through the listings. So, if you have a listing on the Web, the tax department will find you, eventually. I don't think I'm being overly dramatic when I say, "Big Brother is watching."

Here's the good news. Sales taxes are not difficult to file. Some states require monthly filing and others allow quarterly. It takes five minutes to fill out and file the necessary paperwork and today, many states have online filing available. Even a busy person, such as yourself, can handle that! Basically, it's a short form where you write in your property address, tax ID number (each tax department will assign you one), your gross rental revenue, how many days the property was occupied, and the amount of taxes you collected. This is a very simple formula. It does *not* take an accounting agree, just a calculator. You even get to keep a 2%–3% tax allowance! (That's 2%–3% of the sales tax collected, *not* your gross revenue). The only difficult part of filing is remembering to do it each month or quarter. You can set up an automatic reminder on your computer, or simply make a note on the appropriate date on your calendar.

Okay, so I now have you convinced to collect and pay sales tax, but what exactly is taxable? You charge a separate cleaning fee, as well as other fees. Are those fees taxable? Please realize that each governing office may have different rules regarding this so be sure to check with your tax offices. Here's my interpretation. Most sales tax laws say that any fees associated as part of the rental agreement are taxable, meaning any money that you keep. Cleaning fees, if they are charged as an extra fee associated with the rental, are taxable. But your housekeeper should not be charging you tax on her services. That is double taxation. Also, if you charge a pet fee that you keep, that's taxable too. But deposits, including pet deposits that are returned, are *not* taxable since they are being returned, even if there are damages, and you have to withhold money from the deposit. While you certainly don't want to shortchange the government, make sure you don't cheat yourself out of money either.

Here are a couple examples:

+ if you charge $1,000 per week + $75 cleaning fee + $200 refundable deposit, then $1,075 is taxable (the rental rate + cleaning fee) and the $200 is not taxable (since this is just a security deposit that will be refunded).
+ if you charge $1,000 per week + $75 cleaning fee + $200 refundable deposit + $300 pet fee, then the taxable amount is $1,375 (the rental rate + cleaning fee + pet fee).
+ if you charge $1,000 per week + $75 cleaning fee + $200 refundable deposit + $300 pet *deposit* (refundable), then the taxable amount is only $1,075 since the $200 and $300 charges are *refundable*.

Keep in mind that taxes are charged on anything associated with rental, so if you require that they pay per bundle of firewood, for use of your fishing boat, use of a snowmobile, etc., those charges are taxable.

Now what about snowbirds and monthly rentals? Do you have to charge sales tax for these long-term rentals? Though many states vary in their rules, many require more than six months rental in order for it to be considered non-transient. In most cases, you will also have to provide a bona fide written lease for that state's minimum amount of months, along with specific terms. Be sure to check with your local tax office before you tell any renter that you will not have to charge sales tax.

As I said, I think collecting sales taxes is relatively easy. Still, some of you may not want to go through the hassles of setting up your sales tax accounts and/or filing returns monthly or quarterly. Well, you'll be glad to know that there is a service you can hire to do this for you. HotSpotManagement.com, specifically created for vacation property owners, will set up your tax accounts and file all the necessary forms and taxes for you. After all, your mother always dreamed you would be a doctor, *not a tax collector*.

Vacation Rental Bans

Vacation rental bans are when a municipality imposes a restriction against renting your property on a nightly, weekly or even monthly basis. They often restrict any rentals on a transient basis, meaning anything less than a full residential lease of six months or more. These bans are becoming more prevalent. Collecting and paying sales taxes on your vacation rental property is your best defense against this happening in your community.

Vacation property owners all around the country are facing impending bans on transient rentals. If you think that your area is immune, think again. Communities in many states including California, Florida, Maine, Pennsylvania, Hawaii, Oregon, Nevada, New Mexico, Texas, Arizona, New York and even parts of Canada have imposed vacation rental bans.

State and local governments are not the only entities imposing vacation rental bans. Condominium complexes and homeowners' associations (HOA) are also getting into the act. This is why when I advise people who are looking to purchase I always tell them that the first step is to check for HOA and local city or town zoning laws to be sure there are no restrictions.

There Are 3 Main Issues Driving Vacation Rental Restrictions

The permanent residents. It seems that many people who live permanently in the vacation rental areas are upset that people are moving in on their secret little paradises. They don't like to deal with the crowed roads, stores, restaurants, the noise, etc. What usually starts the wheels in motion for such a restriction is a permanent resident filing a formal complaint with his local government or HOA.

The main disadvantage for vacation rental owners, though they do pay property taxes, is that most are not voting members of the community. Even if an area had 25 percent of the homes owned by permanent residents and 75 percent owned by out-of-town residents, it doesn't matter—the out-of-towners have no "vote." The permanent residents win every time.

Economics. With the demand for vacation homes so strong, especially in what used to be sleepy little towns, the prices are driving out the locals. They can no longer afford to live in those areas. Two places that come to mind are Hawaii and the Florida Keys. Both have limited the number of vacation rental licenses they are issuing.

The hotel and bed and breakfast (B&B) industries. Most people who rent by owner think that their main competitors are property managers. While property managers do share the industry, it's really hotels and B&Bs who are our biggest competitors. Vacation rental owners are edging in on their territories. And watch out, hotels especially have deep pockets and plenty of money to lobby against short-term rentals.

The biggest problem vacation rental owners face in this situation is that it's difficult for individual owners to band together to fight the cause. This is when it's imperative that individual owners and property managers work together. For example, Big Bear, California had a group of B&B owners who lobbied against vacation rentals. Thankfully Big Bear had a good number of property managers and they worked with individual vacation homeowners to fight it together. It was an ugly debate, but for now they have been successful in legally having the right to rent their properties on a nightly or weekly basis.

Defense? One thing you may want to consider is networking with other owners and property managers to band together to lobby against any proposed bans. But your number one defense against vacation rental bans in your area is to collect and pay sales taxes! And encourage all other owners in your area to do the same. In every case I have seen regarding vacation rental bans, the sales tax revenue has been a heavily weighted deciding factor on whether or not the bans get passed. The areas where the majority of the property owners collect and pay sales taxes usually don't lose their right to rent. For instances, in 2005, Polk County, Florida reported that the vacation home industry contributed more than $3.5 million in tourism development taxes (sales tax) to their region. That's some serious money for the county. I would venture to guess that Polk County Florida would have a hard time passing a vacation rental ban. Let's face it, once the county, city or town is used to the revenue stream from the sales taxes collected via vacation rentals, no one likes to give it up, especially not politicians.

And probably equally important is to get socially and politically involved in your vacation rental community. Attend meetings, volunteer events, etc. that can help the community get to know you. Let them see that you're not just some monster investor who cares nothing about their community. Be sensitive to their gripes and annoyances and try your best not to add to the problems. Be sure to clearly inform your renters of any parking, noise, or other ordinances within the community. Remember, even though you don't live there full time, it's your community too.

Order home delivery of their local newspaper and be sure to read up on any problems, complaints, or initiatives regarding rentals. While a ban may be imminent, you'll at least go down fighting.

CHAPTER

20

Handling Keys

You live in Indiana, your renters live in Texas, and your property is in Colorado. How do you get the keys to the renters? Don't worry, this is not as complicated as it seems.

You have many options when it comes to keys. First, you can use the old-fashioned method of mailing the keys to your renters. Many owners have been doing this for twenty or thirty or more years.

When my husband and I first got married, we used to vacation at Martha's Vineyard every year. We rented directly from an owner. She would mail us the keys before we left, and then we would mail them back after we returned. It was effective.

Effective, but not necessarily simple. You may not have given it much thought, but mailing keys leaves a lot of room for error. And it means more work than is really necessary. The problem is you have to make numerous sets of keys, send them out in a timely manner so that your renter receives them before they leave home, and then you have to be sure that your renters mail the keys back to you. Forget any one of these steps and you will have a potentially serious problem on your hands. What if the renters forget to bring the keys with them when they leave your rental home? What if they don't send them back? What if they lose them while they are there?

There are two ways to alleviate all this trouble of mailing keys: use a lockbox or buy an electronic keyless lock.

Lockboxes. You can buy a combination key box. A key box attaches to your doorknob, doorframe or somewhere on your property. The most common ones are made by GE, are very inexpensive ($25–$30), and can be found at most hardware stores, from locksmiths, or on the internet (just a note: there are many brands out there, but I like the portable push button made by GE Supra. It holds up to the elements quite well, and I have used the same one for many years). A key box is not a complex piece of equipment. You easily set your own code, hang it on your doorknob, and put the keys inside the box. You then give the renter the combination when you send them the driving directions (they usually don't forget the directions when they leave home, and even if they do, you could always give them the code over the phone). The key box combination is easy to change, but the downside is that you have to be there physically to do it.

Electric keyless locks. Your other option is to buy some sort of keyless entry door lock. While these are the best solution for condominium complexes that prohibit lock boxes, they are also a great solution for any owners who are not too keen on having the same lockbox codes for each guest. Keyless locks have come a long way since the first edition of this book. There are many to choose from and are much less expensive than when they first came out. There are two main types of keyless locks: those with remote access and those without. I've used both but prefer the ones with remote access (I'll explain why in a little while).

The main advantage of the keyless locks is that you and the guests don't have to worry about keys; when you have six people staying in your home but only two keys, no one has to worry about "who has the key". Secondly, you can easily program the locks with different access codes so that you're giving out different, unique codes for each guest. And you can program unique codes for your housekeeping and maintenance staff—this way they can each have their own unique codes. For example, my keyless locks can simultaneously store multiple codes. I use one of the codes as an emergency back-up code, another for my housekeeper, and a third for my renters. For simplicity sake, I code the locks to the last 4 digits of the guest's phone number. This way you have a number that is distinctly unique for all guests, and it's very easy for the renters to remember.

Keyless locks can be found online or through most locksmiths and hardware stores. They are very easy to install, most often will fit right into your existing deadbolt's place and operate on batteries. The main downside to these locks is they are battery operated. If you decide to go with this sort of lock, be sure to change the batteries often and have a lockbox hidden somewhere with your keys in it.

You might also want to consider another type of keyless lock, the kind that offers remote access. These are pretty pricey, but they do offer many conveniences such as the ability to store, change, and create combinations from your home computer or even via cell phone. Most of them require internet in your vacation home. These types of locks also have a monthly service fee associated with them.

I use the Nexia Home Intelligence System (formally known as Schlage Link) in most of my vacation rental properties. I also use the programmable thermostat that connects to this system too. I love these locks for a myriad of reasons. First and foremost, I like it that

I have control of the locks from home—I can set the codes, change the thermostat settings and even unlock the door from my computer, cellphone or iPad. And secondly, I love it that I get an email every time the door is unlocked. I no longer have that lump in my throat wondering if my housekeepers cleaned before the guests arrived because as soon as my housekeeper puts her code into the lock, I get an email notification. Also, since I get an email when the guests arrive, I can also call the guests to welcome them (which is a nice personal touch for your guests—little do they know that I got an email telling me they arrived). And lastly I love these locks because they are time sensitive. I can set the renter's code to activate at check-in time and deactivate at checkout time. This has alleviated early check-ins completely.

The main downside is most of the locks that have the ability to change the codes remotely are internet based. You'll need to have internet connectivity to your home. But they will work even if the internet is down (the only thing you cannot do when the internet is down is add or delete codes). And the second downside is you're dealing with an electronic piece of equipment. Anything could go wrong at any time—it's always best to have a back-up plan. I highly suggest installing a back-up lockbox with a key inside . . . just in case.

Lost Keys

You get the phone call, the one you knew was inevitable: "We went to the beach, a big wave hit, and I lost my keys." What do you do if your renters lose their keys? Well, if you decide to purchase one of the keyless locks, this will not be a problem for you. But if you use either of the other two methods, then you will *most likely* have this happen eventually.

The best way to solve lost keys is to prepare ahead of time. Be proactive. The most logical solution is to turn to your housekeeper for lost key issues (see, I told you they are your lifelines!). Set up fees and protocol ahead of time. Will your housekeeper want your renters to call her directly, or should they call you first? Ahh, now you're thinking, if they locked themselves out, and your phone number and the housekeeper's number are inside the home, then how will they call? You see, I am very crafty and have thought of every angle (not really—actually, I got burned and I learned from my mistake). Simply put a sticker inside the lock box with your contact numbers on it. This way, since the lock box always stays on the door, they can open it and retrieve this information.

Also consider your housekeeper and fees. If she has to come out to help renters, how much would she want for her services? During regular business hours, after hours, or in the middle of the night? Be sure that these fees are on your rental rules.

Next, you should distribute your keys to everyone you can. This way, if your housekeeper is unavailable, you are still covered. Give keys to other owners, association managers, maybe even the real estate agent who sold you the place.

Now, the next thing you should do is hide a key somewhere. If you have a single family dwelling, this is very easy to do. You can even purchase a second lock box, put a different code on it and mount it in a more obscure place (this is good for maintenance people too, since you're giving a different code than your regular lock box code that the renters use). Of course, if you own a condominium, you'll have to be a little more creative. Before I converted to the keyless locks, I became very inventive in avoiding disasters:

It was Fourth of July weekend. I was in upstate New York dealing with the property that my family and I rented for the week after finding it in the newspaper. My cell phone rang, and it was my housekeeper in Florida. She had an accident and was in the hospital (thankfully not badly injured). She was not going to be able to clean my condo. And, of course, I had guests due to arrive in just a few hours. My first thought was oh no, but then I remembered that I am a proactive owner! I have a back-up housekeeper. I called the back-up housekeeper, and she just happened to be at the condo downstairs. No problem, she'll clean my home too. I hung up and thought, good . . . solved. About an hour later, my back-up housekeeper called to tell me that her key does not fit my door. My blood pressure shot through the ceiling! I forgot to give her a key the last time I changed the locks. But again, I had a solution. "No problem, here's my lock box code," I said, "The keys are inside." She called back two minutes later. "Christine, I got the lock box open, and there are no keys inside." By that point, my blood pressure must have been off the chart. My renters either forgot to put the keys inside the lock box, or they left them in the condo. Now what? I thought and thought, then . . . an epiphany! I told her to go upstairs to another owner's condo. I gave her that condo's lock box code. I told her to go inside and go to the utility closet. I told her to feel the backside of the hot water tank (I'm sure she thought I was nuts!). Taped to the backside of the hot water tank was a key to my condo! Luckily, I had remembered to replace that one when I changed the locks. The back-up housekeeper entered my condo and was able to clean my condo before the next guest arrived. Disaster averted.

Liability with Keys

I know that a concern with many owners is the liability associated with keys. First and foremost, be sure that whoever you give your keys to is trustworthy. Do *not* put the address or unit number on any key, especially hidden keys. Also, on your lock boxes, since you cannot change your codes after each renter, be sure to explain to each renter, in writing (on the directions is good place to do so), that the code is not changed after each checkout. Tell them not to use the lock box as a holding spot for the keys while they go out.

For liability purposes, you should install some type of keyless lock on the inside your home in addition to your regular lock. This can either be an old-fashioned chain or a keyless dead bolt. This is for the safety of the people inside. You would not want anyone to be able to use a key and come inside and harm your guests.

Another important task you must do is re-keying your locks (at least once a year). Most often people think of re-keying their locks because of security reasons—when you buy a new property, switch housekeepers, or rent to a vacationer you didn't trust, etc.

Re-keying your lock is a good exception to the rule, "If it ain't broken—don't fix it." It's the best way to avoid bent or broken keys, as well as locks that are hard to turn. It's a simple task, for around $5–$10 per lock including the service and 15 minutes of your time, your lock will be like brand new again. Just take your locks off your door and take them to your local hardware store. This is also good for your locks because when they are re-keyed, they typically take apart the lock, clean and lubricate it. This prevents keys from getting stuck or your locks not working at all.

Like so many issues associated with vacation home rentals, the important thing to remember about keys is that a little bit of planning goes a long way toward avoiding future problems. Just think of me and my housekeeper story. The only reason it had a happy ending was because I had built what NASA would call "redundancy" into my system. When they send a spacecraft millions of miles away from Earth, what if something goes wrong? They solve this problem by building backup systems that cover for any equipment that fails. Think about keys in much the same way. After all, though you're not millions of miles away, you may well be *hundreds* of miles away—bad enough. Of course, a backup system for keys is much easier than fixing a probe sent into deep space, and you don't need to be a rocket scientist.

21

Cleaning and Maintenance

Ask any owner the biggest reason they are hesitant to "rent by owner" and you almost always get the same answer . . . maintenance. Everyone is afraid of managing long distance maintenance. Again, it may sound incredibly simple but things just don't go wrong that often. Think about it, how often do things go wrong at home? And if they do, what do you do? Call a repairman. You can just as easily pick up the phone and call a repairman from your home as an on-site management company can. Throughout this chapter, you will find some very useful tips on how to avoid problems and some quick solutions if they by chance do arrive.

As I said before, your housekeeper service is your lifeline. It is vital. Remember my nightmare that a renter will show up and find the place dirty? Sure, you could have your renters clean the property themselves, but you are giving up control of your home when you do this. Is that something you really want to do? After all, your idea of clean may not be the same as mine. The "clean it yourself" system seems to only work in cottages and cabins when the renters are required to bring all their own bedding and linens. Even then, the owners are generally not too satisfied with the cleanliness . . . and you certainly cannot go and clean your home every time a renter leaves! That leaves you with hiring *somebody* or some *company*.

Finding Housekeepers

Well, you know the old cliché: good help is hard to find. So just how do you find a housekeeper? You're probably not expecting this answer—literally right outside your front door! Visit your property on a weekend and go outside when most renters are usually checking out. I can almost guarantee that your neighbors have cleaning services. Now don't be a stranger. Talk to the people cleaning; ask who they work for. Even if your neighbor uses a management company, these workers are usually willing to pick up a side job. What if the housekeeper you talk to would love to work for you but does not have time? Consider staggering your checkout time so that she can clean both. Remember, you are in control. Take advantage of that. There's no rule that says checkout must be 10 A.M. and check-in must be 3 P.M. Don't rule out the housekeepers that are cleaning your home currently through your management company. If he or she is a subcontractor, not an actual employee, you can possibly hire him or her. It's definitely worth looking into.

Another good, yet overlooked, resource for housekeepers is your local church. Sometimes a pastor will know of someone who is looking for extra work. It pays to be resourceful. Don't give up on the idea of hiring an individual just because "it's impossible to find good help these days." No, it's not impossible. Don't believe that old cliché.

The next question almost always seems to be, should I hire an individual or should I hire a company? I wish there was an easy answer, but there are benefits and potential problems with both.

Cleaning services. Do tend to be more reliable in the sense that yes, they will show up consistently. Because they have multiple crews of employees, if/when someone is out, there is another person to pick up the slack. But the downside is you'll have different people cleaning your home each week, which means they don't have a chance to become familiar with the property. Also, large cleaning services work in volume and tend not to take as much time taking care of your individual needs. They generally have a set list of duties they perform, and they tend not to deviate from that list. An upside is that cleaning services are easily found because they are listed in the phonebook and other directories. Most times, cleaning services are less expensive than individuals.

Individuals. On the other hand, usually take more time to clean and pay attention to details and your specific requests. Most will even do light maintenance such as change light bulbs, change furnace filters, and add personal touches. They also tend to be better at communicating with you about your home.

I have tried both and have just had better luck with individuals. But, as I've said, the right person can be hard to find. Regardless of which you choose, you should always have names and contact information for back-up in case you get into a situation where your cleaning service does not show up.

Be sure to have a list of expectations for your cleaning posted somewhere inside your home. The back of a closet door works well. Don't worry about hiding it from view of your renters, it's OK for them to see that you have high expectations for your cleaning staff. It will make them even more certain that they made the right choice in renting your home.

Daily or Mid-week Cleaning

Should you offer daily or mid-week cleaning for your guests? I do offer daily and mid-week cleaning for an extra charge as an option for my renters. If the renters want it, I'll arrange it. I have found that most people don't want it, however.

Your first step in deciding whether or not to provide daily or mid-week cleaning is to ask your housekeeper if she is available to clean daily or mid-week. Housekeepers often have regular jobs during the week and are not available to clean outside of the weekends.

My thoughts? Well, there are trust issues for the renters when it comes to your cleaning staff. Think about it, how difficult is it to find someone that you trust to clean your primary home? You have to worry about things such as jewelry, money, and other valuables that might be lying around. I think renters worry somewhat about their personal belongings, and that's the main reason they forgo this option. I know when we stay in hotels, I always "wonder" about my personal belongings. I would guess that this is the primary reason renters choose not to have a mid-week clean.

Now on the flip side, my housekeeper does not like to do mid-week cleaning either. First, it's a lot more work for her to clean around the renters' personal belongings. Secondly, it's a matter of personal safety for her. She does not know my renters at all, and closing herself into a home with renters inside can compromise her personal safety.

So with all those things in mind, I don't require or even persuade people to go for mid-stay cleans.

Laundry For Back-to-Back Rentals

Having one guest check-out and your next guest checking-in on the same day is a good thing. It means you're maximizing your rentals, but cleaning between guests in a timely manner can be quite challenging, especially when it comes to getting all the laundry washed.

There is a simple solution: Keep two full sets of linens in your rental. This way the housekeepers can replace the linens without having to wait for the washer and dryer to finish. Often times your housekeeper can take the soiled linens to be cleaned off-site.

This is pretty common practice for housekeepers. More often than not, your housekeeper will incorporate it into the regular fees they charge. Some housekeepers might also have linen service, which will supply fresh sheets and towels each week.

Maintenance

Now ... maintenance. Don't put the book down! This isn't going to hurt. Proper maintenance is imperative, so you just have to be sure to go about it the right way. Remember, this is the thing that's either going to make your rentals run smoothly or make your life hell. Do not view this as your primary residence. By that I mean, when was the last time you had service in your home? Most likely when something was broken. Well, just put aside the old way of thinking, "if it ain't broke don't fix it." With your vacation property, I advocate the exact opposite. You must do preventative maintenance on *everything* that you possibly can. I almost hesitate to say it because I know you've heard it countless times as a kid ... but it bears repeating, so I'll say it again: an ounce of prevention is worth a pound of cure.

You need to try to anticipate all of your problems up front and fix them before they become an issue. This is where you'll really come to view vacation property ownership as a business venture. Don't get worked up about spending $75 twice a year to have your furnace cleaned. Remember all the money you are saving from not having a management company? It's OK to spend some of it here. What is that $75 compared to all the money you're saving. I promise it will make your life easier.

Furthermore, you can hire a maintenance person to oversee your property. This works particularly well for people who live very far from their second home and for those who don't have time to visit more than once or twice a year. The good news is that maintenance people are much easier to find than housekeepers, and you can use the same tactics that you used to find your housekeepers. There are companies and individuals that you can hire. They can do as little or as much as you feel you need. Some people have a maintenance person come to their property each time a guest leaves to check on things such as light bulbs, furnace filters, leaky faucets, etc. Others choose to have their housekeepers police the needs and notify you or your maintenance person if there is a problem. It's your property and your choice. Experiment a little and find out what works best for you.

Don't overlook the fact that your neighbors are also renting. You may be able to pool your resources and find someone you can all hire together. Condominium complexes usually have on-staff maintenance. Check with the complex maintenance person and see if he or she would like to moonlight. One condominium complex where I own has so many self-managing owners (I taught many of them) that the association was able to hire one full-time maintenance person to work for the owners, and each owner simply pays on an hourly basis. Read what this resourceful owner did:

> Ed and his wife live in New York. They own a vacation property on Grand Cayman Island. Ed saw the benefits of renting by owner because a lot of his neighbors were doing it. Ed was apprehensive about joining them, however, because of the maintenance aspect of rentals. After all, how was he supposed to fix anything from New York? Ed came up with an ingenious solution to this problem. Now you must understand that Grand Cayman does have high-season and low-season rates, but most properties are booked 40+ weeks per year. So their rental revenue was quite high, but so were the management commissions. Since there were six other people who were renting by owner, Ed decided that they could band together and

hire one person to oversee maintenance for all their properties. He figured that they could hire one full-time person, and each owner would pay two months of this person's salary. When other owners in the complex heard what these six owners were doing, they also were very interested. In the end, the 12 owners agreed to each pay one month of the maintenance person's salary. They now have a full-time employee, devoted to maintaining their 12 homes, and the satisfaction of renting by owner, without all the worries.

As for me, I am a "by owner" purist. I do it all. Remember, if you follow my book, you will be renting to "friends." For the most part, I don't get calls for little things. Your renters will do quick-solve maintenance themselves, and you'll most likely never even hear about it. Now I am *not* advocating that you have your renters do maintenance for you. You still have to do all of your preventative maintenance up front. For example, I've never gotten a call for a stopped up toilet. No, I don't have a special clog proof toilet, but I do have a plunger, and I think that the renters just use it. They know I live 1000 miles away, so they don't call me for minor maintenance. Other issues such as a broken washing machine, electrical problems, or a leak from the upstairs unit (all of which have happened to me) are the real hurdles. In these cases, I simply call a repairperson. I keep a copy of the area phonebook at my home. The renters, or my cleaning service, let the repairperson into my unit and the work gets done. Yes, it is an inconvenience for your renters but they are almost always very understanding about these things, and the bottom line is these problems do not happen all that often. When the day is done, I compensate them for their inconvenience by either refunding a portion of the rent or taking a percentage off their next stay.

Here's another story that you may find instructive:

Mike and Daphne own a cabin in Pennsylvania in the mountains and they live in New Jersey. They rented their cabin to a family with children. One night, they got a phone call from the renters. It seems that their son had been leaning back in his chair (we've all seen this before) and fell back. The boy was fine, but the chair put a small hole in the wall. The father told Mike that he noticed that there was some drywall spackle under the sink. He was calling to ask if it was all right if he just fixed the hole himself. He also wanted to know if there was some touch up paint somewhere.

To which I say, don't you just love a happy ending? Seriously, there's a great lesson to this story. You see, often when we think about maintenance, we assume that we are just talking about appliances, plumbing, and other such basics. But in reality, more often than not things go wrong because the renters themselves have damaged something, almost always by mistake. Most renters will be responsible and conscientious about the damages they have caused. And, given the proper tools, most would rather just fix or solve the problem themselves. What must have been going through this dad's mind? If I were him, the first thing that I would think is how much is this going to cost us? Especially if it's something I can just fix myself. Renters don't want to get socked with damage charges as much as you don't want the damages.

Below you will find a list of things that you can do to your property for preventative maintenance, as well as items you should have on hand for those accidental damages. Give the renters the chance to fix the problems on their own. Sounds obvious, right? Maybe. Or maybe not. Let me share with you an example from my own experience.:

I was at my condo in Florida one summer. Halfway through the week, my son came in, and said, "Mom, my teacher is here!" We just happened to be vacationing in the same place at the same time. I went out and began talking to her. After a while she said, "Christine, can I ask you a favor? Can I borrow your broom?" She was renting a home on the beach that did not have a broom! How could she as a renter possibly keep it clean? The sand! I was astonished!

Let's take a look at that list. Be sure everything is in working order (especially advertised items), and keep good records of all maintenance. Here are the essentials:

- Write down make, model, and serial numbers of all major appliances. If you need to schedule service, you can have this information on hand.
- Consider purchasing extended warranties on major appliances, especially washers and dryers, since they are appliances that are used above and beyond normal.
- Have your dryer vent cleaned regularly. Or when you visit, take your leaf blower and blow it out yourself.
- Clean the condenser coils on your refrigerator.
- Have your furnace/air conditioner cleaned and checked regularly.
- Change furnace filters at least once a month.
- Schedule regular chimney and fireplace cleaning and inspections. General rule of thumb is after each cord of wood burned.
- Clean out the screens on your faucets and showerheads, especially with wells and hard water areas.
- For properties using wells, consider replacing water consumption appliances with water saving appliances (i.e., toilets, front load washing machines, dishwashers, shower heads).
- Clean out sink/drains regularly. Hair is the most common cause of slow and clogged drains. To do this, unscrew the stopper in sinks and bathtubs and clean out the hair.
- Inspect breaker panels and plug receptacles at least once every two years, especially in salt-water areas. Salt corrodes wiring and causes malfunctions.

- Schedule regular pest control.
- In areas where rodents and pests are a problem, regularly check property for point of entry and plug those areas. These are sometimes included in pest control contracts but be sure it's being done.
- Schedule regular landscape maintenance and snow removal.
- Schedule regular carpet cleaning, or consider installing ceramic, hard wood, or solid surface flooring.
- Schedule a deep cleaning at least once a year, including washing throw rugs, curtains and blinds, ovens, baseboards, and steam clean sofas, etc.
- Wash all blankets and comforters at least once every five rentals.
- Replace things often before they get worn out and dingy, especially coffee makers, toasters, blenders, wash cloths, towels, pillows, and all bedding.
- Set up storm policies with a housekeeper or maintenance person. Have them do whatever is necessary to storm-proof your property for example, pull in patio furniture, turn off appliances, etc.
- For owners who close their property for the winter, schedule maintenance person or housekeeper to check up on your property during the closed season.
- Keep a copy of the local phonebook for your vacation property in your permanent home so you can easily find appropriate maintenance contractors. I know what you're probably thinking: Phonebook? With Google, who uses the phone book anymore? Well, believe it or not, a lot of little mom and pop business in small towns still do not have internet presence. They do things the old fashioned way—they advertise in the yellow pages.

Maintenance Supplies

Be sure to have these items on hand:

+ Broom, mop, and vacuum.
+ Cleaning supplies, including window cleaner and bleach or disinfectant.
+ Plungers near each toilet.
+ Shovel and ice melt, sand or salt.
+ Spackle and trowel.
+ Touch-up paint (in a small jar clearly marked), paintbrush, or disposable sponge brush.
+ Hammer, screwdrivers (flat head and Phillips head), nails and screws, pliers, channel locks, crescent wrench. These tools can be found at dollar stores.
+ Teflon tape for quick plumbing repairs.
+ A tube of silicone.
+ Wood glue.
+ Liquid drain opener.
+ Extra batteries for smoke detectors and TV remotes.
+ Light bulbs, in all sizes and wattage including appliance bulbs.
+ Duct tape (there are millions of uses).
+ Extra furnace filters.

I'm betting you can think of many other items you might want to add to this list, but I think you get the idea. Maintenance is not the nightmare subject you thought it was. Things just don't go wrong that often. Unless, of course, you don't prepare for it. Then all bets are off.

CHAPTER

22

Furnishings and Supplies

Here's an important question: why do people rent vacation homes rather than just stay in a hotel? There are numerous reasons, but I can tell you that convenience is a big part of it. Not only will they have a kitchen, but also they will have furnishings and other amenities that you just won't find in a standard hotel room. In other words, they will feel right at home. So how you furnish your vacation home will make a big difference to your guests. It may be a critical factor in their decision to return next year. They may even tell their friends what a gem they have found and suggest they should try it out too.

Let's start with the kitchen. There is nothing more annoying to a renter than an ill-equipped kitchen. Conversely, I cannot tell you how many times my guests have complimented my well-equipped kitchen. When furnishing your kitchen, be sure to have ample supplies on hand for your renters. The general rule of thumb is have at least double the amount of dishes, cups, glasses, etc., that your property sleeps. So if you sleep 8, have dishes for 16. This serves a couple of purposes. First, it's for the convenience of the renter, especially when they're on vacation. People don't like having to take the dishes they used for breakfast out of the dishwasher and hand wash them to eat lunch.

Secondly, having enough dishes and utensils will conserve water and power. They'll only run the dishwasher when it's full, not because they need a clean plate. Also consider supplying a set of dishwasher safe, hard plastic cups, especially if you have a pool or hot tub. Another thing that renters appreciate is little plastic cups, bowls and plates for little children (and this will also help alleviate spills). Don't overlook the utensils, gadgets, and appliances that are specific to your particular area. If you're on the beach, for example, a big lobster pot and lobster/crab crackers are essential. And if you're in a colder climate, a crock-pot and recipes for your favorite soups or stews would be a nice thing to have.

You also want to be sure to furnish your home in an appropriate manner. By this I mean don't put satin sheets in a cabin that is mainly rented by men's hunting groups, and don't use a plastic outdoor patio set as your dining room table in a place that rents for $3,000 a week. There are certain levels of comfort and furnishings that renters expect in specific markets and price points. Do the best to make your place feel homey and welcoming, not too cluttered and not stuffy or sparsely decorated.

The importance of adding a family photo is often overlooked. Adding your family photo gives your property the personalized feel that renters are looking for. Coincidently, it also serves as a gentle reminder to your guests that they are staying in someone's home.

I once had a friend stay in my vacation rental and she told me she turned my photo upside down. She said she felt as though I was watching her. My response was, "Good!" And for this same reason, you should not put family photos in the bedroom. You *don't* want to your guests to feel like you're watching them in there!

When you are purchasing furnishings, your main concern should be the "look" of the furniture. But be sure to spend your money wisely; you have take into consideration that you will need to replace furnishings more often than you do at home. You might buy the best quality furnishings for your home, but I wouldn't for a rental home. I prefer less expensive, lesser quality furniture, but not the bottom of the barrel. I simply plan to replace them more often. I could spend $3,500 for a sofa that's great quality and looks nice, or I can spend $1,200 for one that looks nice but is only of decent quality. I can replace that one three times for the same amount as the top of the line.

With some items, of course, it is necessary to have the best quality. Kitchen and dining room chairs are the first things that come to mind. I am a relatively small person, so I never thought about this. The first place I owned had nice looking, medium quality chairs. I found that within a couple of years, most of them had broken. Some people are very hard on chairs. And face it, some people are pretty heavy. I recommend all chairs (interior and exterior) have a 300-pound capacity. There are many styles of wrought iron interior dining sets available these days. I highly recommend them.

I got this note from an owner who read the first edition of my book.

Christine, when I read about having good chairs in your book, I have to admit, I rolled my eyes and said, 'OK, I don't have weak chairs.'

My very first renters left Sunday. She wrote me this nice note about how much fun they had and how they want to rent it again next year. I was delighted, until I read the next line of the note. It said, "Friday as I sat down to eat lunch, I heard a crack before the chair broke and I fell to the ground."

Now I'm re-reading your book to see what else I snubbed my nose at the first time around.

One mistake some people make is to just put all their old furnishing from their home into their rental homes and get new stuff for home. But your renters may not necessarily want that old stuff either. So consider bringing it to your local charity and taking a write-off instead. I have used an occasional old piece of furniture here and there, but never without refinishing it or a giving it a nice coat of paint or faux finish. Don't fill your house with your treasured family heirlooms either. Since some people may not remember that coaster under their frosty glass of lemonade, I recommend you purchase glass to cover the tops of wooden dining room and bedside tables.

As for beds, make sure they are firm or extra firm. Comfortable beds are very important. One compromise that renters will rarely make is on bed size. Ask any hotel which rooms are the first to fill up. The answer is always the king-size rooms. If renters have a king-size bed at home, then chances are they will have a tough time sleeping on anything smaller.

And speaking of hotels, have you noticed that they have been playing up quality of their bed linens? It seems like a broad marketing approach that's working for them. And retailers are feeding from it as well. In every major department store and linen stores, you'll find a "hotel collection" of sheets. They're usually crisp colored, luxuriously soft and . . . expensive. While I'm not so sure that having the best linens is going to make or break your rentals, I do think having and advertising top-quality linens does make a difference to some guests.

When shopping for sheets there are so many choices and decisions to make. Most "hotel collections" I found were either Egyptian cotton or Sateen. While price will surely play a big part in which linens you choose to purchase, it's always nice to know what you're shopping for. Below you'll find some explanations of the various and often confusing descriptions of sheets.

Bed Sheets 101

Thread Count. Thread count is the number of threads used to weave one square inch of the fabric. It's often used as a gauge to measure the fabric quality. Higher thread counts mean a tighter weave, a softer and stronger fabric, and a finer quality. Typically 300-thread or above is what you would want to buy for your vacation rental.

Egyptian cotton. Egyptian cotton is a general classification for strong, lustrous, long threaded 100-percent cotton produced mainly in the Nile River Valley. When woven into fabric, it will produce a lush feeling sheet that is not stiff. Egyptian cotton is known to be the highest quality, will have the least amount of pilling and will last for many years. While it will wash well and stand up to occasional bleaching, the downsides are that it tends to be very expensive, running about $200 and up per set, and it tends to wrinkle very easily.

Supima cotton. This is the registered trademark for Pima cotton grown in the U.S. It is a combination of Egyptian cotton and the cotton grown by the Pima Indians of the American Southwest. It is similar to Egyptian cotton in that it is silky, strong and has outstanding durability, but it costs much less.

Pima cotton. Pima is essentially the American, budget version of Egyptian cotton. It is significantly less expensive than Egyptian cotton and won't last as long. But I wouldn't snub my nose at Pima cotton, they are still very nice, soft and more affordable version of the Egyptian cotton and Supima cotton and would work fine in your vacation rentals.

Percale. Percale can be made of any fiber but is usually cotton or a cotton/polyester blend. A minimum thread count of 180 is required to be classified as percale. When it's woven, the threads are much shorter, so the sheets are resistant to wrinkling and dry very quickly. But they're also thinner, tend to pill, don't hold up to bleaching and usually don't last very long. Some vacation rental owners actually prefer blended percale sheets because they dry very quickly and since they are typically inexpensive, making it very affordable to replace sheets if they get stained or damaged.

Sateen. Sateen is a particular weave of cotton that creates a fabric with a silken feel and a very smooth and lustrous surface. They tend to be a nice balance in quality smartly priced in the midrange of all sheets. The downside of Sateen is they tend to not be as breathable as some of the other weaves, therefore I would not recommend them in your warm or hot climates. Because sateen sheets are very popular, they can often be found on sale online and at major department stores.

Don't forget to play up your sheets in your advertisements (just as the hotels do). Advertising "Egyptian Cotton Sheets" will likely brighten a few prospective renters' eyes. And don't worry if you cannot afford the most expensive sheets, you might do just as well buying Sateen sheets and playing up descriptive words. The main point is to show your guests that you have nice bedding that will ensure them a restful night of sleep.

Decorating

Decorating your second home can be a lot of fun for most people—but it's not fun for me. I'll be the first to admit I am no decorator. I get heart palpitations at the sheer thought of having to choose fabrics or paint colors. I really have no business writing one word about decorating.

But what I am good at is marketing and renting vacation homes. So I am going to approach this section from a marketing perspective. When choosing your décor, top-of-mind should always be: how will this look in the photos online? If you approach your décor as an extension of marketing it will force you to look at it differently.

My single piece of advice in the decorating category is: Don't be afraid of color! Throughout my career in the vacation rental industry I bet I have looked at hundreds of thousands of vacation homes online. I cannot tell you how many people use drab colors (or no color at all) when decorating their vacation homes. Colors will be the one thing that will make a significant difference in your advertisements online. If you are uncomfortable choosing colors, then do what I do—hire a decorator to choose the colors for you! For as little as $40–$60 you can hire someone to come to your home and work out an entire color palette of colors for you. It'll be the best money you ever spend.

The first time I bought new furniture for my vacation rental, I went to a local furniture store. I fell in love with a living room suite that they had on the floor in stock. I knew it would look great but it would clash terribly with the wall colors I had. The sales lady overheard me talking to my husband about our dilemma and she said, "Oh, you can just paint the walls a nice coral and then you can accent with amaranth and periwinkle." Now, my color vocabulary consists of exactly eight colors which happen to be the same ones that come in a box of Crayola Crayons—I had no idea what she was talking about! I looked at her and said, "You seem to know colors quite well. I have a deal for you—how about you come over to my condo and pick out the exact colors I should have my walls painted and I will buy this furniture from you right now." She grabbed her keys and off we went. It took her ten minutes to choose the colors. After the new furniture and paint colors were on the walls, my home booked up very quickly and I increased my bookings by more than 50%. Most of the renters who booked told me they chose my place because they loved the colors. From that moment on, I knew that "color" was an important aspect of marketing my vacation rental homes.

I like to shop for quilts and comforters online because the photos on the web will give me a pretty good idea of how my photos will look in my advertisements online. I tend to gravitate toward colorful prints and I pull one color out of the print and accessorize around that color. For example, I bought a zigzag quilt where the main color was blue. It had a faint red line in it so I bought a red throw pillow, red lamp shades and a beach scene piece of artwork that had one red umbrella in it. Those red accessories really stood out when I photographed the bedroom—and it gave the room a completed look.

Now speaking of accessories, any decorator will tell you that it's the accessories that pull everything together and give your rooms that finished look. Don't overlook the importance of adding wall art, accent pieces, throw pillows, etc. But, I caution you here. It is so easy to get caught up buying too much décor for your vacation home. Avoid that cluttered look. When the renter looks at your photos, their initial impression is very important. If they see a lot of stuff, the first impression may be that the place is cluttered or not clean. Whatever you do, do not over-decorate!

Supplies

Besides furnishing your vacation home with the obvious items that renters expect, there are also things you can add that will just make it a more enjoyable place to be. Things that show you have put a lot of thought and personal attention into your home. I am a true believer that every vacation property needs to have relaxing family activities on hand. These items include videos, DVDs, CDs, books, magazines, and games (Yahtzee, Scrabble, and a deck of playing cards are a *must*). If your property is near the beach, other fun activity items might include sand buckets and sand shovels. This will also stop the kids from using your kitchen utensils as digging tools! Even extra hats and mittens from the dollar store would be greatly appreciated by that skier who loses his on the slopes.

I also like to supply my kitchens with additional items that are not necessarily expected but always appreciated by my guests. These items include salt, pepper, tea, coffee, sugar, creamer, spices, foil, plastic wrap, trash bags and cleaning supplies. Then there are various assortments of bathroom items that you can add to your home, such as a blow dryer, shampoo, soap, razors, etc.

The next question that seems to follow this advice is: do these things get stolen? For the most part, these items are not stolen. People appreciate these extras. But don't spend thousands filling your home with things that will be a temptation. Many of these odds and ends can be purchased at the dollar store or at second-hand stores. I have had people take things home, but, believe it or not, they mail them back, or they call and say, "We took this home by mistake." There's more honesty out there than you may realize.

Furnishing your property is a mix of the practical and the aesthetic. A little creativity can go a long way in this department. You don't want to spend a fortune, but you do want to create an atmosphere that is warm, inviting—and safe—for your guests, and for yourself.

HIGHLY RECOMMENDED ITEMS

- ❏ 13x9 baking dish
- ❏ 2 quart pyrex dish
- ❏ basting spoon
- ❏ broom/mop/dust pan
- ❏ can piercer/bottle opener
- ❏ coffee pot (auto shut off)
- ❏ cookie sheet
- ❏ cutting board
- ❏ fire extinguisher

- ❏ large skillet
- ❏ large glass casserole dish
- ❏ measuring spoons
- ❏ medium covered saucepan
- ❏ micro/refrig. dishes
- ❏ paring knife
- ❏ roast knife
- ❏ rubber spatula
- ❏ salad serving spoons

- ❏ slotted spoon
- ❏ spatula
- ❏ toaster (wide slot)
- ❏ vegetable peeler
- ❏ 2 cake pans
- ❏ 3 piece mixing bowl set
- ❏ blender
- ❏ can opener
- ❏ coasters
- ❏ colander
- ❏ cork screw
- ❏ Dutch oven with lid
- ❏ fondue set

- ❏ large covered saucepan
- ❏ lobster pot
- ❏ meat fork
- ❏ medium skillet
- ❏ microwave
- ❏ plastic pitcher
- ❏ roaster w/lid
- ❏ salad bowl
- ❏ salt and pepper shakers
- ❏ soup ladle
- ❏ tea kettle
- ❏ tongs
- ❏ hot pad/trivet

DINNERWARE

You should have twice the amount of plates, cups, etc. that your home accommodates. If your property sleeps 4, have a service for 8, etc.

- ❏ dinner plates
- ❏ bowls
- ❏ saucers
- ❏ salad forks
- ❏ teaspoons
- ❏ steak knives
- ❏ water glasses
- ❏ wine glasses

- ❏ sandwich plates
- ❏ cups/mugs
- ❏ dinner forks
- ❏ tablespoons
- ❏ table knives
- ❏ tea glasses
- ❏ rock glasses

MISCELLANEOUS

- ❏ blankets
- ❏ mattress pads
- ❏ shower liner
- ❏ phones
- ❏ lamps

- ❏ TV (cable ready with remotes)
- ❏ plungers
- ❏ ashtrays (if applicable)
- ❏ iron (auto shut off)

- ❏ phone and phonebook
- ❏ VCR/DVD
- ❏ pillow protectors
- ❏ waste cans
- ❏ alarm clock/radio
- ❏ pictures
- ❏ pillows (two per bed including sofa bed)
- ❏ vacuum cleaner
- ❏ fly swatter
- ❏ ironing board
- ❏ CD player

OTHER ITEMS

Things that are nice to have but not necessary:

- ❏ reading lamp
- ❏ door mats
- ❏ beach chairs/service
- ❏ patio set
- ❏ basketball hoop
- ❏ boogie boards
- ❏ volleyball net
- ❏ napkin holder
- ❏ ice-cream scoop
- ❏ hatchet
- ❏ plastic plates, cups, bowls for children
- ❏ cookbooks
- ❏ porta-crib
- ❏ plug covers
- ❏ rolling pin
- ❏ games (Yahtzee, Scrabble, cards)
- ❏ videos/DVDs
- ❏ BBQ grill and utensils
- ❏ hot tub
- ❏ tennis racquets
- ❏ bikes
- ❏ crock-pot
- ❏ rubber tub mat
- ❏ placemats
- ❏ crab/nut crackers
- ❏ dishwasher safe plastic cups
- ❏ office supplies (PC/printer/ fax)
- ❏ high chair
- ❏ safety locks for cabinets
- ❏ first aid kit
- ❏ hair dryer

Safety. There are certain safety considerations that you should keep in mind when furnishing and supplying your property. Some states even require periodic safety inspections. Check with your state sales tax office, they can tell you if a state safety inspection is required for your property. But even if your property is not subject to a safety inspection, it is a good idea to be sure that you have working smoke detectors and fire extinguishers within easy access. You should also clearly post emergency information such as evacuation plans, poison control centers, etc. As an added safety measure, purchase automatic shut off irons and coffee makers. You may also include first aid kits, and appropriate warnings about area wildlife dangers (raccoons, bears, snakes, jellyfish, ticks, etc.).

On my directions to my renters, I always write: "Keep your eyes open if on the beach at dusk or dawn. We often see dolphins swimming right off shore. If the dolphins come in close, which they do occasionally, do not get in the water, and try to touch them. Please respect the wildlife; it is illegal to touch the dolphins. We humans have germs that harm the dolphins."

Keep in mind when you are decorating, there will most likely be a child occupying the rooms. Glass top coffee tables are durable and look nice, but I shudder to think of the toddler who falls onto the corner of it. Plug covers and safety locks on cabinets should also not be overlooked. And you might want to add a highchair and porta-crib. For liability reasons, I do not recommend you supply car seats. Be careful when supplying any items for infants and small children, as baby items are the number one manufacturer-recalled items (mainly for safety issues).

Owner's Closet

By the way, don't forget yourself! You will need a place to store your own personal things that you wouldn't necessarily want your renters to have. Set a closet aside that is designated as an owner's closet and lock it. I keep all our personal belongings in this closet so that it makes packing up and going to my vacation home a breeze. It is where I keep all of our toiletries, my personal sheets and bedding (I like to have my own that are off-limits to renters), laundry detergent, all sorts of cleaning supplies and extra supplies for my property. I even keep some non-perishable food items there. I installed a lock on the door and always keep it locked. My housekeeper has a key to my owner's closet, and I also hide a key in my home.

Many owners are reluctant to take a closet away from a bedroom for this purpose. Don't be. You should make it as easy and convenient as possible for yourself too. Remember the real reason you bought this vacation home in the first place. I took a closet out of the smallest bedroom and converted into our owner's closet. Then, I purchased a wardrobe at an estate sale and placed it right in front of the closet door. This way my renters still have a place to hang their things, and I still have all my belongings for me too.

More Than Just a Guest Book

Furnishing your property with a guest book is more valuable to you and your guests than just a chronicle of who stayed in your home. They give your renters a chance to share their vacation experience with you and your subsequent guests. They can also provide invaluable feedback about your property and housekeepers, or even offer suggestions for improving your property.

I have always included guest books in my properties. It's so much fun to read about what my guests did and how much they enjoyed their stay. My guest books contain comments on everything from the best attractions to restaurant reviews to the many other fun things in and around our homes.

Guest books can be used as a way for guests to give constructive criticism that they may not feel comfortable telling you in person. Here's an example from one of my guest books: "It sounded like thunder rumbling constantly above your condo." The guest never mentioned this complaint to me. After I read this, I did a little investigating and found out that the condo directly above mine had broken rollers on their sliding glass door, which was the culprit of the thunder-like noise. I informed my upstairs neighbors of the problem and thankfully they got it fixed. Then I wrote this entry in my guest book, "Thanks so much for letting me know. We got the problem resolved." By writing this, it tells all subsequent renters that I do read comments and rectify problems. Since the renter who complained was long gone by the time I read his entry, I picked up the phone and called him. I told him that I had found and solved the problem. He was so delighted that I took action. He said that he otherwise loved our condo but hesitated to ever stay again because of this nuisance. Now he and his family are some of my regular guests.

Aside from being a customer feedback mechanism for you, the guest books are an important resource for your renters as well. I had a repeat renter call me to say that she was disappointed that I had started a new guest book. She said the last time she visited, she used our guest book as a guide to her vacation. She was looking forward to using it again. I called my housekeeper and he helped her locate it (apparently my housekeeper locked up the old one in my owner's closet).

Guest books also offer a nice piece of "home history." It sends chills up my spine when I read the entries from a guest who occupied my property during the tragedy on 9/11, or the people from New Orleans who stayed in my homes while they watched CNN as Hurricane Katrina ravaged their hometown. There is a story of a family that had a near-death experience on a capsized boat, and another story of one of my guests who saved a stranger's life.

And don't forget to sign your own guest book when you visit your own property. By doing this it tells the renters that this is indeed your second home that you use yourself. Be sure to write down any maintenance you did while you were there. I write stuff like, "washed all the baseboards, blew out the dryer vent, had the furnace cleaned," etc. This gives you reference for your subsequent visits. It saves me from the head-scratching, "hmmmm did I replace my sofa in 2011 or was it 2012?" To your renters, adding these entries shows that you care about your home and are actively involved in your property's maintenance.

Furthermore it may encourage them to take extra care of your home while they are staying there.

Lastly, your guest book is an excellent resource for logging the personal use of your property for IRS purposes. Since there are very strict guidelines for properties that are claimed as investment properties on income tax returns, your signed guest book will serve as proof of maintenance vs. personal use of your property in the unfortunate eventuality of an IRS audit.

If you would like to purchase a guest book for your property, my favorite one is available on my website, www.HowToRentByOwner.com. Rather than blank pages, each page has leading questions prompting your guest what to write about.

Local Attraction Book

One of the most appreciated items in my property is something that cost next to nothing to supply. I created my own guidebook. I bought a three-ring binder and some blank clear plastic sleeves. The motivation behind it was twofold:

- To let the guests know about the local restaurants, shopping, attractions, and sights to see;
- To answer questions regarding my property, especially the amenities.

This book has been a timesaver for me because it cut down the number of calls from guests needing to know about my property. Prior to creating my attraction book, I used to get calls from guests asking questions like, "Where do I find the parking passes?" or "Which remote works the satellite TV?" The attraction book serves as an easy-to-find place for answers to my guests' frequently asked questions.

Furthermore, my guests greatly appreciate my local attraction book. They love having an array of restaurant menus, directions to the grocery store, and maps at their disposal. It's easy, inexpensive, and I'm sure your guests will appreciate a local attraction book, too.

To set up your local attraction book, start by going to your local office supply store. Buy a high quality three ring binder (the cheap ones will fall apart too quickly) and some clear vinyl 3-ring binder, top-load sheet protectors. Add a personal touch to your book by inserting a handwritten and signed welcome letter inserted into the front of the book. Collect and add many of the items listed below and slip them into the binder.

Information about the area:

- maps
- menus from local restaurants
- area amusement brochures
- church schedules
- directions to hospitals
- airport information
- shopping information
- discount coupons for shopping or attractions

Information about your property:

- instructions for the DVD player, satellite or cable TV, and DVR
- how to override the programmed thermostat
- how to work controls for swimming pools, boats, or other amenities

Include the following contact information:

- housekeepers
- maintenance staff
- owners
- security officers
- local police/fire
- weather information

Rental rules

- ❑ check-in policy
- ❑ check-out policy
- ❑ complex/subdivision rules
- ❑ quiet times

Don't forget to supply blank insert pages for the guests to share their "local finds" too.

High-speed Internet

When deciding which amenities you should provide for your guests, it's always helpful to know what travelers are looking for when they shop for accommodations.

With the increased demand for internet connectivity, it's become a necessity to provide wireless high-speed internet for your guests. If you decide to forgo providing this amenity, you could be missing out on valuable bookings.

Wireless or not? In my opinion, wireless is a must! With iPhones, smart phones, iPads and tablets people have become dependent on wireless connectivity. Providing a wireless connection for your guests makes it easy to get connected to the internet from anywhere in your home. Furthermore, you wouldn't have to worry about strategically placing your Ethernet connection near a desk. Guests could sit on the sofa, at the kitchen table, on the beds, or even outside by the pool to use their computers. Also, multiple guests can be connected at the same time. Today, you can purchase a wireless router for around $50.

With a wireless router you can set a password so that your neighbors can't piggyback on your competitive advantage. Just provide your guests with a simple password in your rental directions.

A Hot Tub?

Many property owners benefit greatly from having a hot tub on the premises. Investing in a hot tub can help you draw more renters, especially during the off-seasons. Believe it or not, hot tubs are even a draw for renters in Florida, Arizona and Hawaii.

Hot tubs cost anywhere between $1500 and $6000 to purchase. The covers run between $200–$600 and usually have to be replaced every two years. Many property owners boast that the small upfront investment is worth tens of thousands of dollars in bookings over time.

All of my properties have hot tubs, including my Florida properties. Nearly every renter inquiring during the months between September and March ask about the hot tub. Without the hot tubs I believe my occupancy would be much lower.

As for managing and cleaning, be sure to hire a qualified spa specialist to come and clean your hot tub after each guest leaves. The jury is still out as to whether or not you should empty, clean and refill the water after each guest. Hot tubs take 4–8 hours to get up to temperature, and the chemicals cannot be fully tested until the water is up to temperature. I personally think it's good to empty it after each guest. Be sure to check with your state and local laws regarding chemical levels for public swimming pools and spas.

If you have a hot tub, you should add a clause to your rental rules regarding hot tub safety.

Here are a couple of examples:

HOT TUB: We invite you to relax and enjoy the hot tub. Turn the water temperature up an hour prior to use until water is a comfortable temperature. When not in use, remember to turn down the water temperature to a slightly cooler level. Secure the cover over the hot tub by snapping it down on the sides. Please do not add any type of soap products to the water.

HOT TUBS: No children under the age of 12 permitted in hot tubs at any time. The American College of Obstetricians and Gynecologists (ACOG) state that becoming overheated in a hot tub is not recommended during pregnancy. When using the hot tub, remember there is certain health risk associated with this facility. Use at your own risk. Our housekeepers drain, sanitize, refill and replenish chemicals in all tubs prior to your arrival; therefore, it may not be warm till later that evening. Hot tub covers are for insulation purposes and are not designed to support a person or persons. DO NOT STAND ON THE HOT TUB COVERS, they will break and you may be charged for replacement. Remember when not using the hot tub, leave cover on so hot tub will stay warm.

Parking Issues

Parking is one of many logistical issues that you have to deal with when renting your property. For instance, I have a property that has a designated parking spot, another property that's gated, and a third property that requires renters to use parking passes on their cars.

If you are going to allow your guests the use of your garage, then it's nice to offer a garage door opener. But be sure to have a back-up in your owners closet and some batteries (leave the batteries out of it). And to avoid having the guests take the garage door opener home with them, make sure you remind them in their check-out policy.

One owner told me that she kept having problems with her guests forgetting to leave the garage door opener in her home when they departed. She came up with a very simple solution: She painted the opener an obnoxious bright orange. "No one ever took that home," she said.

To save yourself time, confusion and aggravation, be sure to communicate detailed parking instructions to your renters. I suggest adding this information to the directions that you send to your renters.

Here are a few sample directions I use:

+ Parking Pass: Parking passes are located inside the home. Renters must display a parking pass on the rear view mirror at all times. Failure to display may result in towing of the vehicle at renter's expense. Leave the parking passes inside the home upon departure.

+ There is an entrance into (your neighborhood) from the main road through (your street name). The security gate code is 1245 and press the "#" key.

+ Inside the lockbox will be an odd shaped key. This is the key to the parking space. Please go and park your car in the parking garage and use the walkover (on the 3rd floor) to get into the building. We have one reserved parking space. It is space number 123. To get into the parking space, get out of your car and unlock the pole with the odd shaped key. The pole will then fold down and you can pull your car into the spot with the pole folded down. When you leave, please be sure to re-lock the pole so no one else parks in that spot. If you have more than one vehicle, you'll have to find a space in the unreserved area. There are parking passes inside the home, please place one in each vehicle and leave them inside the condo when you depart. When you leave, PLEASE Leave the keys INSIDE the lockbox.

+ Garage Door Openers: A garage door opener is provided for your convenience. When you check out, remember to leave the opener inside the home. Loss or non-return of the garage door opener will result in $X charge.

23

Solving Problems

UGH! This is a topic I hate talking about. Wouldn't it be wonderful if the world were full of *perfect renters?* Well, unfortunately in the real world problems do arise. Thank goodness there are more good people in this world than bad. But you still have to be prepared for those occasional people who give you a major headache. Remember, the best way to avoid problems is to screen your guests as effectively as possible. If you get that phone call from a 35-year-old business executive who's coming for his college fraternity reunion, think twice about whether you will rent to him; it could be fine, or it could be disastrous.

On a positive note, I can say that damages are rarely a problem, and theft is virtually unheard of. In all the years I have been renting, I have never had anything stolen from my property. I also surveyed owners on this and only found 1 out of 150 owners ever experienced any sort of theft. We have had damages, of course, but most were quite minor. Although getting through these issues is not fun, it doesn't have to be a nightmare if you handle it in a calm, professional manner.

When dealing with these difficult issues, it's imperative that you switch modes and become a businessperson. First, don't get into an argument. Keep your emotions out of it. Think of yourself as a gate agent at the airport dealing with irate customers who have just been informed that their flight has been delayed or canceled. I think gate agents are the most skilled group of customer service employees. They are always so calm. I watch them in amazement as they deal with customers. Unlike a lot of other industries, where customer service employees are trained to do whatever pleases the customer (give the meal free at a restaurant, discount a defective product, etc.), gate agents are trained to keep control of the situation without giving in to the customer's unreasonable demands. Let them be your example.

You, the owner, can control the situation without losing the upper hand. Do whatever you feel is fair and reasonable in a given situation. Remember, you only have to compensate when there is a valid reason, not because the customer demands it.

Given every potential problem, as always your best course of action is to be proactive rather than reactive. Set yourself up ahead of time with clearly defined rental rules and check-in policies. Here are some guidelines for the most common problems.

Major Damage

OK, I know that you are thinking, "I live far away. How would I even know if there were any damages to my vacation home?" This is where you need to have good communication with your cleaning staff.

Instruct them take photos, send you the pictures and call you immediately. This is the reason for the damage or theft deposit. (If your housekeeper does not have a camera phone—yes in 2013 there are still people who don't or don't have data plans, then keep disposable camera in your owner's closet along with a self-addressed stamped envelope. Now you have proof of the damage and a way to assess the cost. It should go without saying that you will not refund the deposit until you know what is owed to you. And you certainly won't rent to them again.

I had a situation once where my renters called and said they broke my bed frame (ahem . . . I did not ask how, I didn't want to know!). Now a bed is something that is necessary to have for the next renter. Under this circumstance, I asked the housekeeper to send one of her employees to the local mattress store to purchase a new frame. I told the housekeeper I would be happy to pay that person's hourly salary. They went, bought the bed, and I sent my housekeeper the reimbursement for her time and expenses. And I took the money out of the deposit from that renter. When I sent the unused portion of the deposit, I mailed a nice letter stating that I was keeping $71.54 of their deposit for the bed that was broken. You should also attach receipts for remedied damages. I also sent them a copy of the rental rules that they signed upon booking and highlighted the section referring to damage deposits. I never heard from them again.

Minor Damage or Theft

Should you worry about every little thing like a broken glass or lost silverware? No. You cannot micro-manage your home. In the grand scheme of things, these are just minor expenses you have to figure on as part of owning a rental property. If you're concerned, ask your renters that if they break anything, please replace it. This is much easier than withholding deposit money and this way the items will be there for the next renter. I use a verbal policy for broken items—have renters replace it with equal quality themselves.

I always make it a practice to say something like this to my guests: "This is my second home. I live 1000 miles away. I can't worry about every little broken item. If you break something that you feel the next renter would need, say the coffee pot, I would much rather you just go to Wal-Mart and buy a new one. This way I don't have to try and figure out how much to charge you (out of your deposit), and the main objective is that these things are there for every renter. If you break one plate, don't worry about it, but if you break the whole stack, be sure to replace them." I've found that most renters are quite comfortable with this policy.

Cleanliness Problems

Let's say your renters have checked out, and you get a phone call from your housekeeper saying that your renters left the home a total mess. Beer cans everywhere, crayon on the walls, a huge stain on the carpet. Use your imagination . . . it can be pretty bad. Rather than get upset, however, remember your objective. You need to get the home ready for the people checking in later today. Do whatever it takes. If it means calling a carpet cleaner and having them come out immediately, then do so. If it means the housekeeper has to spend six hours cleaning rather than her usual two hours, then so be it. Have her do it. If your next renters show up, and they are still not done, instruct your housekeepers to tell them to go out to lunch or dinner—on the owner. As for the costs (I think you guessed this one), take them out of the deposit of the messy renter, including the dinner you had to buy for the next renters. It's a cost associated with their damages. But, never consider this as an opportunity for you to make more money, only cover your costs. Here's another example.

My housekeeper showed up at my home, then called immediately and informed me that someone had smoked cigars in my home. There is no excuse for that. Talk about ample warning! The no smoking policy is clearly stated on my websites, in my rental rules, on the sign on my front door, and on the nice framed note that says, "Our home is non-smoking, please respect it, feel free to use the ashtray located under the kitchen sink to smoke outside on the patio." But, apparently, they ignored all of that and smoked anyway. How was I going to get rid of the smell? It was nearly impossible to air out the place in the five hours between checkout and check-in. I followed all the steps above, had everything cleaned, and dinner for the next guests and all. Well, when I sent the letter with the deposit refund, these people called me. They unequivocally denied that they smoked in the home; they admitted they smoked, but claimed they did so outside. They were arguing about having to pay the charges.

Now this becomes a he said/she said situation. Do I believe the renters or my housekeeper? Maybe they *did* smoke outside but left the sliding door open and the smoke blew in. Or, maybe they smoked outside all week long, and then, as they were packing up, Dad had a stogie in his mouth as he was coming in and out. So what did I do? I stood behind my housekeeper! I explained to the renter that I was sorry, but my loyalties have to be with my housekeeper. I explained how she had worked for me for years and had never ever called me before. I explained that since I am not able to be there physically, my housekeeper is the person responsible for making those judgment calls. The renter asked if she could then have my housekeeper's phone number so she could discuss this with her. I said, "No. If you would like, I can have my housekeeper sign a letter stating the damages." In the end, the renter was not pleased, but I stood firm. I still do not know the real story, but I have no reason not to believe my housekeeper.

Cancellations

Cancellations are the second biggest problem that vacation owners face (after cleanliness issue). This is another issue that needs to be clearly defined in your rental rules. Keep in mind; your chances of re-renting a week grow exponentially lower as the date draws nearer. I've learned over the years that I have to be pretty stringent about cancellations. Once it's booked it's booked. No cancellations. As a vacation rental business owner, I cannot "insure" everyone's health, work schedules, or the weather. It may sound harsh but cancellations can pose a high risk to your bottom line. Instead, I encourage my guests to purchase traveler's insurance.

Other owners choose to have a cancellation fee or re-rent fee. This fee would be $100–$500 or a percentage of the total rental amount. Since you set the rules, you can make that figure anything you wish. If someone cancels then keep the deposit and/or any payments that you have received as per your rental rules. If you re-rent and feel so inclined, you can refund all or part of the money that they have prepaid. The bottom line is set up your cancellation policies in your favor.

Lastly, there is also the option of putting that week up on one of the many auction websites, such as eBay. Just be sure to put in your auction notice that the winner must be approved by the property owner and comply with all rental rules and regulations. Otherwise you might end up getting the very kind of renters I've been advising you avoid! Read how one owner, Nadia, solved her cancellation problem:

Nadia had rented her snowbird season (January to March) in April of the previous year for $1,000 per month + $200 damage deposit. In November, these guests stayed at her property for a long weekend. Upon returning, the renters called Nadia and explained that although her home was beautiful, and it was everything that she described, they decided to go to a totally different city for their three-month stay. Nadia's rental rules required her snowbirds to pay in full 60 days prior to their rental date, and her cancellation for snowbird rentals was 180 days. She had every right to keep their full payment (but not the deposit since it was a damage deposit). Nadia explained to the renters that it would be very difficult to re-rent those dates since most snowbirds have secured their rentals by now. The renters clearly understood her dilemma as well as the rental policies. Fortunately for the renters, Nadia is very soft-hearted and felt really bad keeping their money. After all, she had spoken with the renters numerous times up to this point and felt as though they were friends. And they were so sweet. But on the flip side, Nadia could not afford to lose out on $3,000. The renters and Nadia came up with a great solution. Nadia agreed to do everything possible to try to re-rent those three months. One month passed and not a single renter called. When the renters and Nadia spoke next, the renters suggested that Nadia reduce the rental rate to $700 per month. They figured whatever portion of the rent they could recover would be better than nothing. Nadia changed her one-line ad on all her portal sites listings. She did not rent January, but did rent February and March and happily refunded the first snowbirds the $1,400 she received from the new renters.

Telephones

There is a debate amongst vacation rental owners whether or not to provide a landline phone in their vacation rental properties. The theory is with so many people owing cell phones these days, why should owners pay $400–$600 per year to provide telephone services. When evaluating your choices you should look at it from two perspectives—your liability exposure and the costs. To help you determine the best course of actions, you should speak with your accountant and attorney.

While I am not an accountant or attorney, I can tell you what I do. I do provide a landline phone in all of my vacation rental properties because in my opinion, the risks of *not* providing are not worth the costs (which are, by the way, tax deductible if you are claiming your vacation home as a business). While we think everyone has cell phones these days, in reality not everyone does. Furthermore, many vacation rental homes are located in areas where the reception might not be the best—yes cell phone service has improved tremendously over the years but let's face it, we all still get dropped calls.

God forbid anything ever happens to someone while they're in your property and they need to call 911. If they call 911 from a land line, the 911 operator can generally tell what address the call is coming from. If they call from a cell phone the guest would need to know the address where they are. What are the chances in a panic they'll know the address of your home? Slim at best. So for safety, security and expediency, I think it's best to provide a land line phone in your vacation rental home.

Now if you do choose to provide a phone, be sure to put a long-distance blocker on your phone (to avoid long-distance charges). This is available through your local phone company for a small fee. If you choose this option, be aware that it cannot be easily turned on and off. So if you are at your property, you will be forced to either use a calling card or your cell phone, even though you are in your own property.

Some owners are now considering unlimited or one-rate calling plans for their vacation properties. These are very reasonably priced and can be marketed as a selling tool: "free local and long-distance calls." But whatever you do, be sure to block out collect calls, person-to-person calls, and 900 numbers.

Complaints

It's hard to make generalizations about complaints, or give advice without knowing the specifics. However, I will tell you two of the most common complaints: the cleanliness of your home and the weather. Since we cannot control the weather, there's really nothing we can do about that one. "I am sorry it rained or didn't snow, I clearly understand how this could affect your vacation, but if you choose to checkout early due to the weather, you must understand that you forfeit your rent." Clear as that!

Now about cleanliness. This is by far the most common complaint heard by owners. It is also the most frustrating. Our hands are tied as long-distance owners; we must completely rely on our cleaning staff.

The best way I can explain this is: have you ever told your child to go and clean his room? Of course you have. Then you ask, "Did you clean your room?" "Yes Mom!" Then you go up to check (because we know you cannot take *his* word), and you find the empty glasses from the last three nights on the bedside table, the bed still unmade, and dirty laundry draped across his chair! You look at your child and say, "I thought you said you cleaned your room?" And the child looks at you like you are absolutely insane. "Mom, I did clean my room! I vacuumed *and* dusted."

So is junior a liar? Not exactly. Your child did indeed clean ... he just didn't pick up. That is *his perception* of clean. Although this is an exaggerated example, the point is, everyone's perception of *clean* is totally different. But you can't afford to leave any ambiguity about it when it comes to letting your cleaning service know exactly what it is that you expect.

To avoid cleanliness complaints after the fact, establish a check-in policy. In that policy, be sure to tell the renters, when you arrive, please check for cleanliness. If *anything* is not acceptable, then please call the housekeeper immediately. If the renters do not notify you or the housekeeper right away, then there is no way to rectify the problem. If they do not take the necessary steps, it is not your fault.

Since we put in all that time and effort, there is a lot of pride that we as owners have in our vacation homes. Sometimes complaints can be taken as constructive criticism. Keep in mind, for every person that complains about something, there are probably five others who just let it go and say nothing. How many times have you eaten in a restaurant, and your food was not hot? There are some people who would send their plate back every time until it was perfect, and there are others who just wouldn't do anything. So, when you get a complaint, be sure to take it seriously, and if you can, resolve the problem as quickly as possible.

The People You Can Never Please

Unfortunately, there are people you can never please. Read about Matthew's guests who always complain:

> Christopher and his wife Erin come and stay every year at Matthew's ski lodge. They always stay for the first three weeks of the ski season. Every year, Matthew calls Christopher and Erin upon check-in, and every year, they complain and say, "Well, we had to do the usual cleaning before we moved our stuff in." All year, Matthew gets no complaints about the cleanliness and has been using the same housekeeper for five years; he knows she's good. Well, this year Matthew and his wife decided to spend the week before the ski season at their rental home. The whole week, they cleaned everything possible. They pulled out the refrigerator, the stove, cleaned all the baseboards, had the carpets cleaned, the works! When he left, Matthew said to himself, "Ha! No way can Christopher and Erin complain this year." He does his usual phone call after they check-in and sure enough, he gets the same song and dance. The home was not clean!?!

Matthew and his wife shouldn't have wasted their time. Clearly, these renters were never going to be pleased (but I commend them for trying). The important part of the story is that in all those years none of the other guests complained. So if you get one or two renters who seem to be chronic whiners, and you're certain that their complaints are unfounded, just do your best to be a good listener, polite, and concerned. Just let it go in one ear and out the other.

Evictions

This is by far one of the scariest things that comes to mind when dealing with your vacation property. Evictions are even worse than dealing with damages because you are faced with a potential confrontation. This is the only reason that I can think of that would require you to jump on a plane or in your car to go and handle it yourself.

Thankfully, evictions are extremely rare, especially with by owner rentals, because we are screening our guests ourselves. The most common evictions is when there is miscommunication about the check-out time or date, for instance the guest thought they were staying until Sunday but their contract states Saturday and you have new renters due to check in on Saturday (this is another reason it's important to have signed contracts).

Management companies sometimes have to evict due to disturbing the peace (partiers) but remember they don't do as much screening of the renters as a person who is renting by owner.

Last spring break I was enjoying one of my beach properties. While there I stopped into the HOA office, while speaking with our HOA manager, she told me she was extremely frustrated because she had to evict guests on a daily basis. I was astonished. I asked her if she wanted me to call the owners to give them some tips on how to screen their guests more carefully. Her response was, "Yes, I would love you to, unfortunately I'm not certain they'll talk with you because they are all management companies." I asked her if she's had to evict from units that were rented by owner and her response was not that she could ever remember.

When you are faced with the dilemma of having to evict someone, chances are your blood pressure will be at full tilt. Again, it's best to be proactive; do your research now, while you are clear-headed and make notes. Research the local policies on eviction for short-term renters. In most states, short-term and transient rentals fall under the same jurisdiction as your local hotels and motels. These laws tend to be quite different from the long-term lease laws, some of which are very restrictive, stating you cannot evict if the temperature outside is X degrees or lower, or during certain months of the year. Find out ahead of time if the police department will supply an officer for the eviction. If it comes to this, stand your ground.

Withholding Deposits

Now, if you have done due diligence to avoid problems, but you still end up with an instance where you'll need to withhold the deposit, there are a couple of things you need to know.

First don't view damage deposits as a way to nickel and dime your renters out of some more cash. There are just some things that should be referred to as "the cost of doing business." Nor should it be used as a way to recoup money for your pain and aggravation. In other words, if a renter had made you angry, it does not give you the right to keep their deposit.

Second, if you keep a damage deposit or any portion of it, you should keep sound records of your exact costs associated with it. Let's say the renters left your home a filthy mess, you can only keep exactly the amount of money that your housekeeper charges for her extra time. If that time has gone over into the next renter's check in time and you have taken my suggestion to send the arriving inconvenienced guests a free meal, be sure to get a copy of that receipt for the meal for your records. In other words, be sure to keep good documentation!

The purpose of this chapter is not to scare you. Remember, most often, fear comes from ignorance. Now that you've read this chapter and have all of the facts you should realize that there is nothing at all to be afraid of. As I said, most of your guests will not be troublemakers. To the contrary, you are likely to become good friends with some of the people you rent to over the years. And if one of these days you do have a rotten experience with one of the bad apples (like that nasty kid you *still* remember from kindergarten), just deal with it and move on. Don't let it ruin your outlook on what otherwise is a very lucrative and rewarding business for you.

CHAPTER

24

Hurricanes and Natural Disasters

You might live somewhere well-removed from hurricanes, tornadoes, wild fires and other natural disasters, but your second home might be not be so safe. Since I own properties along the Gulf Coast, I have had to deal with hurricanes hitting my vacation homes. As a result I've had to learn to deal with the aftermath of these natural disasters even though I'm miles away from my property.

Before the storm. First and foremost, be considerate of your renters who are scheduled to arrive when a major hurricane or other type of storm is imminent. I think it's best to contact anyone who will be renting at least over the next 2 weeks and possibly beyond. Be accessible via phone and email. It's likely your renters will be seeking information and comfort that

329

their vacation won't be ruined or cancelled. While you may not know much more than they do (because you're getting your information from the same source as they are—CNN or The Weather Channel), it's best to engage them and work out a plan.

Whatever you do, deflect any requests for refunds until you are certain your area is in the path of the storm. I have been in too many situations where a guest called and wanted to cancel their vacation that's a month away because they see a hurricane stirring in the Gulf. In my rental policy, it clearly states that I only give refunds for mandatory evacuations.

Obviously you'll have to take into account your renter's travel to and from your property. For instance, in 2005, Hurricane Dennis was predicted to make landfall on Sunday, July 10. Saturday morning I had guests scheduled to check out and Saturday afternoon I had new ones checking in. My departing guests checked out unaffected. Even though there was not a mandatory evacuation as of Friday night, I called my guests who were scheduled to check in on Saturday afternoon and told them it would be best if they waited a day to check in. At that point, it would have been too risky to have them drive down and possibly have to turn right back around and leave again.

The next step would be to become familiar with your natural disaster insurance policy—pull it out and read it. Contact your insurance company and find out what their process is for claims should you end up with any. In most cases they will advise you to contact their claims department if your home gets damaged, and get a claim or case number before you make any repairs. Remember, if your insurance agent is in your second home area, he is most likely inaccessible. You may have to call the national claims number.

After the storm. If your area sustains damage, at some point you may need to go there and assess the damages yourself. Prior to departing for your property's location, be sure that you can even get in. A lot of areas do not allow anyone to enter until a few days after the storms.

This is for your own safety. Check news, state or county websites for information on accessibility of the area. Also, be sure to bring proof of ownership, such as insurance policy, deed, power bill etc., or you might not be allowed in. Be patient, especially in heavily damaged areas, because they may allow access to permanent residents first.

When you visit, you will want to pack your car with supplies from home because the home improvement stores in damaged areas may have a hard time keeping inventory up to demand. Some things I would bring: a cooler with food and drinks, candles, flashlights and possibly generators, contractor trash bags, fans, shovels, rakes, brooms, hammers, nails screwdrivers, cleaning supplies and paper towels.

Also, take your camera with you. If you have any damages, be sure to take photos of everything before you fix anything. Insurance adjusters will likely be very busy. They'll prioritize their claims and of course, permanent residents take precedence.

Remember, everyone needs help and contract labor will be scarce. If you plan to bring anyone to do paid work, be careful. Florida, for example, requires that all paid help must be licensed in the state of Florida.

And lastly, if you are one of the more fortunate who had little or no damage, you may want to pop an e-mail to your renters, or add something to your website or online ads stating that your property is fine and did not sustain damages.

CHAPTER

25

Networking with Other Owners

It really is true . . . there is strength in numbers. Networking with other owners is much more important than you may have thought. How many times have you borrowed a power tool or a cup of sugar from your neighbors at home? The same is true with your vacation home. And while you may not be swapping sugar, maybe you can bounce ideas off one another. Better yet, you can share lots of useful information, and help each other out. Remember, you share something in common with them, and you're basically in the same boat. Throughout this book, you will notice many references to other owners. In the sections about keys, maintenance, problem solving, pricing . . . come to think of it, I refer to other owners in just about every chapter, and that's not by coincidence. Networking is vital.

So how do you find the other owners? In many cases, you will meet other owners when you are visiting your property. Don't worry if they use a management company, there are always things that these owners need. They will need many of the same things as you. If your property is part of an association, you can obtain a list of owners directly from the association. Often the association will hold an annual homeowners meeting, a great opportunity to meet and socialize with your fellow owners. I also try to find other owners who live in my hometown. This is especially helpful for transporting small items and supplies.

If you are not in an association, you can find other owners from the management companies or directly from their renters. Don't be shy. If you see someone at his or her house, be neighborly, and strike up a conversation. These guests may well know the owner. Or maybe they *are* the owners.

Another great resource for meeting fellow owners is by attending one of my seminars. **My seminars give you a golden opportunity to meet and network with other vacation property owners.** I usually hold the seminars in major metropolitan areas, although I do occasionally go to vacation areas. Also be sure to check my website, www.howtorentbyowner.com, I have a lot of useful information on there too, and I am adding new information all the time.

And lastly, there are a couple of websites devoted to vacation property owners and their networking needs. These websites have a wealth of helpful information for vacation property owners as well as newsletters and discussion boards.

This is my favorite one that I read every day (and often respond):

http://groups.yahoo.com/group/vacation_rentals/

The best way to show you the value of networking is through a real story. Read about how these two owners found each other and how networking has helped them:

Denise lives in Anaheim, California. She owns a vacation home in Lake Tahoe and was eager to meet another owner. She went on the internet and looked up Lake Tahoe. Then she searched for owners who live somewhere in the Anaheim area. That's where she met Sheryl. They conversed first via email, then over the telephone. Coincidentally, it turned out that Sheryl and Denise lived only a few blocks from one another at home too. They met five years ago and, believe it or not, have never been at their vacation homes in Tahoe at the same time. But every time Denise plans the trip, she calls Sheryl to see if she needs anything done, or transported. And, of course, Sheryl does the same for Denise.

These two truly work as a team of owners. They have done many things together and always work out discounts and deals. They take turns overseeing projects too. Sheryl always visits in the fall, so she orders the firewood and is there for delivery. Denise is always there in the spring, so she calls the chimney sweep and has both homes done at the same time. One had all the screens replaced on her home, so the other did too. Their homes, even though very different, were built by the same builder. Denise's air conditioner went out one year, and she had to have it replaced. She informed Sheryl. No, Sheryl didn't go and replace hers too, but since they had the same builder, and the houses were the same age, Sheryl now knew to be on the look-out for this problem. It was very helpful information. They even have renters who call and want to book two places. What a perfect situation! And, naturally, they refer renters to one another too.

The important lesson from this story is that you don't have to do things for other owners with the express purpose of getting something back from them. Help them out simply because it's the right thing to do. And, chances are, you will find other owners who will do the same for you. What goes around truly does come around.

26

Final Notes from the Author

Think of this not as the end of the book, rather the start of a new adventure. This is where my advice ends and your actions begin.

Renting by owner isn't for everyone, but for many people it is the difference between being able to afford a vacation home and not. You now know how to share your dream home with others by managing it yourself, and having the rental income pay the mortgage, taxes, utilities, and maintenance. Oftentimes, owners get caught up in the management aspects of ownership. Don't let this encompass you.

Thanks for taking the time to read this book. As I said in the beginning, it's not just my own experiences, it's yours too. Please share whether you loved, hated or were inspired by this book, I would love to hear your stories. Please email me Christine@HowToRentByOwner.com

I will close with my favorite article that continually inspires me. I read it as poetry, where I find many underlying hidden messages pertaining to all aspects of owning and managing my properties. Take the risk.

Of Risk and Reward

By Jack Simpson, real estate broker, columnist, and vacation homeowner.

"Life is richer and more rewarding for those who take risks to get what they want. Most all truly great achievements involve risk. This applies in the various fields of exploration, competitive sports, business, finance, even love and war. Real estate investing is no exception.

In the course of my business, I meet a lot of people who are looking for something more out of life. For many of them, it's a vacation rental home at the beach. The rewards are there to be had: pride of ownership, free personal use, rental income, and good potential for appreciation. But there are risks too. What if it doesn't rent? What if there's a hurricane? What of the unknown? Most bold, self-confident people go for it all—the risk and the reward. They buy. The timid talk themselves out of it. I feel sorry for them.

I am accustomed to taking risks, not only in real estate investing but in many other facets of life. If I see something I want, I go for it. Sometimes I hit. Sometimes I miss. But at least I am in there swinging. I have learned to savor the success and learn from the ones that don't work out. Along this line, I have some thoughts to share with you:

Control the risk. You can exert control over certain activities such as selecting your own investments or managing your own business. But you have absolutely no control over the spin of a roulette wheel or the draw of the lottery. I take risks but I don't gamble. There's a big difference.

Enjoy the risk. That's right—enjoy it. Risk is a challenge. It excites and sharpens the senses. Most people perform better under pressure. Some thrive on it. Who would play a golf course if it had no sand traps or water hazards? A world without challenge would be downright depressing.

Concentrate on your goal. Don't be distracted by obstacles and negative thoughts. Think about the golf course. You don't hit a hole in one if all you can think about is staying out of the rough. Whether you expect to win or to lose, you are probably right.

Accept all setbacks. Not every venture will be successful, but that doesn't mean it failed either. You fail only if you stop trying. Most every success story is full of setbacks along the way. They build character and make you a strong person.

Consider the alternative. Trying to eliminate the risks often creates other risks. Some people put all their money in a "safe" insured account only to see their buying power taken away by taxes and inflation. Ask yourself, 'What's the worst that can happen?' To me, the worst thing is seeing your life slip by without the risk and reward. That's sad.

We have all heard 'Nothing ventured, nothing gained,' 'Better to have loved and lost . . . ,' and those saddest of words ' . . . it might have been.' But I believe Kris Kristofferson put it best when he wrote the song 'I'd rather be sorry for something I've done than for something I didn't do.'"

1

Forms

Throughout this book, there are many references to proper documentation and forms. It is very important, for both yourself and your renters, that you have these items. This is yet another way to make your business run smoothly. Consult an attorney to review your documents.

I recommend that you build a template for these forms in your word processing program. This can be easily accomplished by using popular programs such as Microsoft Word, Google Docs or similar programs. Save these templates and use them over and over again. All forms, except the deposit refund, which is mailed with your deposit-refund check, can be emailed directly to your guest. If you email the forms as attachments, I recommend you convert them to .pdf files so they cannot be altered by the guest.

You want to be sure to customize your forms to suit your property. Also, you may want to have an attorney look over your forms to be certain that you are properly covered.

* Electronic versions can be found at
  www.HowToRentByOwner.com/RentalRules

Reservation Confirmation

The confirmation forms will be emailed to your renters upon booking. Remember to have your renters print, read sign and fax, scan and email or mail you the signed copy.

Enclosed is our rental contract and rules. Please print, read and sign and either scan and email, mail or fax it back to. Thanks so much. Feel free to contact me if you have any questions.

Thanks again,
Christine
Christine and Tom Karpinski
Your Address
Your city, State and Zip Code
Your Phone number
Email: Christine@HowtoRentByOwner.com
Webpage: www.howtorentbyowner.com

Today's Date,

Dear Mr. and Mrs. Guest,

Thank you for choosing our condominium for your vacation. We hope that you have a pleasant stay. The unit is located in the

My Resort Complex
4567 Scenic Drive, Unit #1234,
Destin, Florida 54321
Phone 850–654–3210.

Your confirmation is as follows:
Check-in date: June 19, 2014 after 3 p.m. CST
(No early check-in please)
Check-out date: June 26, 2014 by 10 a.m. CST
Number of people in party: 2 adults, 2 children
Number of approved pets: 1 small dog

After I receive your $200 down payment, your bill will be as follows:
   Total bill $1,581.75 = $1,350 (rental rate) + $75 (cleaning fee) +
$156.75(11% Florida tax)
   1st payment of $790.87 due April 19, 2014 (60 days prior)
   2nd payment of $790.88 due June 5, 2014 (14 days prior)

As soon as I receive your final payment, I will send the directions and
lock box/key/door code instructions.

Please sign and return 1 copy of this confirmation, and 1 copy of the
rules.

Thanks! Have a great vacation!
   Christine

Signature_____ Date_____

Rental Rules and Regulations

*These will be emailed to your renters upon booking. Remember these forms
are equally important as payment. Use this form only as a model, you will
want to add information regarding your property and it's hazards. Since I
am not an attorney, it is very important to have your attorney review your
rental rules contract to ensure the terms and conditions of your contract
comply with the state and local laws as well as rules and covenants where
your property is located.*

My Resort Complex
4567 Scenic Drive, Unit #1234
Destin, Florida 54321
Phone 850–654–3210

The condo has 2 bedrooms and 2 full bathrooms: 1 has a king-size bed, and the 2nd bedroom has a queen-size bed.

My Resort Complex is a beachfront resort, which owns approximately 300 linear feet of private undeveloped beachfront. All of the condos at My Resort Complex are located across the street from the beach. Our condo is located on the second floor in building #1, which is on the east side, perpendicular to the beach; the condo does not have a beach view. Between March 15-Oct 15, we include daily beach service, 2 chairs and 1 umbrella.

1. CHECK-IN TIME IS AFTER 4 P.M. CST
   CHECK OUT IS 10 A.M. CST.
   No Early Check-ins or late check outs are permitted.

2. SMOKING—This is a NON SMOKING unit.

3. PETS—Pets NOT permitted in rental condo at any time. A $500 penalty will be charged if there is evidence of any unauthorized pets in the property.
   — Or —
   PETS—Pets are permitted in rental condo only with prior approval. $200 per pet fee applies. All pets must be leashed at all times. Pet owners are responsible for cleaning up of any/all pet refuse. Pets are not allowed on furniture at any time. Any evidence of pets on furniture may incur extra cleaning fees. All pets must be up to date on rabies vaccinations and all other vaccinations. Heartworm preventative is highly recommended. All pets are to be treated with Advantage or similar topical flea and tick repellent three (3) days prior to arrival. The condo owners assume no responsibility for illness or injury that may incur to pets while on the premises. Renters must abide by all complex pet rules including but not limited to cleaning up after your dog, not leaving dog unattended on leashes and curb barking.

4. MINIMUM AGE—My Resort Complex has a minimum age for renting. We cannot rent to vacationing students or singles under 25 years of age unless accompanied by an adult guardian or parent.

5. DAMAGE—Charges will be billed to your credit card account for the following:
   a. damages to the condo or its contents;
   b. charges incurred due to contraband, pets or collection of rents or services rendered during the stay;

   c. debris, rubbish and discards left inside the condo;

      d. soiled dishes left in the sink or dishwasher;

      e. lost keys;

      f. damaged, lost or stolen linens;

      g. smoking inside the condo;

      h. parking passes are lost or not left inside the condo upon departure;

      i. check-in early or check-out late;

      j. violations any of the resort rules that incur fines or penalties;

      k. trash not properly disposed of. All trash and refuse must be taken to the dumpsters located to the north end of the condominium complex. No trash is to be left outside doors or on balconies at any time. Strictly enforced. A fine of $X, per day, if trash is left outside the door or on the balcony.

6. PAYMENT—An advance payment equal to 50% of the rental rate is required 90 days before arrival. The advance payment will be applied toward the room rent. The advance payment is not a damage deposit. The BALANCE OF RENT is due thirty (30) days before your arrival date. Unless otherwise specified the subsequent payments will be automatically charged to your credit card on the due dates listed above. The charge will show up on your credit card as "Your Business Name". On occasion your credit card bank might call to verify that you have authorized the charge. Please remember to authorize all payments. Failure to authorize charges that result in falsely reported fraud or unauthorized payments will result in a penalty to the renter up to $100.

If you wish to pay via check or a different credit card you must notify us prior to the due date. If you wish to pay by check, please make payments in the form of bank money orders, cashier's checks or personal checks payable to *Your Name* and mail it to the address listed above. Checks must arrive on or before the due date. If payments are not received on time or if your credit card is declined, the reservation may be cancelled and previous payments become non-refundable in compliance with the cancellation policies listed below.

7. CANCELLATIONS—A ninety (90) day notice is required for cancellation. Cancellations that are made more than ninety (90) days prior to the arrival date are subject to a 10% Cancellation fee or $X whichever is greater. Cancellations or

changes that result in a shortened stay, that are made within 90 days of the arrival date, forfeit the full advance payment and reservation deposit. Cancellation or early departure does not warrant any refund of rent or deposit.

8. MONTHLY RESERVATION CANCELLATIONS—Monthly renters must cancel one hundred twenty (120) days prior to check-in. Monthly renters who make a change that results in a shortened stay must be made at least ninety (90) days prior to check-in.

9. MAXIMUM OCCUPANCY—The maximum number of guests per condominium is limited to X# (X#) persons (any ages; children included). Prior approval is needed for any additional persons. An additional charge or $X per person per night for guests in addition to X# (X#) will be assessed. Unauthorized extra guests could result in eviction.

10. MINIMUM STAY—this property requires a three (3) night minimum stay. Longer minimum stays may be required during holiday periods. If a rental is taken for less than three days, the guest will be charged the three-night rate.

11. INCLUSIVE FEES—Rates include a one-time linen-towel setup. Amenity fees are included in the rental rate.

    a. Swimming Pool . The use of the swimming pool (s) is limited to owners and their houseguests. All bathers are required to observe the posted complex regulations.

12. HOUSEKEEPING—no daily housekeeping service. While linens and bath towels are included in the unit, daily housekeeping service is not included in the rental rate however, is available at an additional rate. We suggest you bring beach towels. We do not permit towels or linens to be taken from the condos.

13. FALSIFIED RESERVATIONS—Any reservation obtained under false pretense will be subject to forfeiture of advance payment, deposit and/or rental money, and the party will not be permitted to check in or may be evicted.

14. WRITTEN EXCEPTIONS—Any exceptions to the above mentioned policies must be approved in writing in advance.

15. PARKING/PARKING PASSES: Parking is limited to two (2) vehicles. Vehicles are to be parked in designated parking areas only. Any illegally parked cars are subject to towing; applicable fines/towing fees and is the sole responsibility of the vehicle owner. Parking passes are located inside the unit. Renters must display parking pass on the rear view mirror at all times. Failure

to display may result in towing of vehicle at renter's expense.
Leave the parking passes inside the unit upon departure.

16. HURRICANE OR STORM POLICY: No refunds will be given, we highly recommend you purchase travel insurance.

17. TRAVEL INSURANCE: We highly recommend your purchase travel insurance. If you wish to purchase travel insurance, go to www.InsureMyTrip.com for details and to purchase.

18. CONDITIONS—The condo will be in clean and working condition. No compensations will be given for non-working items outside the owner's control, including but not limited to power outages, cable TV outages, internet outages, etc. For items inside the owner's control, the owners will make every attempt to rectify problems that may occur while you are in the condo. It is the renter's responsibility to notify the owner immediately if there are any problems. No refunds or any other compensation will be given for the problems that the owner is able to rectify within a reasonable time frame.

19. LIABILITY—The condo is privately owned; the owners are not responsible for any accidents, injuries or illness that occurs while on the premises or its facilities. The Homeowners are not responsible for the loss of personal belongings or valuables of the guest. By accepting this reservation, it is agreed that all guest are expressly assuming the risk of any harm arising from their use of the premises or others whom they invite to use the premise.

I hereby give permission to charge my credit card for the amounts above. I agree that all rental monies are non-refundable per cancellation policy above. I have read my rights to purchase travel insurance. I also agree damage charges can be charged to my credit card if damages are incurred during my stay. By Signing Below, I agree to all terms and conditions of this agreement.

Signature_____ Date_____

Pet Policy

If you accept pets in your property you can simply add pet rules to your existing rental rules.

PETS—Pets are permitted in rental home only with prior approval. $X per pet fee applies.

1. This property accepts dogs only. No cats, birds, snakes, potbelly pigs, hamsters, ferrets, or other animals allowed at any time.
2. All pets must be on leashes at all times.
3. Pet owners are responsible for cleaning up any/all pet refuse.
4. Pets are not allowed on furniture at any time. Any evidence of pets on furniture may incur extra cleaning fees.
5. All pets must be up to date on rabies vaccinations and all other vaccinations. Heartworm preventative is highly recommended.
6. All pets are to be treated with Advantage or similar topical flea and tick repellent three (3) days prior to arrival. Fleas and ticks are very rampant in this area and can cause harmful or fatal illness to humans and pets. All items above are the sole responsibility of the pet owner.
7. The homeowners assume no responsibility for illness or injury that may incur to pets while on the premises.
8. "Vicious or Dangerous Dogs" trained for dog fighting or with any tendency or disposition to attack any dog other domestic animals or humans without provocation, are not permitted at any time.

For other sample pet policy addendums visit the Humane Society's website at www.hsus.org or www.rentwithpets.org

Directions & Arrival Policy

Send directions, arrival policy, departure information, and emergency information as one document to the guests at least two weeks prior to their check-in date. Give clear directions from all points, north, south, east, west, airport, etc. Be sure to include landmarks before and after your property (in case they passed it).

I received your final payment. Thanks! Enclosed are all the directions you will need to get to and into the condo.

Have a great time,
Christine

Directions To My Resort—My Resort Complex is located at 4567 Scenic Drive, Destin, Florida 3254, Unit #12345. The resort between the Wal-Mart and the Outlet Mall.

There is an entrance into My Resort Complex from the main road through Destin, Hwy 98, or you can access the resort from Scenic Drive. The security gate code is 123456.

Coming from the Airport—take a right out of the airport, go to the end of the road, and turn left onto *State Rt 31*. Once you pass the *Burger King*, take a right on to the *Mid-Bay Bridge* (toll road $2). At the end of the bridge, take a left, and follow directions coming from west.

Coming from the west—you'll pass *Wal-Mart (on left) and Home Depot (on left)*. After signs for *Miramar Beach* watch for the *My Resort Complex* sign on the right. If you get to the *Silver Sands Outlet Mall*, you've gone too far. Once in the complex, take your first right, then proceed to the condo buildings.

Coming from the east—pass Sandestin, then turn left, at the first sign for the beaches, onto Scenic Drive (*Silver Sands Outlet mall on right*). Stay on Scenic Drive, aprox. 2 miles. My Resort Complex will be on the right (just passed *Neighbor*).

Once in the Resort—proceed to Condo Bldg #1. We're unit #1234 (second floor).

The lock box code—XXXX, take the keys out, and keep them with you at all times. Do not use the lockbox as a holding spot while you are staying in the condo as the code is not changed after each guest.

—Or—

Door code—we have an electronic lock on the door which will be coded to the last four digits of your cell phone number. Enter the code and turn the toggle in the center of the lock to disengage the deadbolt. Turn the door handle to enter the door. To lock, press the *Schlage* button and turn the toggle to engage the deadbolt. Troubleshooting—if you hear a long beep you have entered the wrong code.

Initial walk through—when you arrive, please inspect the condo for cleanliness, broken or damaged items. You must report any such issues to the owners or housekeeping staff within two hours of check-in.

Beach, pool, tennis courts, work out facilities—the amenities areas are locked at all times. The code to enter the amenities area is 9876.

Thanks and have a great vacation!

Departure Information

It's important to make sure your guests know what you expect them to do before they check out and in order to get a full refund of their deposit.

Before departure please be sure to do the following:

- Sign our guestbook.
- Take out all trash.
- Load and run the dishwasher.
- Close and lock all windows. Close all blinds and drapes.
- In summer months turn the air to 79°, in the cooler months turn heat to 60°.
- Check all drawers, closets and cupboards for personal belongings.
- Check all outlets for phone, tablet, and game chargers.
- Leave the keys, garage door openers, and amenities passes on the kitchen table.
- Turn off all the lights.
- Lock the doors.
- Leave by 10 A.M.
- Have a safe journey home.

Emergency Information

Be sure to have all the following information on both your directions and posted somewhere in your property. I copied mine on pretty paper, framed it, and put it near my telephone in my unit.

In case of emergency, dial 911.
Poison Control 789-654-3210
You are in Walton County.
My Resort, in Destin, Florida
The address is:
4567 Scenic Drive,
Destin, Florida 32541
Unit #1234
Phone 850-654-3210

If you have trouble with the unit, call the owners—
Tom and Christine Karpinski. Call collect, 512-123-4567.

We can also be reached on our cell phones :
512-123-4567 (Christine) or 512-345-6789 (Tom)

Vacation Tips

You will want to include some useful vacation area tips. Notice I have covered, shopping, restaurants, recipe for local food, attractions as well as some area dangers.

You can find many local area tips in a book on my coffee table. Here are a few personal favorites for the area:

When you go to the outlet mall, make your first stop the mall office, open until 6:30 P.M. (located behind the mall). They have a booklet called the "passport book," which is full of all sorts of coupons for most of the stores … also if the men decide to go shopping too and get tired, they have a billiard room in the upstairs of the food court. If you take the kids along, there's also has a game room. In the passport book, there's usually a coupon for buy $5 worth of tokens—get $5 free!

Deep-sea fishing is great in Destin. If the guys like deep sea fishing, this is a "must" for them.

Seaside is a nice little village heading east down 98, watch for the signs, you'll take a right. Seaside is a very upscale area that's fun to go to "dream" about when you win the lottery. They have a bunch of artsy shops, but things are very expensive, it's just a fun place to look around.

Keep your eyes open if on the beach at dusk or dawn, we very often see dolphins swimming right off shore. If the dolphins come in close, which they do occasionally, do not get in the water and try to touch them. Please respect that they are wildlife. It is illegal to touch the dolphins (we humans have germs that harm the dolphins).

A fun "cheap" thing to do is to rent the ocean kayaks off the beach. Morning is usually the best time; the waters are generally calmer. The kayaks are very easy to maneuver, and it's only around $10/hour.

Food and Restaurants—There are a lot of great restaurants in the area. The Back Porch is one of our favorites. It's located in Destin. Depending on the season, it can be very crowded, so be prepared to wait. They do have a playground on the beach for the kids to play in while waiting. I recommend you bring a change of clothes for the little ones; it's tough to resist the temptation to play near the water, and it's better to be prepared than to get upset when they inevitably get wet. Remember you're on vacation, there's no use stressing about it!

If you want to cook up a seafood feast, my favorite store is called Shrimper's. To get there, go east on 98, past the outlet mall about 6 or 8 miles, and it's on the left-hand side, past Bayou Bill's ... They have the freshest fish and shrimp and great prices ... A local "specialty" is the smoked tuna dip; it's great on crackers as an appetizer. Also, if you can get your hands on "red shrimp," they're a must try! Boil them in water for 90 SECONDS (no more, no less!), and then dip them in drawn butter, and you'll think you're eating lobster ... Typically "reds" are only available on Tuesdays. Shrimper's also has the "best" key lime pie around!

There is also another seafood market that has now hired a full-time chef to prepare things that you can cook at home. It is supposed to make it easy to make "home cooked gourmet food." It's called Destin Ice, and it's located on Hwy 98 to the west on the right, almost all the way down to the bridge to the island.

I recently discovered there is a new Dollar store on HWY 98 that has a lot of useful items all for $1. It's a great place to pick up odds and ends along with sand toys. It's located west of the condo, just beyond the Home Depot on the right, in the shopping center with Office Depot.

Warnings—Over the past few years, there have been some ocean related deaths along the gulf coast. Please pay attention to the flags on the beach. If there is a RED FLAG do NOT swim. The rip tides (rip currents) have been very strong. If you by chance do get caught in a rip tide, swim parallel to the beach. Our Resort does NOT have lifeguards.

And one last precaution, sharks are in the gulf. Use common sense whenever in the water, especially in the evening (when sharks do most of their feeding).

Sand Dunes—Please make everyone in your group aware that it is illegal to walk on or across the sand dunes along the beach. They are there to protect from hurricanes. If you are caught walking on the dunes there are heavy fines. Don't walk on the Dunes!

Property Instructions

You will want to also include instruction on how to use everything in your home.

Inclement Weather Road Closings For these in area information call the National Park Service at 865-436-1200 or visit http://www.nps.gov/grsm/.

FIRE SAFETY—Due to the great and always present risk of fire, we ask that you not have any open flames, such as candles, inside the cabin. Other than the outside grill, please do not have open fires on the property. There is a fire extinguisher located in the kitchen.

TV & DVD PLAYER—in the drawer of the coffee table, you will find operating instructions for the TV and DVD player. Press the "Guide" button on the remote for the TV guide.

HOT TUB—We invite you to relax and enjoy the hot tub. Turn the water temperature up an hour prior to use until water is a comfortable temperature. When not in use, remember to turn down the water temperature to a slightly cooler level. Secure cover over the hot tub by snapping it down on the sides. Please do not add any type of soap products to the water.

FIREPLACE—The fireplace is a non-vented propane gas log fired firebox. Please do not throw any paper or other combustible materials in the fireplace. Do not remove or adjust logs. There is NO need to open the damper. Below are brief instructions, and full operation instructions are located on the metal instruction sheet by the fireplace.

Instructions: The pilot light should already be lit and simply turn knob to the level of flame desired.

To turn flame off, turn knob only to the "Pilot" position. Do not turn whole system to "Off" as this will extinguish the pilot light.

Lighting the Pilot Light: If the pilot light is not lit, please follow instructions below.

1. Turn black knob to "Pilot." Then push knob in and while

continuing to push in press the "Igniter" knob until pilot lights. (You may have to press knob several times.)

2. Check to see if the pilot is lit.

3. Once lit, continue pressing in pilot knob for approx. 30 seconds. Release and make sure pilot is still lit. Should pilot not light, make sure knob is on "Pilot" setting and continue to push in to bleed any air that might have accumulated in gas lines. While continuing to push in, click the starter button and the pilot will light.

GRILL—A grill is provided for your use on the outside porch. As a fire safety precaution, please do not remove the charcoal ash debris after use. We will safely dispose of the ashes after you visit.

TELEPHONE—You may make local calls and use your telephone credit card for long distance calls. Because we are in the mountains cell phones may not have the best reception in the cabin.

DISHWASHER—Because of the very cold water temperatures in this area, please run water in the sink until it is hot just prior to running dishwasher. This will ensure cleaner dishes.

HEATING AND AIR—Feel free to keep the thermostat at a comfortable setting. We do ask that you not run the unit at any time when the windows or doors are open. When you leave, please set the thermostat to 60 degrees in the cooler months and in the warmer months, turn the air-conditioning to 79.

SEPTIC SYSTEM—The septic system is very effective, however, it will clog up if improper material is flushed.

INSECTS—As a product of country living, it is possible that you may see a few insects in the cabin. If your children play in the woods, you may want to check them for ticks nightly.

Deposit Refund Letter—Full Refund

Send the deposit refund letter with the refund check after you have confir-
mation from your housekeeper that there was no damage or theft. A nice
personal touch would be to hand-write this in a thank you card and send a
business card magnet so your renters can contact you again. You can also
use this opportunity to request they write a review of your property online.

Your name
Your address
Your City, State, Zip
Your Phone Number
Your email address
Your webpage address http://your websiteaddress.com

Today's date

Dear Mr. and Mrs. Renter,

Thank you for choosing our condominium for your vacation.
We hope that you had a pleasant stay. Thanks for taking care of our
home during your stay. The condo was left in good condition, therefore, enclosed you'll find your full $XXX deposit refunded.

I was wondering if you can do us a favor. Can you write a quick
review about our condo and/or your experience renting from us?
Reviews from past guests mean a lot when choosing a vacation
rental from the many condos online. Furthermore, many websites
give priority placement to ads that have 5 star reviews, so we would
of course appreciate 5 stars.

Here's the link where you can write your review
http://www.mywesbite.com/reviews/write

If you wish to rent again, feel free call or email me directly. This
property generally books six months in advance so just keep that in
mind if you're set on particular dates.

Thanks again for staying with us. We look forward to hosting
you and your family again.

Christine

Deposit Refund Letter—Partial Refund

Send the deposit refund letter with the refund check and copies of receipts for damages after you have taken care of the damages. Note: I do not recommend soliciting a review from people who caused damages.

Your name
Your address
Your City, State, Zip
Your Phone Number
Your email address
Your webpage address http://your websiteaddress.com

Today's date

Dear Mr. and Mrs. Renter,

Thank you for choosing our condominium for your vacation. We hope that you had a pleasant stay.

Enclosed you'll find a check for $XXX which is your deposit refund minus the cost of replacing the blender which was broken during your stay. Also enclosed is the bill for the housekeeper's time to go to the store and purchase a new blender. Thanks again for notifying me that the blender was broken.

If you wish to rent again, just call/email me. I do book up quickly so just keep that in mind if you're set on particular dates.

Looking forward to hearing from you again.

Thanks again!

Christine

Cleaning Checklist

When dealing with your housekeepers and cleaning staff, it's best to have a clear, concise list of duties. It's best to be as specific as possible. Post these somewhere in your property; the inside of a closet door works well. Don't worry about hiding it from your guest's view—it's okay for them to see that you have high expectations for your cleaning staff.

Kitchen

- ❑ Clean appliances, counters, cabinets, table, and chairs.
- ❑ Clean, scrub, and sanitize sinks, countertops, and backsplashes.
- ❑ Clean range top and wipe out inside of oven.
- ❑ Clean appliance exteriors, including the inside of toaster and coffee maker.
- ❑ Clean inside and outside of refrigerator and microwave oven.
- ❑ Wash floor.
- ❑ Empty dishwasher, and quickly organize cupboards.
- ❑ Restock auto dish detergent, liquid dish soap, coffee filters, and trash bags.
- ❑ Put out 2 clean dishtowels, and a new dish rag/sponge.

Living Room

- ❑ Clean, dust, and vacuum.
- ❑ Dust window sills and ledges.
- ❑ Dust furniture, blinds, picture frames, knickknacks, ceiling fans, and lamps.
- ❑ Vacuum carpets or wash floor.
- ❑ Vacuum furniture, including under seat cushions.
- ❑ Check sofa bed for dirty linens.
- ❑ Wash windows on sliding glass doors.
- ❑ Empty and clean wastebaskets.
- ❑ Be sure to leave clean linens for the sofa bed.

Bathrooms

- ❏ Clean, scrub and sanitize showers, bathtubs, vanity, sinks, and backsplashes.
- ❏ Clean mirrors.
- ❏ Clean and sanitize toilets.
- ❏ Polish chrome.
- ❏ Wash floors and tile walls.
- ❏ Empty wastebasket.
- ❏ Replenish liquid hand soap.
- ❏ Supply clean linens:
  X# hand towels,
  X# washcloths,
  X# bath towels, and
  1 shower mat.

Other areas

- ❏ Be sure washer and dryer are empty; clean out lint trap.
- ❏ Check light bulbs, change if necessary.
- ❏ Once per month, change furnace filter.
- ❏ Wipe off patio set, clean barbeque grill.
- ❏ Notify owner immediately if you notice any damages, missing items, or if the place was left excessively dirty

2

State Sales Taxes by State

Most states require you to collect and remit sales tax on vacation rental transactions. Additionally, some states require you to have tax and/or business licenses (often renewable annually). And to further complicate matters, some counties and cities require you to collect and remit additional taxes on top of the sales taxes required by the state—these taxes may be referred to as sales, lodging, bed, hotel, room, tourist, or transient accommodations taxes. Bottom line: no two states or counties are the same.

Because the sales tax information changes so frequently, there's no way to have a complete, comprehensive list of every city, county and state requirement in the United States. Unfortunately, you will have to do some research on your own to make sure you are complaint with your state and local sales tax laws. Below is a list of state sales tax office which is a good place to start your research for the sales tax rules specific to your property.

If this is all too overwhelming, there is a company you can use to take care of all of your sales tax needs. You can find them online at www.hotspottax.com or you can call them at 877-589-0207. Please be sure to tell them that Christine Karpinski recommended them!

Alabama	http://www.ador.state.al.us/salestax/index.html
Alaska	http://www.dced.state.ak.us/dca/LOGON/tax-sales.htm
Arizona	http://www.revenue.state.az.us
Arkansas	http://www.state.ar.us/dfa/odd/salestax_index.html
California	http://www.boe.ca.gov/sutax/faqscont.htm
Colorado	http://www.revenue.state.co.us/TPS_Dir/wrap.asp?incl=salestaxforms
Connecticut	http://www.ct.gov
Delaware	http://www.state.de.us/revenue/index.htm
Florida	http://www.myflorida.com/dor/taxes/sales_tax.html
Georgia	https://etax.dor.ga.gov/bustax_salestax.aspx
Hawaii	http://www.state.hi.us/tax
Idaho	http://tax.idaho.gov/i–1049.cfm
Illinois	http://www.revenue.state.il.us
Indiana	http://www.in.gov/dor/3504.htm
Iowa	http://www.state.ia.us/tax/taxlaw/taxtypes.html#sales
Kansas	http://www.ksrevenue.org
Kentucky	http://revenue.ky.gov/business/salesanduse.htm
Louisiana	http://www.rev.state.la.us/sections/business/sales.asp#sales
Maine	http://www.state.me.us/revenue/salesuse/homepage.html
Maryland	http://taxes.marylandtaxes.com/Business_Taxes/Business_Tax_Types/Sales_and_Use_Tax/
Massachusetts	http://www.mass.gov/dor/
Michigan	http://www.michigan.gov/treasury
Minnesota	http://www.revenue.state.mn.us/businesses/sut/Pages/File-and-Pay.aspx

Mississippi	http://www.dor.ms.gov
Missouri	http://www.dor.mo.gov/tax/business/sales
Montana	http://mt.gov/
Nebraska	http://www.revenue.ne.gov/salestax.htm
Nevada	http://tax.state.nv.us
New Hampshire	http://www.revenue.nh.gov
New Jersey	http://www.state.nj.us/treasury/revenue/
New Mexico	http://www.tax.newmexico.gov/Pages/TRD-Homepage.aspx
New York	http://www.tax.ny.gov
North Carolina	http://www.dor.state.nc.us/taxes/sales
North Dakota	http://www.nd.gov/tax/salesanduse/
Ohio	http://www.tax.ohio.gov/sales_and_use/faqs.aspx
Oklahoma	http://www.oktax.state.ok.us/btforms.html
Oregon	http://www.oregon.gov/Pages/index.aspx
Pennsylvania	http://www.revenue.state.pa.us/portal/server.pt/community/sales,_use___hotel_occupancy_tax/14487
Rhode Island	http://www.tax.ri.gov/taxforms/sales_excise/sales_use.php
South Carolina	http://www.sctax.org/Forms+and+Instructions/salesUse/default.htm
South Dakota	http://www.state.sd.us/drr2/businesstax/st/salestax.htm
Tennessee	http://www.state.tn.us/
Texas	http://www.window.state.tx.us/taxinfo/sales/new_business.html
Utah	http://www.tax.utah.gov/sales
Vermont	http://www.state.vt.us/tax/index.htm
Virginia	http://www.tax.virginia.gov/site.cfm?alias=HowToFileSales
Washington	http://dor.wa.gov/content/FindTaxesAndRates/OtherTaxes/tax_hotelmotel.aspx
Washington D.C.	http://otr.cfo.dc.gov/
West Virginia	http://www.wv.gov/
Wisconsin	http://www.dor.state.wi.us/salesanduse/
Wyoming	http://revenue.wyo.gov/home

APPENDIX

3

Recommendations

There are people and companies that have given me permission to use their copyrighted information in this book. I have only contacted people and companies that I truly believe in and feel very comfortable recommending them to you. Some have even given a "special offer" to readers of this book. Feel free to contact them directly and be sure to tell them that you heard about them from Christine Karpinski.

HomeAway.com

HomeAway is the #1 vacation rental company in the world, with more than 48 million visits per month to our network of sites including #1 sites in the U.S., UK, France, Germany, Italy, Spain, and Brazil.

Use code upon checkout to receive $50 off your subscription. RAFHRIB0654

VRBO.com

VRBO is the #1 vacation rental site in the world, with more than 12 million visits per month.

Use this code upon checkout to receive $50 off your subscription. RAFHRIB-A2AC5

Flipkey.com

It's Free to List your Property on FlipKey and TripAdvisor!
Sign-up at www.flipkey.com/freelisting/ and get a $50 Amazon.com gift card when you make $1,000 in bookings on FlipKey.

Email "HTRBO" to memberservices@flipkey.com to redeem.

GulfCoastRentals.com

Since 1997 GulfCoastRentals.com has been serving property owners and travelers along the Gulf Coast.

Receive a 10% discount on a new property listing when you include "(Karpinski)" on the signup form (on the property name line).

PerfectPlaces.com
*Your resource for vacation
rental properties worldwide.* Vacancy

PerfectPlaces.com

To receive $30 off your one year subscription, use "karpinski" as your promo code.

Equity Trust Company
225 Burns Road
Elyria, OH 44035
440-323-5491
http://trustetc.com

The Equity Trust Company is a leading provider of truly self-directed Individual Retirement Accounts (IRAs) and small business retirement plans. Clients at Equity Trust have the option to invest their retirement funds in areas where they have knowledge and expertise. Equity Trust IRA investment options include real estate IRAs, mortgages/deeds of trust, and private placement IRAs.

Amy Ashcroft Greener
Amy Greener Photography
amygreenerphotography@gmail.com
www.amygreenerphotography.com
www.facebook.com/amygreenerphotography

Writing and photography services for vacation rental property owners.

Supra, Division of GE Interlogix
4001 Fairview Industrial Drive SE
Salem, OR 97302
503-589-8660
www.ge-keysafe.com

Manufacturers of KeySafe - C3 Portable lock boxes.

Broderick Perkins

San Jose, CA
info@deadlinenews.com
www.deadlinenews.com

Broderick Perkins, is founder and executive editor of San Jose, CA-based DeadlineNews.Com, a real estate news-based editorial content provider, who also offers editorial content consulting. Perkins is a Pulitzer Prize winning journalist and has been a consumer and real estate journalist for 35 years.

Andy Sirkin

250 Montgomery Sutter Street, Suite 1200
San Francisco, CA 94104
www.andysirkin.com
DASirkin@earthlink.net

D. Andrew Sirkin is a recognized expert in co-ownership forms including condominiums, tenancy in common, equity sharing and co-housing. He is an accredited instructor with the California Department of Real Estate, and frequently conducts co-ownership workshops for attorneys, real estate agents, corporations, and prospective homebuyers. He is the Author of *The Equity Sharing Manual,* (John Wiley and Sons, 1994, ISBN: 0471587338) and The Condominium Bluebook, (Piedmont Press, 2004, ISBN: 1882889215).

Tom Kelly

PO Box 4719
Rolling Bay, WA 98061
www.tomkelly.com
news@tomkelly.com
@tomkellywriter

Tom Kelly, a nationally syndicated columnist and the lead author of *How a Second Home Can Be Your Best Investment, Cashing in on a Second Home in Mexico, Cashing in on a Second Home in Central America*, has also published *Bargains Beyond the Border, Real Estate for Baby Boomers and Beyond,* and *The New Reverse Mortgage Formula.* His newest book, *Cold Crossover,* a novel about the disappearance of a former basketball star and featuring a real estate agent who sells second homes, is the first in a series of mystery novels.

Dottie DeHart

DeHart & Company
The Piedmont Center
1375 Lenoir Rhyne Blvd. SE,
Suite 109
Hickory, NC 28602
Direct Phone: (828) 325-4967
dottie@dehartandcompany.com

DeHart & Company is a full-service public relations firm with more than 15 years of experience. We have a solid background in serving the non-fiction industry. We enjoy long-term relationships with big publishers, smaller publishers, and self-published authors alike. And, yes, on occasion we work with clients who have no book at all, but hire us to promote their products and services or to grow their business.

Barry Kerrigan

Desktop Miracles, Inc.
barry@desktopmiracles.com
802-253-7900
www.desktopmiracles.com

Desktop Miracles is the premiere independent publishing studio for entrepreneurial authors. We provide bestseller-quality book design, production and manufacturing services for speakers, consultants, and business professionals. We create a customized plan for each client and project, and then assemble a team of industry experts to help authors achieve their specific business and professional goals.

Christine Karpinski

Christine@howtorentbyowner.com
www.howtorentbyowner.com

Private consultations available for but not limited to: purchasing properties that will have positive cash flow, advertising your vacation rental, copywriting, equipping and decorating vacation rentals.

Index

due diligence, 77
dwelling, in homeowner's insurance coverage, 63–64

E

Easypano, 188
Egyptian cotton, 299
809 Area Code Scam, 225
electric keyless locks, 276–278
email, 148–149, 204–205
email address, 155
email scams, 219–220
emergency information form, 352
Equity Trust Company, 367
evictions, 325–326
exchanges, 111–112, 201–202
existing properties, new building vs., 74–77
exit strategy, with co-ownership, 101
expenses, of co-ownership, 90–91

F

Fair Housing Act, 214
family room, staging, 176–177
Fannie Mae, 37, 41
features
    in ad copy, 168
    security, 60
financing, 13, 33–48
    adjustable rate mortgages, 36, 40, 42, 78
    cash purchases, 44
    for co-ownership, 89–90
    down payments, 44
    fixed-rate, fixed-term, 39–40
    interest-only loans, 40
    as investment property, 37–39
    jumbo loans, 40–41
    mortgage payments, 41–42
    with multiple properties, 109–111
    pre-approval for, 45–48
    pre-qualification for, 45
    as second home, 37–38
    securities backed, 42–43
    with self-directed IRAs, 43–44
    term of, 36–37

tips for getting, 34–35
    types of mortgages, 35–36
fines, for damage or theft, 260–261
Fireman's Fund, 62
fire station, distance to, 60–61
fixed-rate, fixed-term financing, 39–40
fixer-uppers, 70–72
Flipkey, 149, 366
Florida, 57, 58, 122, 197, 331
Fly Fisherman Magazine, 144
focal point (for photos), 179–180
forms
    cleaning checklist, 359–360
    departure information, 351
    deposit refund letters, 357–358
    directions and arrival policy, 349–350
    emergency information, 352
    pet policy, 348
    property instructions, 355–356
    rental rules and regulations, 343–347
    reservation confirmation, 342–343
    vacation tips, 353–354
fractional ownership. *See* co-ownership
Freddie Mac, 37, 41
friend rates, 200–201
furnishings, 74, 295–300
    of co-owned properties, 95–96
    selling, with home, 115

G

Generation Y, 125
godaddy, 147
Google Maps, 144–145
Greener, Amy Ashcroft, 163–164, 171, 367
guest book, 159, 307–309
GulfCoastRentals, 366

H

handicapped accessibility, 237–238
hard-to-please people, 324–325
high-speed Internet, 311
HomeAway, 149, 157–158, 366
homeowner's associations (HOA), 64, 73, 272

About the Author

Vacation rental properties are rarely big moneymakers for their owners; more often than not, they're a money pit. So when Christine Karpinski discovered you really could make money with vacation homes, she knew she had to share her knowledge with others. For nearly twenty years, she has done just that at her seminars with thousands of owners. From helping an individual purchase their very first property to training a whole team of employees for an owner of nearly 200 properties to anyone in between, Christine's seminars have transformed vacation property ownership into a lucrative investment.

Shortly after moving to Atlanta in 1996, Christine went to Destin, Florida where she fell in love with the beaches and dreamed of owning a vacation property. But there was one problem: the little one- and two-bedroom condos were pricier than she realized, costing more than their home in Atlanta. Christine even considered rental income, but just couldn't seem to make the numbers work. For most people, this is where the dream ends.

Being determined, Christine didn't give up and realized the only factor that could make a vacation property on the beach possible was eliminating property management commissions (which are generally 20-50% of the rental income). From there she started researching "renting by owner". And yes, she did end up buying that dream home on the beach and had positive cash flow from day one!

Hearing of Christine's success, other owners wanted to know why she had so many more bookings than they did and made twice as much money! Fellow owners were also intrigued that she never had damage by guests and she wasn't paying commission to the management company.

Clearly, Christine had figured out how to profitably manage vacation rentals, so she started setting up seminars to teach other owners. Now Christine has become one of the most respected voices in vacation property ownership. Today, she can be found speaking all over the country at seminars, on radio, trade shows and she is a regular contributor to industry magazines and many online newsletters.

In March of 2004, Christine completed her first two books, *How To Rent Vacation Properties By Owner—The Complete Guide to Buy, Manage, Furnish, Rent, Maintain and Advertise Your Vacation Rental Investment* and *The Vacation Rental Organizer*, which were both on the best-sellers list and have sold thousands of copies and many print runs.

In July of 2005, Christine's second book was released, *Profit from Your Vacation Home Dream, The Complete Guide to a Savvy Financial and Emotional Investment* which earned an honorable mention in the Bob Bruss, "Best Real Estate Books of 2005" awards.

In January of 2007, Christine released a full rewritten second edition, *How to Rent Vacation Properties by Owner, 2nd Edition: The Complete Guide to Buy, Manage, Furnish, Rent, Maintain and Advertise Your Vacation Rental Investment* which has been on the Best Seller's list for six years.

In September 2013, Christine released a full, rewrtiten third edition, *How to Rent Vacation Properties by Owner, 3rd Edition: The Complete Guide to Buy, Manage, Furnish, Rent, Maintain and Advertise Your Vacation Rental Investment.*

Christine has taught countless sold-out seminars throughout the country including The Real Estate Expo in NYC with Donald Trump, Suze Orman and Robert Kiyosaki. She has been a frequent guest on television and radio shows such as CNN, Fox News, Bloomberg's "Personal Finance," CBS MarketWatch Radio, and HGTV Radio and is often interviewed on real estate topics for Realty Times, The Wall Street Journal, Kiplinger's Personal Finance and many daily newspapers. Her books, combined with her seminars and media appearances, have helped thousands of people manage and profit from their second homes.

In February of 2005, Brian Sharples of WVR Group, Inc. (now HomeAway, Inc.) asked her to consult for his new company he was starting. In July of 2005, Christine became a full time employee and served as Director, Owner Community for HomeAway, Inc. In this roll she created an extensive resource center for vacation rental owners. Under her direction, she conducted countless seminars for vacation owners, a weekly podcast series, over a thousand articles, and championed and executed HomeAway's first-ever owners conference.

During her tenure at HomeAway, Christine also served as an internal consultant for products and services pertaining to vacation rental owners. She was also she was also a trusted advisor to the executive team—who relied on Christine's perspective for a myriad of key decisions that helped shape and influence what HomeAway has become today. One of her greatest accomplishments during her tenure at HomeAway was the work she did for the acquisition of VRBO. com.

In February of 2011, Christine left HomeAway Inc.

Today Christine is enjoying working as an independent author, speaker and advisor in the vacation rental industry. She and her family reside in Austin, Texas. She owns multiple vacation rental properties that she still rents "By Owner" and is often referred to as "The Most Respected Voice in the Vacation Rental Industry."

Still have questions about buying or renting a vacation home?

Contact Christine!

Christine Karpinski
Christine@howtorentbyowner.com

www.howtorentbyowner.com

facebook.com/OwnerCommunity

Private consultations available for but not limited to:
purchasing properties that will have positive cash flow, advertising your
vacation rental, copywriting, equipping and decorating vacation rentals.

Join the conversation with 5000 other vacation rental owners.
Subscribe to the vacation rentals chat forum.

WEB: http://groups.yahoo.com/group/vacation_rentals/
EMAIL: vacation_rentals-subscribe@yahoogroups.com